WESTERN ALLIED FORCES

OF

WWII

ORDER OF BATTLE
WESTERN ALLIED FORCES
OF
WWII

MICHAEL E. HASKEW

amber
BOOKS

First published in 2009 by
Amber Books Ltd
Bradley's Close
74–77 White Lion Street
London N1 9PF
www.amberbooks.co.uk

ISBN: 978-1-906626-54-9

Project Editor: Michael Spilling
Design: Hawes Design
Picture Research: Terry Forshaw

Printed in Dubai

PICTURE CREDITS

Amber Books: 24, 36, 45
Art-Tech/MARS: 60
Art-Tech/Aerospace: 90, 106, 128
Cody Images: 6, 14
Corbis: 25
Library of Congress: 125
Public Domain: 91
U.S. Department of Defense: 75, 170

ARTWORKS
Alcaniz Fresno's S.A.: 23, 39, 151, 179
Art-Tech/Aerospace: 117, 141, 160

All maps Cartographica © Amber Books
Except page 99, Patrick Mulrey © Amber Books

CONTENTS

Pre-War British & Commonwealth Forces   6

Defence of Poland: 1939   14

Scandinavia and the Low Countries   24

Battle of France: 1940   36

North Africa: 1940–43   60

The Balkans: 1941–45   90

Sicily and Italy: 1943–45   106

Northwest Europe: 1942–45   128

Invading the Reich: 1945   170

Glossary of Key Abbreviations   186

Acknowledgements   186

Index   187

Pre-War British & Commonwealth Forces

The experience of World War I led British military commanders to reconsider the doctrine and tactical employment of troops which had cost the nation so dearly during the conflict of 1914–18.

British Vickers light tanks train somewhere in England before the commencement of hostilities.

While one faction asserted that the only way the war could have been won was by the infantry launching a head-on assault against an entrenched enemy, another considered that the cost of charging into machine-gun and rifle fire, and contending with fortified positions and barbed wire, was too great. The primary discussion centred around enhanced fire support for the troops versus improved mobility for the infantry itself. In the former case, the infantry would move forward following artillery bombardment and with the tank and aircraft assets available softening the enemy positions. The latter involved an effective combination of fire and manoeuvre with rapid tank and troop movement. A major complication of an evolving military doctrine was the proper use of the tank in battle.

Innovative tank concepts

Some military planners, such as J.F.C. Fuller, Basil Liddell and Percy Hobart, embraced the concept that the tank would either become the primary offensive weapon of the army or even possibly entirely supplant the infantry and cavalry as the sole winner of future ground wars. In contrast, General Sir Douglas Haig, commander of Britain's Home Army, as well as a number of other senior officers considered the tank to be an integral component of modern combat but believed that the infantry would, in the final analysis, continue to be the primary instrument of warfare.

Amid the debate, the inter-war strength of the British Army dwindled in comparison to its peak during World War I. Based on a plan adopted in 1920, the army consisted of five infantry divisions organized into three brigades, each with four battalions; 12 cavalry regiments formed into two brigades; engineer and logistical formations; and a single brigade of artillery. A separate Machine Gun Corps was also dissolved, and these weapons were added to the organic infantry battalions. By the 1930s, the economic constraints of the Great Depression had contributed to the need to balance combat efficiency with cost effectiveness.

Debate about the use of small arms, particularly the machine gun, had continued for years, but the war games of 1931 and 1932 resulted in the beginnings of an armoured warfare doctrine within the British Army.

BRITISH ARMY: INFANTRY DIVISIONS (3 SEPT 1939)			
Div	Commander	HQ	Brigades
1 Inf	Maj-Gen H.R.L.G. Alexander	Aldershot	1, 2, 3 Inf
2 Inf	Maj-Gen H.C. Loyd	Aldershot	4, 5, 6 Inf
3 Inf	Maj-Gen B.L. Montgomery	Bulford	7, 8, 9 Inf
4 Inf	Maj-Gen D.G. Johnson	Colchester	10, 11, 12 Inf
5 Inf	Maj-Gen H.E. Franklyn	Catterick Camp	13, 15 Inf
7 Inf	Maj-Gen R.N. O'Connor	Underway in Egypt	Cairo
8 Inf	Maj-Gen A.R. Godwin-Austen	Jerusalem, Palestine	14, 16 Inf
9 Inf	Maj-Gen G.M. Lindsay	Perth	26, 27, 28 Inf
12 Inf	Maj-Gen R.L. Petre	Woolwich	35, 36, 37 Inf
15 Inf	Maj-Gen R. Le Fannu	Glasgow	44, 45, 46 Inf
18 Inf	Maj-Gen T.G. Dalby	Hertford	53, 54, 55 Inf
38 Inf	Maj-Gen G.T. Raikes	Shrewsbury	113, 114, 115 Inf
42 Inf	Maj-Gen W.G. Holmes	Manchester	125, 126, 127 Inf
43 Inf	Maj-Gen A.N. Floyer-Acland	Salisbury	128, 129, 130 Inf
44 Inf	Maj-Gen E.A. Osborne	Woolwich	131, 132, 133 Inf
45 Inf	Maj-Gen F.V.B. Witts	Salisbury	134, 135, 136 Inf
46 Inf	Maj-Gen A.L. Ransome	York	137, 138, 139 Inf
48 Inf	Maj-Gen F.C. Roberts	Oxford	143, 144, 145 Inf
49 Inf	Maj-Gen P.J. Mackesey	York	146, 147, 148 Inf
51 Inf	Maj-Gen V.M. Fortune	Perth	152, 153, 154 Inf
52 Inf	Maj-Gen J.S. Drew	Glasgow	155, 156, 157 Inf
53 Inf	Maj-Gen B.T. Wilson	Shrewsbury	158, 159, 160 Inf
54 Inf	Maj-Gen J.H.T. Priestman	Hertford	161, 162, 163 Inf
61 Inf	Maj-Gen R.J. Collins	Oxford	182, 183, 184 Inf
66 Inf	Maj-Gen A.W. Purser	Manchester	197, 198, 199 Inf

COMMANDS AND DISTRICTS, UNITED KINGDOM (3 SEPT 1939)

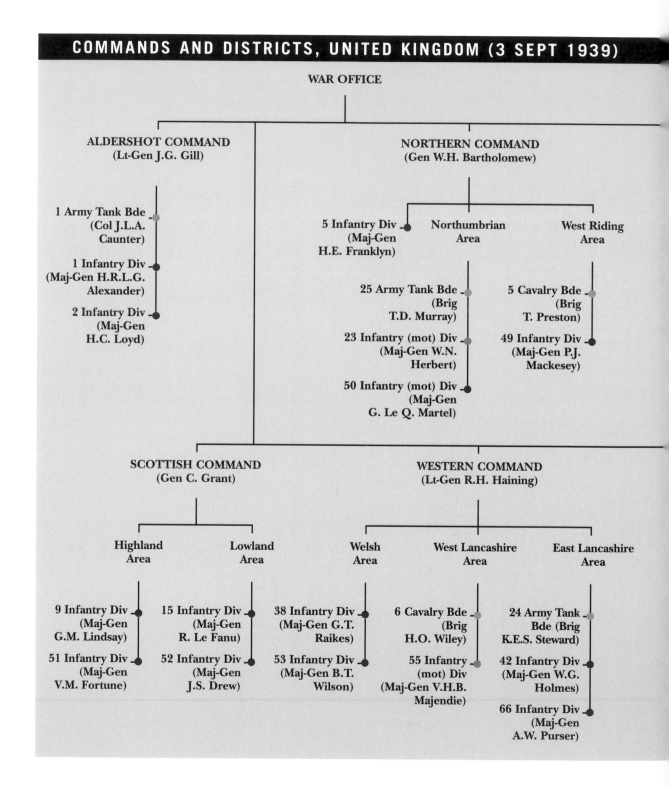

WAR OFFICE

ALDERSHOT COMMAND
(Lt-Gen J.G. Gill)

1 Army Tank Bde
(Col J.L.A.
Caunter)

1 Infantry Div
(Maj-Gen H.R.L.G.
Alexander)

2 Infantry Div
(Maj-Gen
H.C. Loyd)

NORTHERN COMMAND
(Gen W.H. Bartholomew)

5 Infantry Div
(Maj-Gen
H.E. Franklyn)

Northumbrian
Area

West Riding
Area

25 Army Tank Bde
(Brig
T.D. Murray)

23 Infantry (mot) Div
(Maj-Gen W.N.
Herbert)

50 Infantry (mot) Div
(Maj-Gen
G. Le Q. Martel)

5 Cavalry Bde
(Brig
T. Preston)

49 Infantry Div
(Maj-Gen P.J.
Mackesey)

SCOTTISH COMMAND
(Gen C. Grant)

Highland
Area

Lowland
Area

9 Infantry Div
(Maj-Gen
G.M. Lindsay)

51 Infantry Div
(Maj-Gen
V.M. Fortune)

15 Infantry Div
(Maj-Gen
R. Le Fanu)

52 Infantry Div
(Maj-Gen
J.S. Drew)

WESTERN COMMAND
(Lt-Gen R.H. Haining)

Welsh
Area

West Lancashire
Area

East Lancashire
Area

38 Infantry Div
(Maj-Gen G.T.
Raikes)

53 Infantry Div
(Maj-Gen B.T.
Wilson)

6 Cavalry Bde
(Brig
H.O. Wiley)

55 Infantry
(mot) Div
(Maj-Gen V.H.B.
Majendie)

24 Army Tank
Bde (Brig
K.E.S. Steward)

42 Infantry Div
(Maj-Gen W.G.
Holmes)

66 Infantry Div
(Maj-Gen
A.W. Purser)

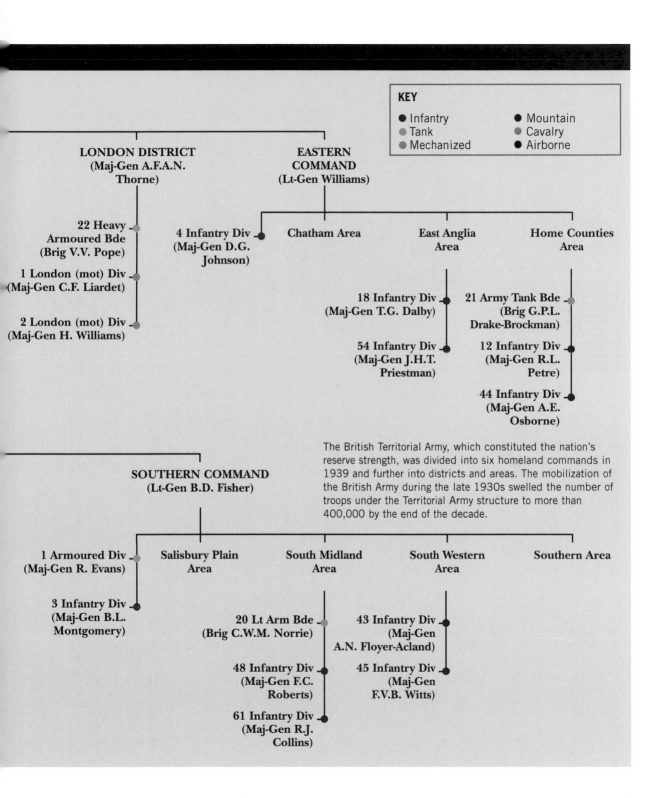

KEY

- ● Infantry
- ● Tank
- ● Mechanized
- ● Mountain
- ● Cavalry
- ● Airborne

LONDON DISTRICT
(Maj-Gen A.F.A.N. Thorne)

22 Heavy Armoured Bde (Brig V.V. Pope)

1 London (mot) Div (Maj-Gen C.F. Liardet)

2 London (mot) Div (Maj-Gen H. Williams)

EASTERN COMMAND
(Lt-Gen Williams)

4 Infantry Div (Maj-Gen D.G. Johnson)

Chatham Area

East Anglia Area

18 Infantry Div (Maj-Gen T.G. Dalby)

54 Infantry Div (Maj-Gen J.H.T. Priestman)

Home Counties Area

21 Army Tank Bde (Brig G.P.L. Drake-Brockman)

12 Infantry Div (Maj-Gen R.L. Petre)

44 Infantry Div (Maj-Gen A.E. Osborne)

The British Territorial Army, which constituted the nation's reserve strength, was divided into six homeland commands in 1939 and further into districts and areas. The mobilization of the British Army during the late 1930s swelled the number of troops under the Territorial Army structure to more than 400,000 by the end of the decade.

SOUTHERN COMMAND
(Lt-Gen B.D. Fisher)

1 Armoured Div (Maj-Gen R. Evans)

3 Infantry Div (Maj-Gen B.L. Montgomery)

Salisbury Plain Area

South Midland Area

20 Lt Arm Bde (Brig C.W.M. Norrie)

48 Infantry Div (Maj-Gen F.C. Roberts)

61 Infantry Div (Maj-Gen R.J. Collins)

South Western Area

43 Infantry Div (Maj-Gen A.N. Floyer-Acland)

45 Infantry Div (Maj-Gen F.V.B. Witts)

Southern Area

Communications among armoured vehicles were improved with radios and signal flags, while it was recognized that tanks were only a component of the overall employment of armoured vehicles. Therefore, three sections of such vehicles emerged: transport and towing vehicles; carriers without armour, such as trucks; and armoured fighting vehicles including tanks, which offered firepower and mobility to formations in the field. The first documented field manual in the British Army about the use of armoured vehicles was published in 1928. Contrary to the misconception that the German Army was highly mechanized on the eve of World War II, in 1939 it was the British Army that was the most highly mechanized fighting force in the world.

Infantry revitalization

During the late 1930s, British infantry strength was augmented, as was the mechanization of units down to

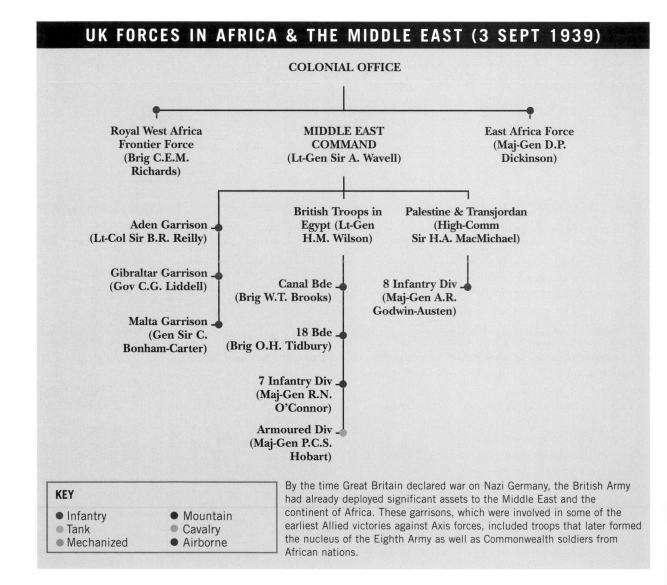

UK FORCES IN AFRICA & THE MIDDLE EAST (3 SEPT 1939)

COLONIAL OFFICE

Royal West Africa Frontier Force (Brig C.E.M. Richards)

MIDDLE EAST COMMAND (Lt-Gen Sir A. Wavell)

East Africa Force (Maj-Gen D.P. Dickinson)

British Troops in Egypt (Lt-Gen H.M. Wilson)

Palestine & Transjordan (High-Comm Sir H.A. MacMichael)

Aden Garrison (Lt-Col Sir B.R. Reilly)

Gibraltar Garrison (Gov C.G. Liddell)

Malta Garrison (Gen Sir C. Bonham-Carter)

Canal Bde (Brig W.T. Brooks)

8 Infantry Div (Maj-Gen A.R. Godwin-Austen)

18 Bde (Brig O.H. Tidbury)

7 Infantry Div (Maj-Gen R.N. O'Connor)

Armoured Div (Maj-Gen P.C.S. Hobart)

KEY
- Infantry
- Tank
- Mechanized
- Mountain
- Cavalry
- Airborne

By the time Great Britain declared war on Nazi Germany, the British Army had already deployed significant assets to the Middle East and the continent of Africa. These garrisons, which were involved in some of the earliest Allied victories against Axis forces, included troops that later formed the nucleus of the Eighth Army as well as Commonwealth soldiers from African nations.

BRITISH ARMY: ARMY TANK BRIGADES			
Brigade	Commander	HQ	Regiments
1 Army Tank	Col J.L.A. Caunter	Aldershot	4, 7, 8 RTR
21 Army Tank	Brig G.P.L. Drake-Brockman	Chipperfield	42, 44, 48 RTR
23 Army Tank	Brig W.F. Murrogh	Liverpool	40, 46, 50 RTR
24 Army Tank	Brig K.E.S. Steward	Leeds	41, 45, 47 RTR
25 Army Tank	Brig T.D. Murray	Newcastle upon Tyne	43, 49, 51 RTR

BRITISH ARMY: CAVALRY BRIGADES		
Brigade	Commander	HQ
5 Cavalry	Brig T. Preston	Bootham, York
6 Cavalry	Brig H.O. Wiley	Leicester

battalion size. Along with the introduction of light Vickers-Carden-Loyd troop carriers, which were utilized for reconnaissance and armed with machine guns, the manpower of some regiments was raised with the addition of a second infantry battalion. The British foot soldier's primary defensive weapon against enemy armour was a pair of 7.62cm (3in) mortars along with the Bren gun and a Boys anti-tank rifle, which rapidly became obsolete during the war and was replaced by the PIAT (Projector Infantry Anti-Tank).

When the BEF was transported to the European continent in 1939, the standard British Army infantry regiment consisted of two battalions of four rifle companies each, further divided into four platoons. During that year, the size of the army expanded rapidly from 227,000 troops in the standing army and 204,000 in the Territorial Army, which constituted the reserves, to a Territorial Army of nearly 430,000 organized into 10 divisions and a cavalry brigade. The Territorial Army was divided into six command districts: Scottish, Western, Southern, Aldershot, Eastern and Northern.

Canada and the Commonwealth

Within 10 days of Great Britain's declaration of war against Nazi Germany, the major nations of the Commonwealth were committed to the struggle. The response from the governments of Australia and New Zealand was immediate, but some debate occurred in Canada and South Africa, where large numbers of citizens were not of British descent. The South African prime minister was actually ousted from office in favour

of a vote to join with Britain. Notably, Ireland, which remained a part of the Commonwealth, declared itself neutral in the wake of Home Rule, which had been granted in the 1920s.

In the summer of 1939, the Canadian Army consisted of 4300 active duty personnel, while the reserve, largely without formal training, numbered less than 52,000. On 1 September, the Canadian Active Service Force came into being, and more than 60,000 volunteers enlisted within weeks. By October, liaison troops had arrived in Britain. Two divisions of the burgeoning Canadian Army were authorized with the understanding that this commitment could grow to six if necessary. In mid-September, one division was earmarked for service overseas, although Canadian troops participated on only a limited scale in operations during the early months of the war. Remarkably, at peak strength just before D-Day, the Canadian Army numbered more than 495,000.

Australia, without a standing army in September 1939, fielded a militia of 35,000 soldiers. The newly constituted Australian Imperial Force eventually rose to 700,000. Its troops distinguished themselves during combat in the Middle East, North Africa and Greece; however, the threat of war with Japan was a continual concern, and by 1943 virtually all Australian Army units were fighting in the Pacific.

BRITISH & COMMONWEALTH MILITARY MANPOWER		
Country	Manpower mobilized, September 1939	Manpower mobilized, May 1945
Australia	91,700	575,100
Canada	63,100	759,800
India	197,000	2,159,700
New Zealand	13,800	192,800
South Africa	19,000	250,000
UK	681,000	4,683,000

CANADIAN ARMY (SEPTEMBER 1939)

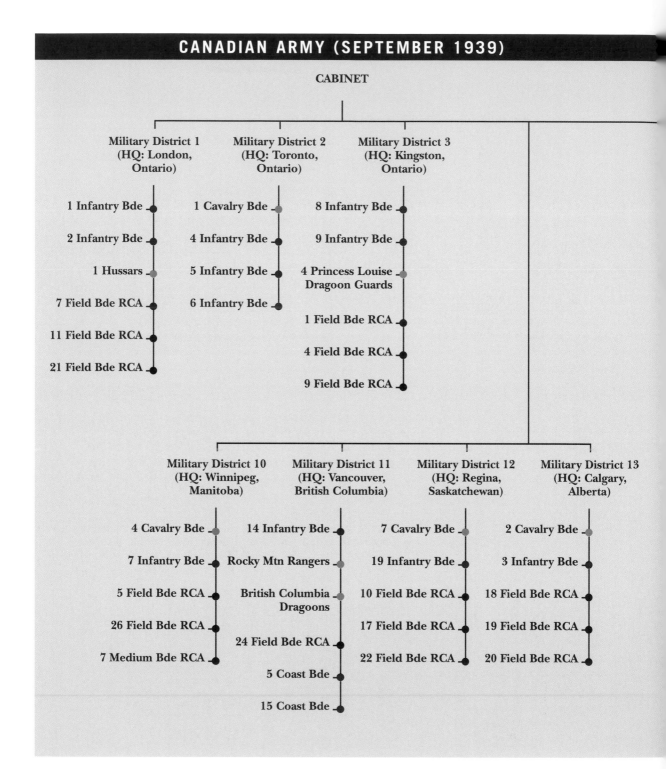

CABINET

Military District 1
(HQ: London, Ontario)

1 Infantry Bde
2 Infantry Bde
1 Hussars
7 Field Bde RCA
11 Field Bde RCA
21 Field Bde RCA

Military District 2
(HQ: Toronto, Ontario)

1 Cavalry Bde
4 Infantry Bde
5 Infantry Bde
6 Infantry Bde

Military District 3
(HQ: Kingston, Ontario)

8 Infantry Bde
9 Infantry Bde
4 Princess Louise Dragoon Guards
1 Field Bde RCA
4 Field Bde RCA
9 Field Bde RCA

Military District 10
(HQ: Winnipeg, Manitoba)

4 Cavalry Bde
7 Infantry Bde
5 Field Bde RCA
26 Field Bde RCA
7 Medium Bde RCA

Military District 11
(HQ: Vancouver, British Columbia)

14 Infantry Bde
Rocky Mtn Rangers
British Columbia Dragoons
24 Field Bde RCA
5 Coast Bde
15 Coast Bde

Military District 12
(HQ: Regina, Saskatchewan)

7 Cavalry Bde
19 Infantry Bde
10 Field Bde RCA
17 Field Bde RCA
22 Field Bde RCA

Military District 13
(HQ: Calgary, Alberta)

2 Cavalry Bde
3 Infantry Bde
18 Field Bde RCA
19 Field Bde RCA
20 Field Bde RCA

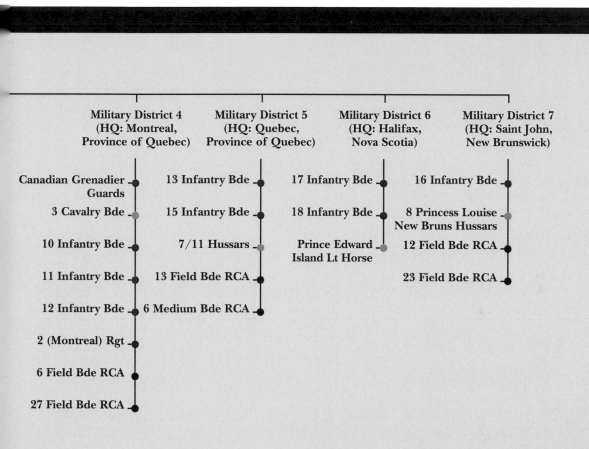

Military District 4 (HQ: Montreal, Province of Quebec)	Military District 5 (HQ: Quebec, Province of Quebec)	Military District 6 (HQ: Halifax, Nova Scotia)	Military District 7 (HQ: Saint John, New Brunswick)
Canadian Grenadier Guards	13 Infantry Bde	17 Infantry Bde	16 Infantry Bde
3 Cavalry Bde	15 Infantry Bde	18 Infantry Bde	8 Princess Louise New Bruns Hussars
10 Infantry Bde	7/11 Hussars	Prince Edward Island Lt Horse	12 Field Bde RCA
11 Infantry Bde	13 Field Bde RCA		23 Field Bde RCA
12 Infantry Bde	6 Medium Bde RCA		
2 (Montreal) Rgt			
6 Field Bde RCA			
27 Field Bde RCA			

KEY

- Infantry
- Tank
- Mechanized
- Mountain
- Cavalry
- Artillery

Although the Canadian Army consisted of fewer than 4300 soldiers of all ranks during the summer of 1939, while reserves numbered only about 51,000, the nation began to mobilize rapidly, expanding training capacity and transporting 23,000 troops to Great Britain by February 1940. Within a month of the declaration of war, more than 60,000 volunteers had enlisted for active service. To assist the war effort further, approximately 700 Canadian officers were temporarily assigned to the British Army.

The territorial administration of the Canadian Army was divided into numerous military districts, and while an infantry division was preparing for deployment to Europe, three further divisions were authorized for defence of the homeland.

The 1st Canadian Infantry Division was the first unit to be fully mobilized on 1 September 1939. The division was sent to the UK in late 1939, and one brigade did briefly cross to France in the wake of the Dunkirk evacuation in June 1940, before being recalled almost immediately. The division then spent the next three years training in England before being transferred to the Mediterranean theatre for the assault on Sicily in July 1943.

Defence of Poland: 1939

In early 1939, although the menace of Soviet Russia was initially of greater concern, the Polish Army developed *Plan Zachód*, or Plan West, in response to the threat of war with Germany.

A unit of Polish cavalry prepares to move out. Amazingly, in a war dominated by mechanized forces, Poland deployed 11 cavalry brigades against German forces. These were not intended to fight on horseback, but functioned as a mobile reserve.

Prior to autumn 1939, the Polish government and military establishment considered the threat of invasion by Germany as secondary to the potential for war with the Soviet Union. During the mid-1930s, Poland had invested in the industrialization of the central region of the country. In 1936, the government initiated the National Defence Fund to raise money to modernize the armed forces. A degree of military modernization had been undertaken, but the prospect of war with Germany was considered remote and was not expected before the early 1940s. Therefore, much of the military equipment produced in Poland was exported.

War clouds gather

However, as German influence and territorial expansion approached the Polish frontier, it became apparent that the threat of invasion by the mechanized German Army was real – even imminent. The Poles were destined to fight briefly on two fronts as Germany ignited World War II in Europe on 1 September 1939, and the Soviet Red Army attacked two weeks later. Under *Plan Zachód* (Plan West), the Polish Army was to field up to 39 infantry divisions, two mountain divisions, 11 cavalry brigades and two mechanized brigades. Nine of the infantry divisions were designated as reserves, while limited numbers of tanks and armoured vehicles were not organized into independent armoured divisions, remaining in brigade strength. Many were allocated to smaller units designated as 'operational groups'. The Polish land forces were organized into six armies under the command of Marshal Edward Smigly-Rydz.

The Polish Army numbered more than one million men, but only partial mobilization had occurred, perhaps around 500,000 soldiers, when hostilities began. Preparations for defence were incomplete when the Germans surged forward along a 1600km (994-mile) front. Great Britain and France had pledged to come to their aid in the event of war with Germany, but had not guaranteed the integrity of Poland's borders and could offer only limited military assistance. The Poles knew too that both nations had signed away the sovereignty of Czechoslovakia. These factors, and the location of dense population and heavy manufacturing centres in the western area of the country, meant that the Poles deployed their forces to defend the western border.

It was a deployment that played into German hands. Some Polish strategists had advocated occupying defensive lines east of the natural barriers of the Vistula and San rivers, believing their forces might hold out against the Germans for as long as six months without major assistance.

However, Polish forces were stretched dangerously thin, particularly in the south where the main German penetrations were to take place. Lengthened reinforcement and supply lines were also exposed to relentless air attack from the *Luftwaffe,* which was both numerically and technologically superior to the Polish Air Force.

ARMOURED FIGHTING VEHICLES (SEPTEMBER 1939)	
Vehicle	**Strength**
TK and TKS Tankettes	440
7TPs	130
Vickers Es	30
R-35s	49
Renault FT-17s	55
wz.29 and wz.34 Armoured Cars	95

POLISH ARMY (SEPTEMBER 1939)	
Unit	**Strength**
Divisions	41
Infantry	39
Armoured	–
Mountain	2
Brigades	13
Cavalry	11
Mechanized	2
Armoured	–
Airborne	–
Automatic Weapons	41,000
Anti-Tank Weapons	4700
Artillery	3388
Reconnaissance Tanks	574
Light Tanks	211
Other Vehicles	6000
Soldiers	1.2 million approx

The Polish Army

Inadequately equipped, partially mobilized and poorly deployed, the Polish Army faced an efficient, mechanized juggernaut in the German *Wehrmacht* when war commenced on 1 September 1939.

In the autumn of 1939, the six Polish armies facing the Germans relied heavily on horse-drawn transportation and obsolete weaponry. Infantry divisions primarily moved on foot, while tanks and armoured units were often dispersed among the infantry formations, rendering them virtually useless in mounting coordinated defensive efforts or counterattacks.

In the spring of 1939, several Polish armies were organized and assigned specific roles in the overall defensive posture of the armed forces. Commanded by General Antoni Szylling, the *Kraków* Army included five infantry divisions, a mountain brigade, a motorized cavalry brigade and a cavalry brigade, while the *Lódz* Army, led by General Juliusz Rómmel, consisted of four infantry divisions and two cavalry brigades, and the *Modlin* Army, under General Emil Krukowicz-Przedrzymirski, fielded two infantry divisions and two cavalry brigades. The *Pomorze* Army, commanded by General Wladyslaw Bortnowski, included five infantry divisions, two so-called national defence brigades and a cavalry brigade. Led by General Tadeusz Kutrzeba, the *Poznan* Army included four infantry divisions and two cavalry brigades.

The *Kraków* Army was intended to resist initial German thrusts while actively retiring eastwards to the north of the Carpathian Mountains, while the *Pomorze* Army was to defend the Polish Corridor in the north, particularly around the towns of Torun and Bydgoszcz. The *Lódz* Army was to provide flank protection between the *Kraków* Army and the *Poznan* Army, which was to fight delaying actions and then fall back to the Warta River. The *Modlin* Army was to defend north of Warsaw near the border with East Prussia and methodically fall back towards the Narew River.

In the summer, two mountain brigades formed the *Karpaty* Army after Germany began to occupy Czechoslovakia beyond the Sudetenland. Its primary task was to secure mountain passes in the Carpathians. The *Prusy* Army, led by General Stefan Dab-Biernacki, was created with six infantry divisions, a battalion of tanks and a cavalry brigade as a reserve to support the *Poznan* and *Kraków* armies. Operational groups were

POLISH TANK FORMATIONS (SEPTEMBER 1939)			
Formation	Sub–Unit	Vehicle	Strength
WBP–M	11 sk	TKS	13
WBP–M	12 sk	TKS	13
25 DP	31 sk	TKS	13
10 DP	32 sk	TKS	13
30 DP	41 sk	TK	13
Kresowa BK	42 sk	TK	13
GO Bielsko	51 sk	TK	13
GO Slask	52 sk	TK	13
GO Slask	61 sk	TKS	13
20 DP	62 sk	TKS	13
8 DP	63 sk	TKS	13
26 DP	71 sk	TKS	13
14 DP	72 sk	TKS	13
4 DP	81 sk	TK	13
26 DP	82 sk	TK	13
10 DP	91 sk	TK	13
10 DP	92 sk	TK	13
10 BKM	101 sk	TK	13
10 BKM	121 sk	TKS	13
	1 bcl	7TP	49
	2 bcl	7TP	49
	21 bcl	R-35	45
	111, 112, 113 kcl	FT-17	45
WBP–M	12 kcl	Vickers	17
10 BKM	121 kcl	Vickers	17

POLISH ARMY: MOBILIZED REGULAR INFANTRY DIVS		
Division	Commander	Regiments
1 Infantry	Maj-Gen W. Kowalski	1, 5, 6
2 Infantry	Col E. Dojan-Surówka	2, 3, 4
3 Infantry	Col M. Turkowski	7, 8, 9
4 Infantry	Col T. Niezabitowski	14, 63, 67
5 Infantry	Maj-Gen J. Zulauf	19, 26, 40
6 Infantry	Maj-Gen B. Mond	12, 16, 20
7 Infantry	Maj-Gen J.T. Gasiorowski	25, 27, 74
8 Infantry	Col T. Furgalski	13, 21, 32
9 Infantry	Col J. Werobej	22, 34, 35
10 Infantry	Maj-Gen F. Dindorf-Ankowicz	28, 30, 31
11 Karpaty Inf	Col B. Prugar-Ketling	48, 49, 53
12 Infantry	Maj-Gen G. Paszkiewicz	51, 52, 54
13 Infantry	Col W. Zubosz-Kalinski	43, 44, 45
14 Infantry	Maj-Gen F. Wlad	55, 57, 58
15 Infantry	Maj-Gen Z. Przyjalkowski	59, 61, 62
16 Infantry	Col S. Switalski	64, 65, 66
17 Infantry	Col M. Mozdyniewicz	68, 69, 70
18 Infantry	Col S. Kossecki	33, 42, 71
19 Infantry	Maj-Gen J. Kwaciszewski	77, 85, 86
20 Infantry	Col W. Liszka-Lawicz	78, 79, 80
21 Mountain	Maj-Gen J. Kustron	3, 4 Mountain 202 Reserve
22 Mountain	Maj-Gen L. Endel-Ragis	2, 5, 6 Mountain
23 Infantry	Col W. Powierza	11, 73, 75
24 Infantry	Maj-Gen B. Krzyzanowski	17, 38, 39
25 Infantry	Maj-Gen F. Alter	29, 56, 60
26 Infantry	Maj-Gen A. Brzechwa-Ajdukiewicz	10, 18, 37
27 Infantry	Maj-Gen J. Drapella	23, 24, 50
28 Infantry	Maj-Gen W. Boncza-Uzdowski	15, 36, 72
29 Infantry	Col I. Oziewicz	41, 76, 81
30 Infantry	Maj-Gen L. Cehak	82, 83, 84

POLISH TANK FORMATIONS (SEPTEMBER 1939)			
Formation	Sub–Unit	Vehicle	Strength
Mazowiecka BK	11 dp	TKS wz.29	13 8
Wolynska BK	21 dp	TKS wz.34	13 8
Suwalska BK	31 dp	TKS wz.34	13 8
Podlaska BK	32 dp	TKS wz.34	13 8
Wilenska BK	33 dp	TKS wz.34	13 8
Krakowska BK	51 dp	TK wz.34	13 8
Kresowa BK	61 dp	TKS wz.34	13 8
Podolska BK	62 dp	TKS wz.34	13 8
Wielkopolska BK	71 dp	TKS wz.34	13 8
Pomorska BK	81 dp	TK wz.34	13 8
Nowogrodzka BK	91 dp	TK wz.34	13 8

Armoured strength

On the eve of battle, the Polish Army included roughly 800 reconnaissance and light tanks. These were primarily obsolete Renault FT-17 light tanks, French Renault R-35s, British-designed Vickers 6-ton (Mark E) tanks and Hotchkiss H-35s, along with the Poles' own 7TP light tanks (which were improved and upgunned versions of the British Vickers), and nearly 600 Polish TK and TKS tankettes, variants of the British Carden-Loyd tankette. While some of these models could hold their own against the German panzers, they were few in number and poorly utilized. Most of the tankettes were armed only with machine guns.

Germany strikes

The swiftness and coordination of the German offensive against the Polish Army proved to be the defenders' undoing. Stuka dive bombers and heavy artillery pounded Polish positions as mechanized infantry units

attached to the armies from time to time, and later ad hoc armies were formed from the remnants of units that retreated before the rapid German advance.

POLISH ARMY (SEPTEMBER 1939)

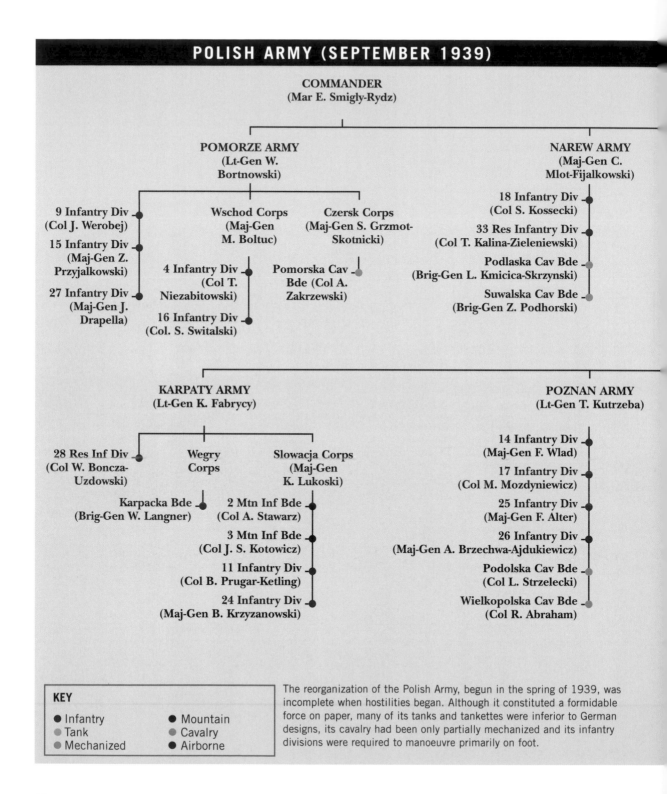

COMMANDER
(Mar E. Smigly-Rydz)

POMORZE ARMY
(Lt-Gen W. Bortnowski)

NAREW ARMY
(Maj-Gen C. Mlot-Fijalkowski)

9 Infantry Div
(Col J. Werobej)

15 Infantry Div
(Maj-Gen Z. Przyjalkowski)

27 Infantry Div
(Maj-Gen J. Drapella)

Wschod Corps
(Maj-Gen M. Boltuc)

Czersk Corps
(Maj-Gen S. Grzmot-Skotnicki)

4 Infantry Div
(Col T. Niezabitowski)

16 Infantry Div
(Col. S. Switalski)

Pomorska Cav Bde (Col A. Zakrzewski)

18 Infantry Div
(Col S. Kossecki)

33 Res Infantry Div
(Col T. Kalina-Zieleniewski)

Podlaska Cav Bde
(Brig-Gen L. Kmicica-Skrzynski)

Suwalska Cav Bde
(Brig-Gen Z. Podhorski)

KARPATY ARMY
(Lt-Gen K. Fabrycy)

POZNAN ARMY
(Lt-Gen T. Kutrzeba)

28 Res Inf Div
(Col W. Boncza-Uzdowski)

Wegry Corps

Slowacja Corps
(Maj-Gen K. Lukoski)

Karpacka Bde
(Brig-Gen W. Langner)

2 Mtn Inf Bde
(Col A. Stawarz)

3 Mtn Inf Bde
(Col J. S. Kotowicz)

11 Infantry Div
(Col B. Prugar-Ketling)

24 Infantry Div
(Maj-Gen B. Krzyzanowski)

14 Infantry Div
(Maj-Gen F. Wlad)

17 Infantry Div
(Col M. Mozdyniewicz)

25 Infantry Div
(Maj-Gen F. Alter)

26 Infantry Div
(Maj-Gen A. Brzechwa-Ajdukiewicz)

Podolska Cav Bde
(Col L. Strzelecki)

Wielkopolska Cav Bde
(Col R. Abraham)

KEY

- ● Infantry
- ● Tank
- ● Mechanized
- ● Mountain
- ● Cavalry
- ● Airborne

The reorganization of the Polish Army, begun in the spring of 1939, was incomplete when hostilities began. Although it constituted a formidable force on paper, many of its tanks and tankettes were inferior to German designs, its cavalry had been only partially mechanized and its infantry divisions were required to manoeuvre primarily on foot.

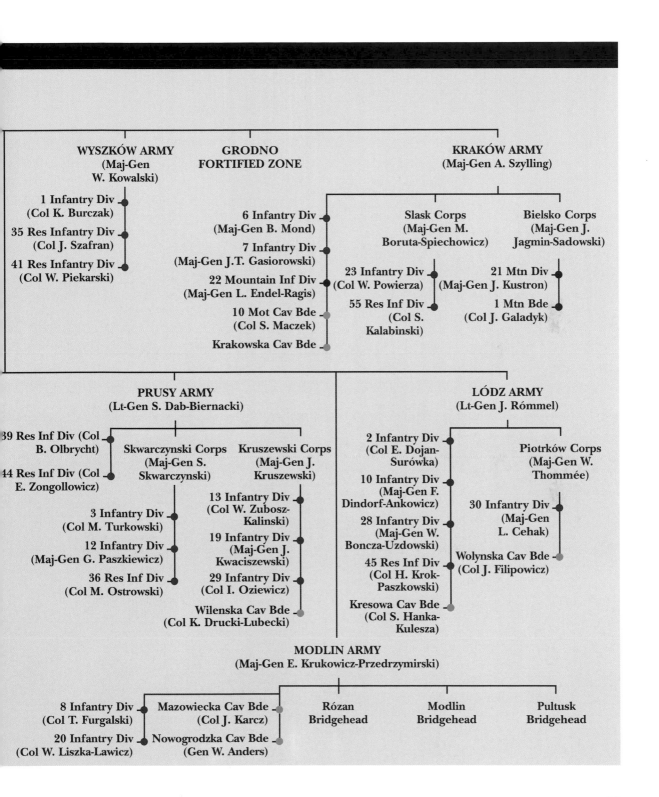

WYSZKÓW ARMY
(Maj-Gen W. Kowalski)

1 Infantry Div
(Col K. Burczak)

35 Res Infantry Div
(Col J. Szafran)

41 Res Infantry Div
(Col W. Piekarski)

GRODNO FORTIFIED ZONE

6 Infantry Div
(Maj-Gen B. Mond)

7 Infantry Div
(Maj-Gen J.T. Gasiorowski)

22 Mountain Inf Div
(Maj-Gen L. Endel-Ragis)

10 Mot Cav Bde
(Col S. Maczek)

Krakowska Cav Bde

KRAKÓW ARMY
(Maj-Gen A. Szylling)

Slask Corps
(Maj-Gen M. Boruta-Spiechowicz)

23 Infantry Div
(Col W. Powierza)

55 Res Inf Div
(Col S. Kalabinski)

Bielsko Corps
(Maj-Gen J. Jagmin-Sadowski)

21 Mtn Div
(Maj-Gen J. Kustron)

1 Mtn Bde
(Col J. Galadyk)

PRUSY ARMY
(Lt-Gen S. Dab-Biernacki)

39 Res Inf Div (Col B. Olbrycht)

44 Res Inf Div (Col E. Zongollowicz)

Skwarczynski Corps
(Maj-Gen S. Skwarczynski)

3 Infantry Div
(Col M. Turkowski)

12 Infantry Div
(Maj-Gen G. Paszkiewicz)

36 Res Inf Div
(Col M. Ostrowski)

Kruszewski Corps
(Maj-Gen J. Kruszewski)

13 Infantry Div
(Col W. Zubosz-Kalinski)

19 Infantry Div
(Maj-Gen J. Kwaciszewski)

29 Infantry Div
(Col I. Oziewicz)

Wilenska Cav Bde
(Col K. Drucki-Lubecki)

LÓDZ ARMY
(Lt-Gen J. Rómmel)

2 Infantry Div
(Col E. Dojan-Surówka)

10 Infantry Div
(Maj-Gen F. Dindorf-Ankowicz)

28 Infantry Div
(Maj-Gen W. Boncza-Uzdowski)

45 Res Inf Div
(Col H. Krok-Paszkowski)

Kresowa Cav Bde
(Col S. Hanka-Kulesza)

Piotrków Corps
(Maj-Gen W. Thommée)

30 Infantry Div
(Maj-Gen L. Cehak)

Wolynska Cav Bde
(Col J. Filipowicz)

MODLIN ARMY
(Maj-Gen E. Krukowicz-Przedrzymirski)

8 Infantry Div
(Col T. Furgalski)

20 Infantry Div
(Col W. Liszka-Lawicz)

Mazowiecka Cav Bde
(Col J. Karcz)

Nowogrodzka Cav Bde
(Gen W. Anders)

Rózan Bridgehead

Modlin Bridgehead

Pultusk Bridgehead

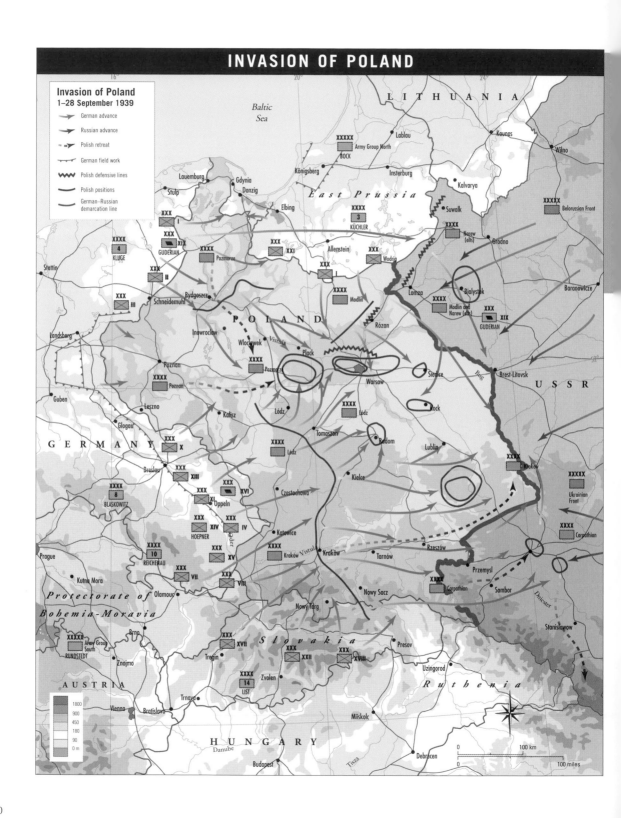

INVASION OF POLAND

Invasion of Poland
1–28 September 1939

German advance
Russian advance
Polish retreat
German field work
Polish defensive lines
Polish positions
German–Russian
demarcation line

1–28 September 1939

With only about half of its one million troops mobilized, the Polish Army deployed defensively along its borders to face the German invasion. Following the initial German incursions, the Poles were obliged to defend against coordinated attacks on their western, northern and southern frontiers, each thrust eventually targeting the capital city of Warsaw. Caught off-guard by the surprise and mobility of the German assault, a number of Polish units, even at army strength, were compelled to withdraw to avoid encirclement. Significant Polish forces west of the Vistula River were surrounded, and on 17 September the Soviet Red Army invaded from the east. Within the month, organized Polish resistance had dwindled. Besieged for two weeks, Warsaw surrendered on 28 September.

penetrated defensive lines and panzers exploited the breakthroughs. Entire Polish armies were often unable to manoeuvre rapidly enough in response and fell back in disorder, to prevent being cut off and encircled. A planned Polish counterattack on 6 September failed to materialize, primarily because the reserve *Prusy* Army was not fully mobilized. Within hours, the Germans were therefore able to enter Kraków, its defending army having been forced to retreat to avoid being surrounded. By 8 September, swiftly advancing *Wehrmacht* panzers had reached the outskirts of the Polish capital of Warsaw, having rolled 225km (140 miles) in seven days.

Generally, Polish forces became fragmented and unable to fight coordinated defensive actions. The largest battle of the campaign in Poland took place at Bzura, west of Warsaw, on 9–19 September. The *Poznan* and *Pomorze* armies counterattacked the flank of the German Eighth Army with some success. However, the attack eventually failed due to lack of supplies and ammunition as well as pressure in other areas of the front.

Defence of Warsaw

While the *Luftwaffe* rained destruction on Warsaw, the *Warszawa* Army was created for the defence of the Polish capital as German spearheads raced eastwards, reaching the gates of the city within a week.

Within a couple of days, nearly two full divisions of infantry and more than 60 artillery pieces augmented the force which Rómmel and Czuma pieced together. Some of these soldiers had been drawn from the Modlin Fortress, a nineteenth-century citadel 80km (50 miles) north of Warsaw, which held out against the Germans until 29 September. Others were from the *Lódz* Army or had retreated from the Vistula and Narew River lines.

German attacks

Initial German assaults on Warsaw were thrown back with severe casualties around the suburbs of Wola and Ochota. Though relatively few in number, Polish anti-tank guns proved effective against German armour, while the citizens constructed barricades across the streets. The German 4th Panzer Division lost nearly 37 per cent of its armour, approximately 80 tanks, in heavy fighting.

While the *Poznan* and *Pomorze* armies began their counter-offensive against the left flank of the German Eighth Army pushing towards Warsaw, the Poles utilized the time to strengthen their defences. Reservists were organized into new units such as the 36th Infantry Regiment 'Academic Legion' and the 8th Infantry Division, consisting of citizens of Warsaw.

The remnants of the *Prusy* Army, which had been quickly shattered by the Germans, filtered into the capital as well. When the fighting at Bzura ended in defeat on 19 September, what was left of the *Poznan* and *Pomorze* armies escaped encirclement and fell

DEFENCE OF WARSAW (10 SEPTEMBER 1939)

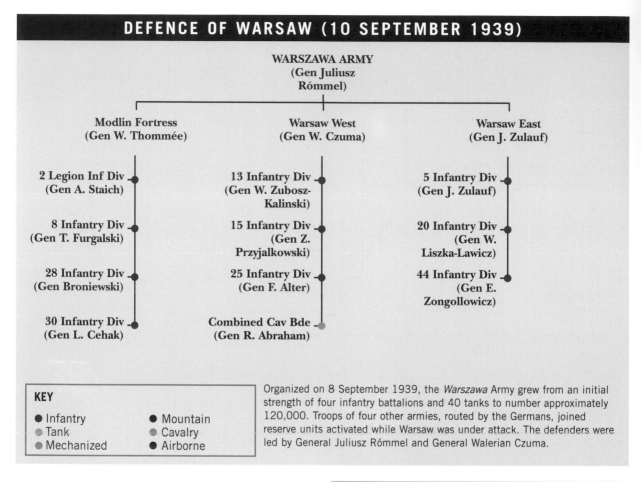

WARSZAWA ARMY
(Gen Juliusz Rómmel)

Modlin Fortress
(Gen W. Thommée)

Warsaw West
(Gen W. Czuma)

Warsaw East
(Gen J. Zulauf)

2 Legion Inf Div
(Gen A. Staich)

8 Infantry Div
(Gen T. Furgalski)

28 Infantry Div
(Gen Broniewski)

30 Infantry Div
(Gen L. Cehak)

13 Infantry Div
(Gen W. Zubosz-
Kalinski)

15 Infantry Div
(Gen Z.
Przyjalkowski)

25 Infantry Div
(Gen F. Alter)

Combined Cav Bde
(Gen R. Abraham)

5 Infantry Div
(Gen J. Zulauf)

20 Infantry Div
(Gen W.
Liszka-Lawicz)

44 Infantry Div
(Gen E.
Zongollowicz)

KEY

● Infantry
● Tank
● Mechanized
● Mountain
● Cavalry
● Airborne

Organized on 8 September 1939, the *Warszawa* Army grew from an initial strength of four infantry battalions and 40 tanks to number approximately 120,000. Troops of four other armies, routed by the Germans, joined reserve units activated while Warsaw was under attack. The defenders were led by General Juliusz Rómmel and General Walerian Czuma.

back to Warsaw and Modlin. At peak strength, the Polish defenders of Warsaw numbered about 120,000.

By mid-September, German forces had closed in on Warsaw from three sides and effectively besieged the city. Continuous air attack and artillery bombardment took their toll on the defenders, who nevertheless put up stiff resistance. The 21st Infantry Regiment 'Children of Warsaw' repelled a German attack against the suburb of Grochów, while an assault in the vicinity of Praga was also beaten back.

Stout defence

During the following two weeks, successive German attacks were repulsed by the Poles, including a general assault along the Warsaw perimeter on 25 September, which engaged nine German infantry divisions

POLISH ARMY: ARMOURED BATTALIONS (SEPT 1939)		
Unit	Commander	Cavalry Brigade
11th Armoured Btn	Maj S. Majewski	Mazowiecka Bde
21st Armoured Btn	Maj S. Glinski	Wolynska Bde
31st Armoured Btn	Cpt B. Bledzki	Suwalska Bde
32nd Armoured Btn	Maj S. Szostak	Podlaska Bde
33rd Armoured Btn	Cpt W. Lubienski	Wilenska Bde
51st Armoured Btn	Maj H. Swietlicki	Krakowska Bde
61st Armoured Btn	Cpt A. Wojcinski	Kresowa Bde
62nd Armoured Btn	Cpt Z. Brodowski	Podolska Bde
71st Armoured Btn	Maj K. Zolkiewicz	Wielkopolska Bde
81st Armoured Btn	Maj F. Szystowski	Pomorska Bde
91st Armoured Btn	Maj A. Sliwinski	Nowogrodzka Bde

1 *KRAKOWSKA BRYGADA KAWALERII*

The *Kraków* Cavalry Brigade, formed on 1 April 1937, opposed the German invasion along with other units of the *Kraków* Army near Zabkowice and Czestochowa. Following the Battle of Tomaszów Lubelski, the remnants of the *Kraków* Army surrendered. Equipped with 13 Polish-made TK tankettes armed with 7.92mm (0.31in) km wz.25 or Hotchkiss 7.7mm (0.3in) machine guns, and eight *Samochód pancerny* wz.34 armoured cars armed with machine guns or 37mm (1.45in) SA-18 Puteaux guns, the Poles were overmatched in armoured strength.

TK tanks x 13

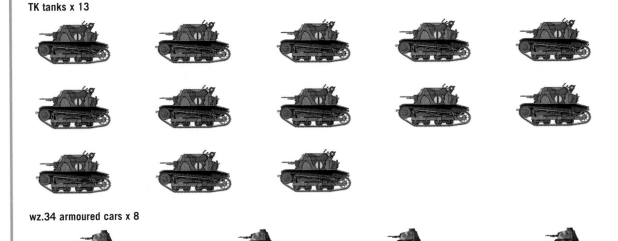

wz.34 armoured cars x 8

supported by aircraft, artillery and armour. Two days later, a second attempt to breach the Warsaw defences on a broad front failed. To their dismay, the Germans discovered that their superiority in tanks was to a large extent neutralized by the confines of urban warfare.

Fall of Warsaw

Polish counterattacks met with some success, particularly in the areas of Praga and Mokotów; however, these served only to postpone the inevitable. With civilian casualties mounting and the infrastructure of Warsaw seriously degraded, Tadeusz Kutrzeba, commander of the Poznan Army, requested surrender talks with the Germans. Meanwhile, some artillery and other weaponry were destroyed or hidden. Several units refused to

consider surrender and escaped into the countryside. Others were personally visited by Rómmel or Czuma in an effort to honour the cease-fire, which went into effect at noon on 27 September.

With the Soviet Red Army advancing from the east, German troops entered Warsaw on 1 October. Nearly 100,000 Polish prisoners were taken, and the defenders suffered 24,000 casualties, including 6000 killed. The toll in civilian dead exceeded 25,000. Before and during Poland's tribulation, a number of soldiers, sailors and airmen escaped to the West. Polish combat units were established and later fought against the Germans. Following the Nazi invasion of the Soviet Union in 1941, other Polish troops were incorporated into the Red Army.

Scandinavia and the Low Countries

In the spring of 1940, the armies of Denmark, Norway, Holland, and Belgium were ill-prepared to fend off the invading Germans, who rapidly swept through their countries during campaigns that concluded in scarcely three months' time.

Belgian horse-drawn artillery taking part in manoeuvres in the summer of 1939.

The outbreak of World War II did not necessarily shock the governments of Scandinavia and the Low Countries, but nor does it appear to have stirred them to immediate action against the threat of invasion by German forces should the attention of their militaristic neighbour turn westwards.

Politics and protection

Tradition, treaty, economic influences and the dependence on Great Britain and France for protection contributed to the lack of preparedness among the military organizations of Denmark, Norway, Holland and Belgium during the opening weeks of World War II. The political and military leaders of these nations were well aware in 1940 that the Germans coveted their lands for several reasons. The presence of valuable natural resources, such as iron and tungsten ore, access to the North Sea and the Atlantic, and the establishment of a staging area for future operations against Germany's traditional enemy, France, weighed heavily in Hitler's plans for conquest.

The assurance of military cooperation with the principals of the alliance that had emerged victorious from World War I may have fostered a false sense of security, but economic recession diverted funding for military expansion and modernization to other seemingly more pressing needs. Sovereignty was also guaranteed by treaty; however, the Nazis' history of disregard for such accords made their future solidity somewhat dubious. Regardless of the theoretical reasons for their lack of preparation, the stark reality was simply that Scandinavia and the Low Countries were faced with long odds from the beginning. Germany's military colossus dwarfed their combined number of men under arms, and political and military leaders were so cowed by the strength of their overbearing neighbour that even hinting at full mobilization, the appropriation of additional funds to the armies, or any overtures involving greater strength of their forces were quelled for fear of antagonizing the Germans.

In 1940, the combined strength of the active armies of Scandinavia and the Low Countries, excluding those of neutral Sweden and of Finland, which had been engaged in a bitter war with the Soviet Union, numbered somewhat more than 420,000. However, these were often poorly equipped and indeed only partially mechanized.

OTTO RUGE (1882–1961)

A career officer of the Norwegian Army, Ruge was an instructor at the National Military Academy from 1929 to 1933, and was later Chief of the General Staff. He was Inspector General of Infantry from 1938 to 1940.

- Controversial for his role in the reduction in size of the Norwegian Army in the 1930s and his criticism of its mobilization capabilities, Ruge was quickly promoted from Colonel to Major-General after the German invasion, replacing General Kristian Laake.
- Ruge advocated a strategy of delaying actions and retiring to the north, defending the city of Trondheim and awaiting assistance from Great Britain.
- Criticized for not allowing his troops to stand and fight more often, he nevertheless prevented his limited forces from being overwhelmed.
- Ruge signed the documents surrendering the Norwegian armed forces on 10 June 1940, and was a prisoner of the Germans until the end of the war.

He died at his residence in the commandant's quarters of Hoytorp Fortress after serving as commander-in-chief of Norway's post-war armed forces.

Denmark

The Royal Danish Army was hopelessly inadequate to confront the invading Germans when Hitler set Operation *Weserübung*, or Weser Exercise, in motion.

'…In order to counter British preparations to take away the neutrality of Denmark and Norway, the German *Wehrmacht* has taken over the armed defence of both nations,' read a communiqué from the German High Command on the morning of 9 April 1940. While the Germans were simultaneously assaulting Norway, the German ambassador to Denmark delivered an ultimatum to the Danish government to accept occupation by German troops or face the destruction of their capital, Copenhagen, from the air.

Within hours, the Danes surrendered, having offered little resistance and for the loss of only 26 dead and 23 wounded. More than 40,000 German troops were already on the march up the Jutland peninsula and disembarking from a merchant ship against little opposition in the harbour of Copenhagen, while airborne troops assaulted Aalborg airport and the Madneso fortress, which had already been abandoned.

Swift surrender

At the time, the Royal Danish Army consisted of only two divisions, Jutland and Zealand, and totalled less than

15,000 troops. Many of these soldiers had been drafted only weeks earlier and were essentially untrained. The Danes fielded no operational tanks. Mechanization consisted of motorcycles, light trucks and a few armoured cars. Eight infantry regiments were formed, with some companies actually employing bicycles, while two cavalry and three artillery regiments were operational. The Germans in Copenhagen quickly overwhelmed the city's garrison and marched towards Amalienborg Palace, the residence of King Christian X. The Danish Life Guard responded in defence, and a sharp clash ensued while the king and his ministers were inside assessing their limited options. In short order, the situation was recognized as futile, and the Life Guard surrendered. King Christian X remained in Copenhagen for the duration of the war.

For Danish honour

At other locations across the Danish-German frontier, sharp skirmishes occurred. One of the earliest of these involved the platoon-sized Lundtoftebjaerg Detachment, which was armed with a pair of 20mm (0.78in) cannon,

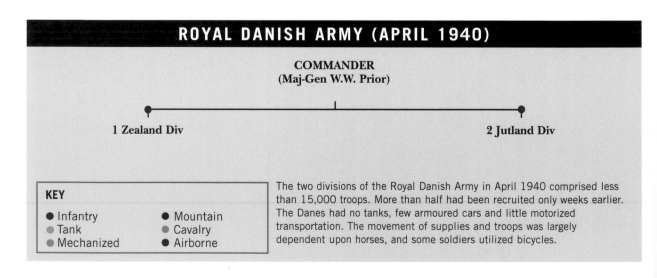

ROYAL DANISH ARMY (APRIL 1940)

COMMANDER
(Maj-Gen W.W. Prior)

1 Zealand Div   2 Jutland Div

KEY
- Infantry
- Tank
- Mechanized
- Mountain
- Cavalry
- Airborne

The two divisions of the Royal Danish Army in April 1940 comprised less than 15,000 troops. More than half had been recruited only weeks earlier. The Danes had no tanks, few armoured cars and little motorized transportation. The movement of supplies and troops was largely dependent upon horses, and some soldiers utilized bicycles.

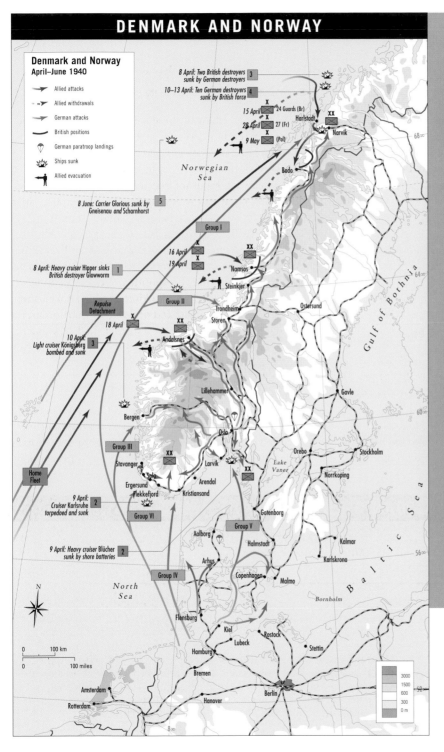

DENMARK AND NORWAY

Denmark and Norway
April–June 1940

- Allied attacks
- Allied withdrawals
- German attacks
- British positions
- German paratroop landings
- Ships sunk
- Allied evacuation

8 April: Two British destroyers sunk by German destroyers **3**

10–13 April: Ten German destroyers sunk by British force **4**

15 April ⊠ X 24 Guards (Br)
28 April ⊠ X 27 (Fr) Harlstadt
9 May ⊠ X (Pol) Narvik ⊠ XX

Norwegian Sea

Bodo

8 June: Carrier Glorious sunk by Gneisenau and Scharnhorst **5**

Group I

16 April ⊠ X
19 April ⊠ X ⊠ XX Namsos
Steinkjer

8 April: Heavy cruiser Hipper sinks British destroyer Glowworm **1**

Group II

Trondheim
Storen
Ostersund

Gulf of Bothnia

Repulse Detachment

18 April ⊠ X
Andalsnes ⊠ XX

10 April: Light cruiser Königsberg bombed and sunk **3**

Lillehammer
Gavle

Bergen

Oslo

Group III

Stavanger ⊠ XX
Egersund
Flekkefjord
Arendal
Kristiansand
Larvik ⊠ XX
Orebo
Lake Vanen
Stockholm
Norrkoping

Home Fleet

9 April: Cruiser Karlsruhe torpedoed and sunk **2**

Group VI

Gotenborg

9 April: Heavy cruiser Blücher sunk by shore batteries **2**

Group V

Aalborg
Halmstadt
Kalmar
Arhus
Karlskrona

Group IV

Copenhagen
Malmo

Baltic Sea

Bornholm

North Sea

N

0   100 km
0   100 miles

Flensburg
Kiel
Rostock
Lubeck
Stettin
Hamburg
Bremen
Berlin
Hanover
Amsterdam
Rotterdam

3000
1500
600
300
0 m

April–June 1940

Opposed by vastly superior German forces on 9 April 1940, a relative few troops of the Royal Danish Army fought briefly against the invaders in the harbour of Copenhagen, at the Amalienborg Palace and in southern Jutland. Under the threat of devastating air attack by the *Luftwaffe* as well, Denmark capitulated within hours.

Simultaneously, German troops invaded Norway at multiple locations. Oslo (the capital), Bergen, Trondheim and Narvik far to the north were assaulted by air and from the sea. Within three weeks, German forces were in control of much of southern Norway. Under the command of General Otto Ruge, the Royal Norwegian Army fought delaying actions in the centre and northern areas of the country and received some assistance from British and French expeditionary contingents. However, the collapse of France in May precipitated the withdrawal of Allied troops and the flight of the government of King Haakon VII, leaving the Royal Norwegian Army to fend for itself.

General Ruge's delaying tactics and skilful withdrawal proved effective, allowing him to hold out against overwhelming German forces for more than two months.

a light machine gun and other small arms, and took up positions astride one of the main roadways in eastern Jutland.

At approximately 4.50 a.m., a German column including armoured cars and motorcycles approached and opened fire on the Danish positions. The Danes replied, knocking out two armoured cars and three motorcycles before being outflanked by German tank and infantry support. A short time later, the Danes were cut off and forced to surrender, one soldier having been killed and another wounded. To the west, in the predawn hours of 9 April, about 50 soldiers who garrisoned the Non-commissioned Officer School at Toender were alerted minutes before German troops reached their barracks. Following a narrow escape, they turned on the German 11th Motorized Regiment near the towns of Abild and Soelstad. At both locations, 20mm (0.78in) guns of the auto-cannon platoon knocked out and damaged German armoured cars and thwarted an attempt to move around their flanks. After being stymied for nearly an hour, the German commander summoned air support, finally driving the stubborn Danes back to Bredebro, where they received the news that their government had capitulated.

Norway

Having relied heavily on a neutral political stance and assurance that Britain would come to its aid, Norway reeled before the onslaught of German arms before rallying to resist the invaders for weeks.

The geographic location of Norway played a key role in the prosecution of World War II. The Germans recognized the value of its iron ore and the ice-free port of Narvik from which it could be transited to Germany. They further realized that Allied occupation of Norway would mean a blockade of German shipping in the Baltic Sea. Norway could also provide Germany access to the Atlantic and a base of operations against Great Britain. For their part, the Norwegians chose butter over guns during the 1930s and maintained a relatively small

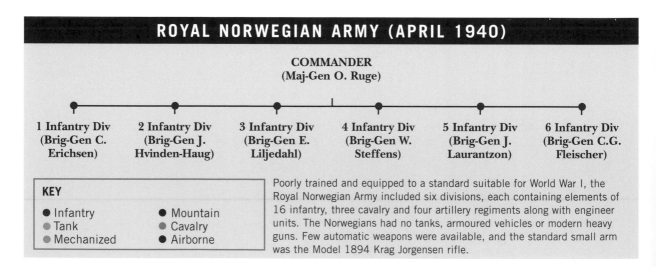

ROYAL NORWEGIAN ARMY (APRIL 1940)

COMMANDER
(Maj-Gen O. Ruge)

| 1 Infantry Div (Brig-Gen C. Erichsen) | 2 Infantry Div (Brig-Gen J. Hvinden-Haug) | 3 Infantry Div (Brig-Gen E. Liljedahl) | 4 Infantry Div (Brig-Gen W. Steffens) | 5 Infantry Div (Brig-Gen J. Laurantzon) | 6 Infantry Div (Brig-Gen C.G. Fleischer) |

KEY

● Infantry   ● Mountain
● Tank   ● Cavalry
● Mechanized   ● Airborne

Poorly trained and equipped to a standard suitable for World War I, the Royal Norwegian Army included six divisions, each containing elements of 16 infantry, three cavalry and four artillery regiments along with engineer units. The Norwegians had no tanks, armoured vehicles or modern heavy guns. Few automatic weapons were available, and the standard small arm was the Model 1894 Krag Jorgensen rifle.

army of approximately 15,000 experienced soldiers and reservists. Training for the Norwegian soldier was the shortest for any of the armed forces of Europe, as little as 48 days.

Desperate defence

At its peril, the government of Norway had neglected to modernize its army during the 1930s. Consequently,

when the German invasion came on 9 April 1940, Norway possessed no tanks or armoured vehicles and no weapons to repel those of an invader. The government itself, after receiving a warning of invasion from Great Britain, failed to authorize full mobilization.

Initially under General Kristian Laake and later General Otto Ruge, who conducted an admirable defensive campaign of delaying actions, the Royal

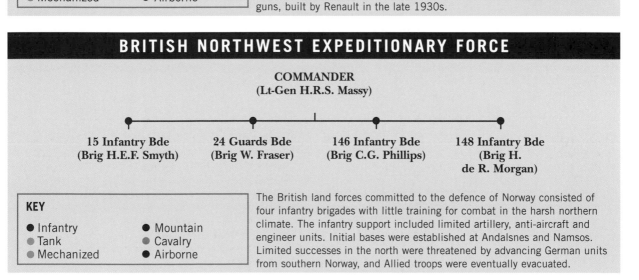

CORPS EXPEDITIONNAIRE FRANCAIS EN SCANDINAVIE

COMMANDER
(Lt-Gen S.G. Audet)

13e Demi Brigade Légion Etrangère (Col Magrin-Verneret)

1re Division Légère de Chasseurs (Gen M.A. Bethouart)

2e Division Légère de Chasseurs (Col Durand)

1re Division Légère d'Infanterie (Maj-Gen F.G.A. Duchemin)

BACP/SBSP

KEY
- Infantry
- Tank
- Mechanized
- Mountain
- Cavalry
- Airborne

Initially organized to provide assistance to Finland during its Winter War with the Soviet Red Army, the French Expeditionary Corps in Scandinavia was redirected to Norway in 1940, following the surrender of the Finns. The French force included the Char D2 tank, a second generation of the design armed with a 47mm (1.8in) cannon and 7.5mm (0.29in) machine guns, built by Renault in the late 1930s.

BRITISH NORTHWEST EXPEDITIONARY FORCE

COMMANDER
(Lt-Gen H.R.S. Massy)

15 Infantry Bde (Brig H.E.F. Smyth)

24 Guards Bde (Brig W. Fraser)

146 Infantry Bde (Brig C.G. Phillips)

148 Infantry Bde (Brig H. de R. Morgan)

KEY
- Infantry
- Tank
- Mechanized
- Mountain
- Cavalry
- Airborne

The British land forces committed to the defence of Norway consisted of four infantry brigades with little training for combat in the harsh northern climate. The infantry support included limited artillery, anti-aircraft and engineer units. Initial bases were established at Andalsnes and Namsos. Limited successes in the north were threatened by advancing German units from southern Norway, and Allied troops were eventually evacuated.

Norwegian Army was organized in six divisions with the designation relating more to a geographic region of operational control than to the size and strength of the unit.

Perhaps the division which most closely resembled that of other Allied fighting entities was the 2nd, based in the south at Ostlandet. Composed of three regiments of infantry, one each of artillery and engineers, two of dismounted dragoons and a pair of attached ad hoc infantry battalions, the 2nd Division surrendered to the Germans on 3 May, two weeks after the first British troops arrived at Lillehammer, when southern Norway was abandoned. In addition, the 1st and 5th Divisions were based at Holden and Oslo respectively, with the 3rd and 4th at Kristiansand and Bergen.

In the event, Norway's major cities, including its ports, were captured by six concurrent German assaults, while Oslo, the capital, was declared an open city and fell to a force of only 1500 airborne troops on the first day of fighting. In the north, combined Allied forces put up stiff resistance to the invaders but were unable to sustain any advantage gained.

Narvik gained

On 27 May, a force of 1250 Allied troops assaulted Narvik, capturing the city the following day. However, the fall of France made the lodgement untenable. Scarcely a month after their arrival, Allied soldiers were withdrawn from Norway. On 9 June 1940, the Royal Norwegian Army surrendered.

Holland

Unable to preserve their neutrality as they had done a quarter century earlier, the Dutch were overwhelmed by superior German forces after only four days of intense fighting.

The forlorn hope that Holland would be able to remain neutral during World War II was shattered on 10 May 1940, when Hitler unleashed *Fall Gelb* (Case Yellow), the invasion of France and the Low Countries. During the inter-war years, Dutch military spending had dwindled. Indeed, manpower consisted of a professional soldiery numbering only about 8000. It was not until April 1940 that the government finally authorized mobilization, at which point more than 100,000 new recruits and additional reservists raised troop levels to about 280,000.

The Dutch had formulated a series of defensive plans in the event of invasion, each of these involving fixed fortifications, tactical flooding of some areas, the use of natural barriers such as numerous rivers, and the defence of a national redoubt called 'Fortress Holland', which bordered the cities of Rotterdam in the south, Haarlem in the north and Utrecht to the east. In the centre of the country, the Grebbe Line would be heavily

Phoney War: 1939–40

The Phoney War, or *Sitzkrieg*, was characterized by a pronounced lack of combat activity on the Western Front from the German invasion of Poland on 1 September 1939, until Hitler launched *Fall Gelb* (Case Yellow), the invasion of France and the Low Countries (Holland, Belgium, Luxembourg), on 10 May 1940.

Although some skirmishing took place, direct confrontations were limited following the short-lived French Saar Offensive. Both sides engaged in extensive propaganda campaigns. While approximately 23 German divisions occupied their Siegfried Line fortifications, French and British troops opposed them behind the fixed defences of the Maginot Line. During the Phoney War, the presence of the British Expeditionary Force grew steadily on the European continent, and Allied troop strength swelled to 110 divisions.

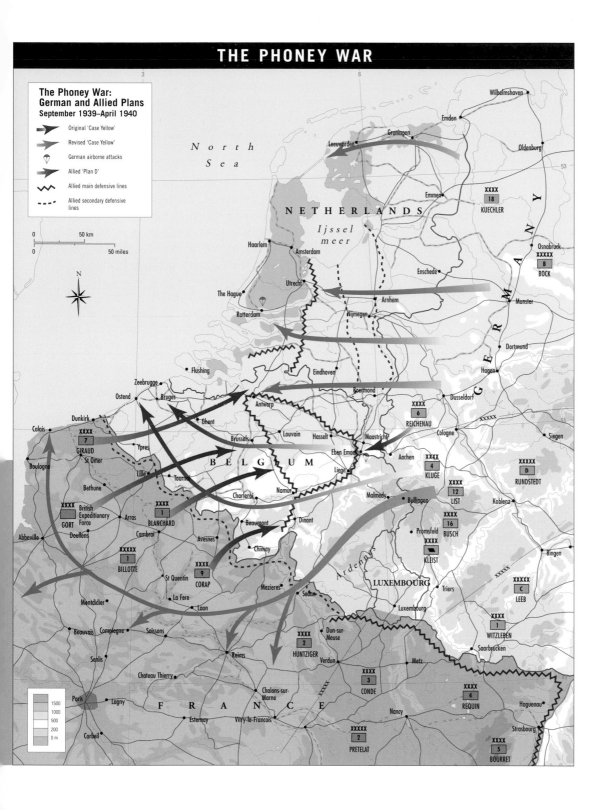

THE PHONEY WAR

**The Phoney War:
German and Allied Plans
September 1939–April 1940**

- Original 'Case Yellow'
- Revised 'Case Yellow'
- German airborne attacks
- Allied 'Plan D'
- Allied main defensive lines
- Allied secondary defensive lines

0   50 km
0   50 miles

N

*North
Sea*

Wilhelmshaven

Emden

Oldenburg

Groningen

Leeuwarden

Emmen

53

NETHERLANDS

*Ijssel
meer*

Haarlem

Amsterdam

Enschede

XXXX
18
KUECHLER

Osnabrück

XXXXX
B
BOCK

Utrecht

Arnhem

Münster

The Hague

Nijmegen

Dortmund

Rotterdam

Hagen

Flushing

Eindhoven

Roermond

Düsseldorf

Zeebrugge

Ostend

Bruges

Ghent

Antwerp

XXXX
6
REICHENAU

Cologne

Siegen

Dunkirk

Calais

XXXX
7
GIRAUD

St Omer

Ypres

Lille

Brussels

Louvain

Hasselt

Maastricht

Eben Emael

Aachen

XXXX
4
KLUGE

XXXXX
D
RUNDSTEDT

Boulogne

Bethune

Tournai

BELGIUM

Charleroi

Namur

Liège

Malmedy

Bullingen

XXXX
12
LIST

Koblenz

XXXX
British
Expeditionary
Force
GORT

Arras

XXXX
1
BLANCHARD

Beaumont

Dinant

Promsfeld

XXXX
16
BUSCH

Bingen

Abbeville

Doullens

Cambrai

Avesnes

Chimay

XXXX
KLEIST

XXXX
1
BILLOTTE

St Quentin

XXXX
9
CORAP

Mezieres

Sedan

Ardennes

LUXEMBOURG

Triers

XXXXX
C
LEEB

Montdidier

La Fere

Laon

Luxembourg

XXXX
1
WITZLEBEN

Beauvais

Compiegne

Saissons

Dun-sur-
Meuse

XXXX
2
HUNTZIGER

Reims

Verdun

Metz

Saarbrücken

Senlis

Chateau Thierry

Chalons-sur-
Marne

XXXX
3
CONDE

XXXX
4
REQUIN

Haguenau

Paris

Lagny

F R A N C E

Esternay

Vitry-le-Francois

Nancy

Strasbourg

XXXX
5
BOURRET

Corbeil

XXXXX
2
PRETELAT

1500
1000
500
200
0 m

31

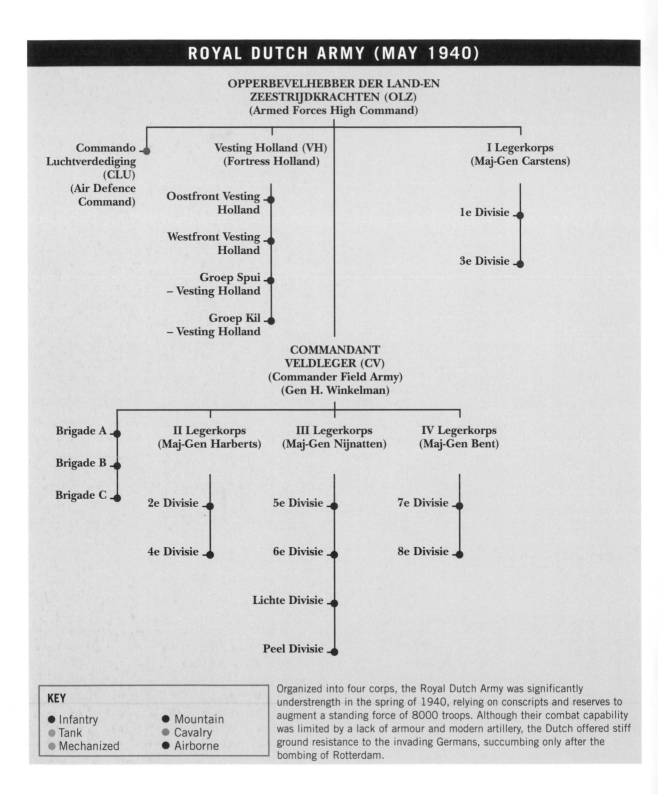

ROYAL DUTCH ARMY (MAY 1940)

OPPERBEVELHEBBER DER LAND-EN ZEESTRIJDKRACHTEN (OLZ)
(Armed Forces High Command)

Commando Luchtverdediging (CLU)
(Air Defence Command)

Vesting Holland (VH)
(Fortress Holland)

I Legerkorps
(Maj-Gen Carstens)

Oostfront Vesting Holland

Westfront Vesting Holland

Groep Spui – Vesting Holland

Groep Kil – Vesting Holland

1e Divisie

3e Divisie

COMMANDANT VELDLEGER (CV)
(Commander Field Army)
(Gen H. Winkelman)

Brigade A

Brigade B

Brigade C

II Legerkorps
(Maj-Gen Harberts)

III Legerkorps
(Maj-Gen Nijnatten)

IV Legerkorps
(Maj-Gen Bent)

2e Divisie

4e Divisie

5e Divisie

6e Divisie

Lichte Divisie

Peel Divisie

7e Divisie

8e Divisie

KEY

- Infantry
- Tank
- Mechanized
- Mountain
- Cavalry
- Airborne

Organized into four corps, the Royal Dutch Army was significantly understrength in the spring of 1940, relying on conscripts and reserves to augment a standing force of 8000 troops. Although their combat capability was limited by a lack of armour and modern artillery, the Dutch offered stiff ground resistance to the invading Germans, succumbing only after the bombing of Rotterdam.

ROYAL DUTCH ARMY: INFANTRY DIVISIONS		
Division	**Commander**	**Regiments**
1e	Col W.F.K. Bischoff v. Heemskerk	Grenadiers, Jagers, 4
2e	Col A.M.M. v. Loon	10, 15, 22
3e	Col L.H. Kraak	1, 9, 12
4e	(not known)	8, 11, 19
5e	(not known)	2, 13, 17
6e	(not known)	3, 6, 14
7e	Col F.B.A.J. Jansen	7, 18, 20
8e	Col A. de Vries	5, 16, 21

defended. The strategy was complicated by political considerations, including concerns about unduly antagonizing the Germans.

Dutch dilemma

In reality, the Royal Dutch Army was significantly overmatched when the Germans crossed the border. Organized into four corps, located at Amersfoort, Arnhem, Breda and Amsterdam, the army was commanded by General Henri Winkelman. It included eight infantry divisions; a few heavy artillery regiments; a light brigade of bicycle troops, armoured cars and cavalry; two anti-aircraft regiments; and a few independent reconnaissance battalions.

Dutch weaponry was woefully inadequate. When the need to modernize was recognized, several orders for updated equipment went to Germany, which, naturally, did not deliver. Artillery consisted primarily of antiquated howitzers, some firing only black powder shells. Twelve Landsverk and 12 DAF M39 armoured cars, along with five Carden-Loyd Mark VI tankettes comprised the bulk of the Royal Dutch Army's armour. A single Renault FT-17 tank had been used to test anti-tank obstacles.

Stiff resistance

Despite its shortcomings in men and materiel, the Royal Dutch Army fought valiantly during its brief confrontation with the German *Wehrmacht*. An airborne assault on The Hague, intended to capture the city and take the Dutch royal family into custody, was embarrassingly unsuccessful, while the German offensive ground to a halt before the Grebbe Line and other fixed fortifications.

In the south, the Germans made rapid progress and reached the outskirts of Rotterdam, while the Grebbe Line was finally overrun on 13 May. Although the situation was obviously hopeless, the Dutch refused to surrender. Furious, Hitler ordered the terror bombing of Rotterdam on 14 May and warned that the other major cities of Holland would suffer a similar fate if resistance persisted. The Dutch capitulated that evening.

Belgium

A battleground for centuries during European conflicts, Belgium was drawn into World War II despite its policy of neutrality.

Overrun by the German Army during World War I, Belgium maintained close military and political ties with France until the mid-1930s, when the government of King Leopold III announced a firm policy of neutrality. Concurrently, a programme of military modernization was undertaken and the length of service for draftees was extended to 17 months. Although the Belgians were alarmed by the rise of Nazi militarism, their armed forces did not participate in military exercises with either Britain or France after 1936. Some lingering distrust of the French persisted, with a number of Belgian leaders believing that the primary French strategy for defence involved fighting the Germans on Belgian territory.

On 10 May 1940, Belgium fielded an army of 100,000 regular troops and a fully mobilized strength of 550,000.

These were organized into five active corps and two reserve corps, which included attached artillery regiments and battalions of engineers. Two cavalry divisions were partially mechanized; however, the bicycle remained a prevalent form of transportation.

As with others of Western Europe and Scandinavia, the Belgian Army was severely lacking in armoured strength. Only 42 operational tanks were available in 1940. These consisted of the British-built T-13 and T-15, variants of the Vickers-Carden-Loyd Model 1934. Weighing about 5.4 tonnes (6 tons), the T-13 was armed with a 47mm (1.8in) cannon, while the T-15 mounted a French Hotchkiss 13.2mm (0.5in) machine gun. Eight of the tanks were the French Renault Model 1935 ACG-1, armed with a 47mm (1.8in) cannon and a secondary machine gun. Additionally, much of the artillery, small arms, and other equipment were either antiquated or in short supply.

The Belgian Army resisted the Germans for 18 days, often engaging in sharp battles. However, the issue was never seriously in doubt. A daring assault by German glider-borne troops captured Fort Eben Emael, considered one of the strongest fixed defensive positions in all of Europe, during the opening hours of the invasion. Other defences along the Albert Canal were breached as the Germans quickly established bridgeheads. Some British and French troops crossed into Belgium to offer assistance. Chaos reigned, and when the first British troops arrived on 11 May, they were promptly fired on by Belgian soldiers.

German armoured spearheads raced through the Ardennes and to the English Channel at Abbeville, France, by 21 May, threatening to cut off and encircle Allied troops to the north. Having suffered nearly 16,000 dead and wounded, Belgium surrendered on 28 May.

BELGIAN ARMY (MAY 1940)	
Weapon/Unit	Strength
Troops	550,000
Automatic Weapons	8640
Anti–Tank Weapons	324
Heavy Artillery	384
Tanks	42
CORPS	
Infantry	7
Cavalry	1
DIVISIONS	
Infantry	20
Cavalry	2
Bicycle Battalions	3

BELGIAN ARMOURED DISTRIBUTION (MAY 1940)			
Unit	T-13	T-15	ACG-1
1re Division d'Infanterie	12	–	–
2e Division d'Infanterie	12	–	–
3e Division d'Infanterie	12	–	–
4e Division d'Infanterie	12	–	–
7e Division d'Infanterie (R)	12	–	–
8e Division d'Infanterie (R)	12	–	–
9e Division d'Infanterie (R)	12	–	–
10e Division d'Infanterie (R)	12	–	–
11e Division d'Infanterie (R)	12	–	–
1re Division des Chasseurs Ardennais	48	3	–
2e Division des Chasseurs Ardennais	–	3	–
Compagnie Ind de l'Unité Cyclistes Frontière	12	–	–
8e Compagnie de l'Unité Cyclistes Frontière	12	–	–
Compagnie PFL de l'Unité de Forteresse	12	–	–
1re Division de Cavalerie			
1er Régiment de Guides	6	6	–
2e Régiment de Lanciers	6	6	–
3e Régiment de Lanciers	6	6	–
2e Division de Cavalerie			
1er Régiment de Lanciers	6	6	–
1er Régiment de Chasseurs	6	6	–
2e Régiment de Chasseurs	6	6	–
Escadron d'Autoblindées	–	–	8

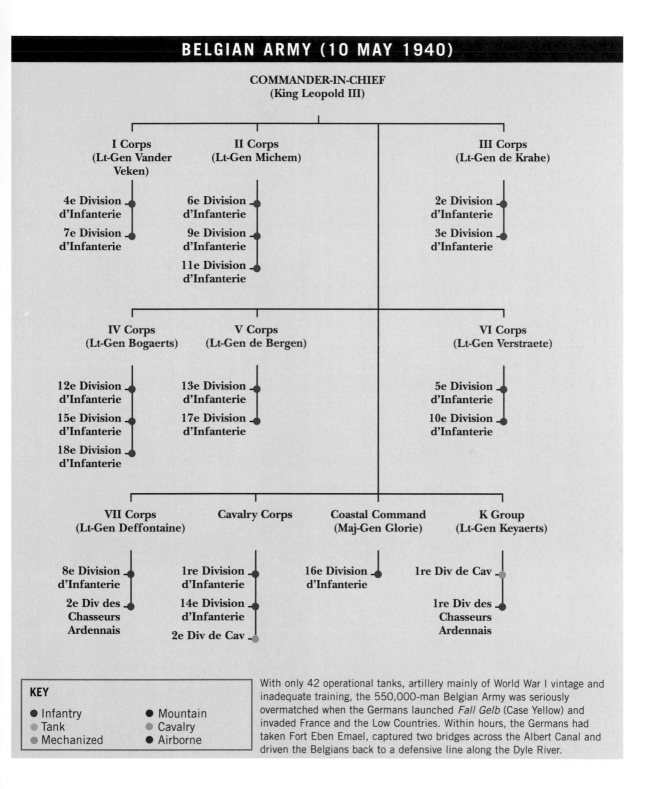

BELGIAN ARMY (10 MAY 1940)

COMMANDER-IN-CHIEF
(King Leopold III)

I Corps
(Lt-Gen Vander Veken)

- 4e Division d'Infanterie
- 7e Division d'Infanterie

II Corps
(Lt-Gen Michem)

- 6e Division d'Infanterie
- 9e Division d'Infanterie
- 11e Division d'Infanterie

III Corps
(Lt-Gen de Krahe)

- 2e Division d'Infanterie
- 3e Division d'Infanterie

IV Corps
(Lt-Gen Bogaerts)

- 12e Division d'Infanterie
- 15e Division d'Infanterie
- 18e Division d'Infanterie

V Corps
(Lt-Gen de Bergen)

- 13e Division d'Infanterie
- 17e Division d'Infanterie

VI Corps
(Lt-Gen Verstraete)

- 5e Division d'Infanterie
- 10e Division d'Infanterie

VII Corps
(Lt-Gen Deffontaine)

- 8e Division d'Infanterie
- 2e Div des Chasseurs Ardennais

Cavalry Corps

- 1re Division d'Infanterie
- 14e Division d'Infanterie
- 2e Div de Cav

Coastal Command
(Maj-Gen Glorie)

- 16e Division d'Infanterie

K Group
(Lt-Gen Keyaerts)

- 1re Div de Cav
- 1re Div des Chasseurs Ardennais

KEY

- Infantry
- Tank
- Mechanized
- Mountain
- Cavalry
- Airborne

With only 42 operational tanks, artillery mainly of World War I vintage and inadequate training, the 550,000-man Belgian Army was seriously overmatched when the Germans launched *Fall Gelb* (Case Yellow) and invaded France and the Low Countries. Within hours, the Germans had taken Fort Eben Emael, captured two bridges across the Albert Canal and driven the Belgians back to a defensive line along the Dyle River.

Battle of France: 1940

The French Army stood as the primary deterrent to Nazi aggression in Western Europe; however, it proved no match for the highly mobile, mechanized *Wehrmacht* and collapsed within weeks.

A French anti-aircraft crew undergo training on the Franco-German border during the 'Phoney War' period.

Changing military doctrine, along with political and economic influences, contributed greatly to the Allied debacle on the Western Front in the spring of 1940. A generation earlier, Great Britain and France had been victorious in World War I. The cost in lives and resources, however, had been tremendous. France alone had suffered nearly 1.5 million dead and more than four million wounded. The legacy of the war cast a lengthy shadow across the French military and political landscape during the 1920s and 1930s.

French military leaders, many of whom had risen to prominence during World War I, were haunted by the horror of the slaughter at Verdun and the Marne. A repeat was too terrible to contemplate. Therefore, the military dictum of *attaque á l'outrance,* or attack to extreme, which had led to orders for massed infantry assaults against a well-entrenched enemy, was discarded.

The Maginot Line

Constructed during the 1930s at a cost of three billion francs, the Maginot Line was a series of fixed fortifications extending from Basel on the Swiss frontier to the border of France and Belgium. The Maginot Line exemplified the changing French doctrine of the continuous front or static defence. Rather than absorbing the staggering casualties of offensive warfare, French commanders opted to confront their traditional enemy, Germany, with a formidable line of fortifications that would be extremely costly to assault. However, the line did not extend along the French-Belgian border to the English Channel coast. The French reasoned that the Maginot Line would deter a direct assault from the west and northwest, while the central region of the Ardennes, with its rolling terrain and heavy forest, provided a natural barrier against invasion. Should the Germans come again, the French expected a repeat of the 1914 Schlieffen Plan, in which the attackers overran Belgium and then pivoted into French territory. Thus, the French Army would advance northwards into Belgium and defend a line along the Dyle River.

Complicating factors

A critical element of the French defensive plan was the continued cooperation of Belgium, which had been an ally during World War I. In 1936, however, following the German occupation of the Rhineland, the Belgians adopted an official policy of neutrality. When the Germans invaded four years later, the two nations had not participated in joint military exercises and had no formal military lines of communication. Further, a number of high-ranking French officers failed clearly to comprehend the imminent threat posed by Nazi Germany and considered the rise of the Soviet Union and communism of greater concern.

The Great Depression meant that funds appropriated to the military for a rearmament programme in the mid-1930s were not always fully or properly utilized by the French High Command, who were elderly and in the twilight of their careers as World War II approached, their minds closed to the complexities of modern warfare. For example, while the French Army did possess some modern equipment, its primary means of communication were of World War I vintage: the French Army continued to rely primarily on the antiquated telegraph, dispatch runners and riders, and even carrier pigeons. Each of these was susceptible to the hazards of the modern battlefield and considerably less reliable than radio communications technology available at the time. As with overall military strategy, the senior commanders were slow to grasp the importance of efficient troop movement and the deployment of support forces, which could have been greatly enhanced with better communications capabilities.

FRENCH ARMY: DIVISIONAL STRENGTH (1940)	
Division type	**Strength**
Infantry	63
North African & Colonial Infantry	21
Armoured	6
Light Mechanized	3
Motorized	9
Mountain	3
Light	10
Cavalry	5
Fortress	13
Artillery Guns	10,700
Tanks	3254

The French Army

Although France possessed the largest army in Western Europe, the illusion of its military might was shattered by the onslaught of the German *Wehrmacht* and the new *Blitzkrieg* tactics practised by Generals Heinz Guderian and Erich von Manstein.

When the Nazis invaded Poland, the greatest concern for Adolf Hitler may well have been the powerful French Army. Firm action by the French would place Germany in a precarious position, fighting a defensive war in the west while the bulk of its army was engaged in the conquest of Poland hundreds of kilometres to the east. The *Führer*'s greatest fear actually began to take shape within days. However, France's Saar Offensive was short-lived. French troops advanced only eight kilometres (five miles) into Germany and were soon ordered to withdraw.

One of the reasons for the withdrawal may have been the Maginot Line mentality, the emphasis on fighting a defensive war. Such a strategy seems ironic given that, in the spring of 1940, the French Army fielded 84 infantry divisions (including 21 made up of colonial troops), along with six armoured, three light mechanized and nine motorized divisions. Nearly 140,000 active and reserve officers led an army of 900,000 in 1939, swelling to more than five million with full mobilization.

Formidable strength

The standard French infantry division on the eve of World War II consisted of three regiments totalling roughly 17,500 men. Four reconnaissance squadrons and two regiments of artillery were attached along with a complement of anti-tank weapons. The French began forming an initial armoured division in 1939, organizing the prototype around a battalion of mechanized infantry, towed artillery and two battalions each of the capable Char B and Hotchkiss light tanks.

By 1940, three major army groups defended France against invasion. The 22 divisions of the First Army Group occupied positions on the Belgian frontier between Longuyon and Maulde, while the 43 divisions of the Second and Third Army Groups garrisoned the Maginot Line and the surrounding area. The Seventh

Army Group, consisting of seven divisions, protected the major English Channel ports of Calais and Dunkirk, while 22 divisions were ostensibly held in reserve.

Although its manpower was second to none, the French Army's combat efficiency was severely degraded during the eight months of the Phoney War. Conscripts resented their countrymen who were not yet in

FRENCH ARMY: LT CAVALRY DIVISIONS (MAY 1940)		
Division	**Regiments**	**Subordinate unit**
1re DLC	2e BC	1e Chasseurs 19e Dragoons
	11e BLM	1re RAM 5e RDP
	75e RATT	10e BDAC
2e DLC	3e BC	18e Chasseurs 5e Cuirassiers
	12e BLM	2e RAM 3e RDP
	73e RATT	10e BDAC
3e DLC	5e BC	4e Hussards 6e Dragoons
	13e BLM	3e RAM 2e RDP
	72e RATT	10e BDAC
4e DLC	4e BC	8e Dragoons 31e Dragoons
	14e BLM	4e RAM 14e RDP
	77e RATT	–
5e DLC	6e BC	11e Cuirassiers 12e Chasseurs
	15e BLM	5e RAM 15e RDP
	78e RATT	10e BDAC

1RE *DIVISION LÉGÈRE MÉCANIQUE* (1RE DLM), 4E CUIRASSIERS

The 4th Cuirassiers regiment of *1re Division Légère Mécanique* (1st Light Mechanized Division) included 48 Somua medium tanks armed with a 47mm (1.8in) cannon and 7.5mm (0.29in) machine gun, along with 47 Hotchkiss H-35 light tanks armed with a 37mm (1.45in) cannon and a 7.5mm (0.29in) machine gun. The 4th Cuirassiers fought in Flanders along the Dyle River line and during the evacuation at Dunkirk. The Somua was a match for any German or Allied tank in service. The Hotchkiss H-35 was rejected by French infantry commanders and accepted by the cavalry.

Somua medium tanks x 48

Hotchkiss H-35 light tanks x 47

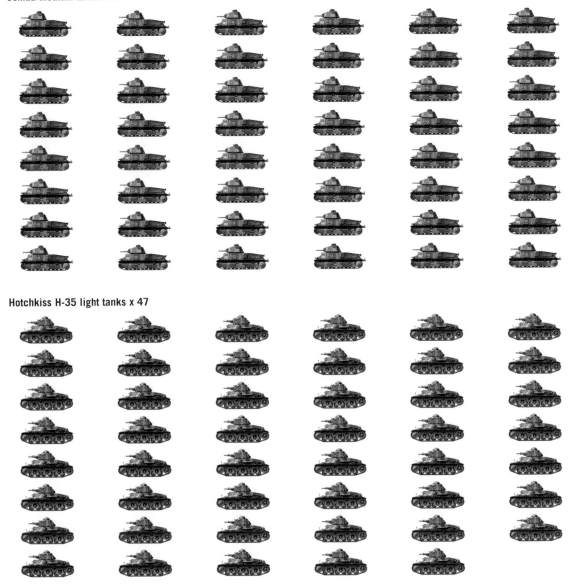

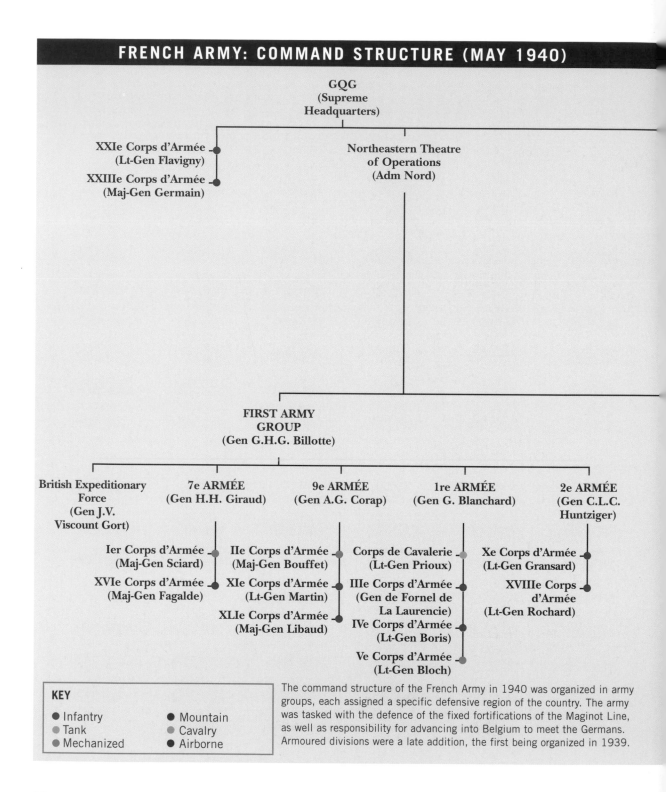

FRENCH ARMY: COMMAND STRUCTURE (MAY 1940)

GQG
(Supreme
Headquarters)

XXIe Corps d'Armée
(Lt-Gen Flavigny)

XXIIIe Corps d'Armée
(Maj-Gen Germain)

Northeastern Theatre
of Operations
(Adm Nord)

FIRST ARMY
GROUP
(Gen G.H.G. Billotte)

British Expeditionary
Force
(Gen J.V.
Viscount Gort)

7e ARMÉE
(Gen H.H. Giraud)

9e ARMÉE
(Gen A.G. Corap)

1re ARMÉE
(Gen G. Blanchard)

2e ARMÉE
(Gen C.L.C.
Huntziger)

Ier Corps d'Armée
(Maj-Gen Sciard)

XVIe Corps d'Armée
(Maj-Gen Fagalde)

IIe Corps d'Armée
(Maj-Gen Bouffet)

XIe Corps d'Armée
(Lt-Gen Martin)

XLIe Corps d'Armée
(Maj-Gen Libaud)

Corps de Cavalerie
(Lt-Gen Prioux)

IIIe Corps d'Armée
(Gen de Fornel de
La Laurencie)

IVe Corps d'Armée
(Lt-Gen Boris)

Ve Corps d'Armée
(Lt-Gen Bloch)

Xe Corps d'Armée
(Lt-Gen Gransard)

XVIIIe Corps
d'Armée
(Lt-Gen Rochard)

KEY

● Infantry
● Mountain
● Tank
● Cavalry
● Mechanized
● Airborne

The command structure of the French Army in 1940 was organized in army groups, each assigned a specific defensive region of the country. The army was tasked with the defence of the fixed fortifications of the Maginot Line, as well as responsibility for advancing into Belgium to meet the Germans. Armoured divisions were a late addition, the first being organized in 1939.

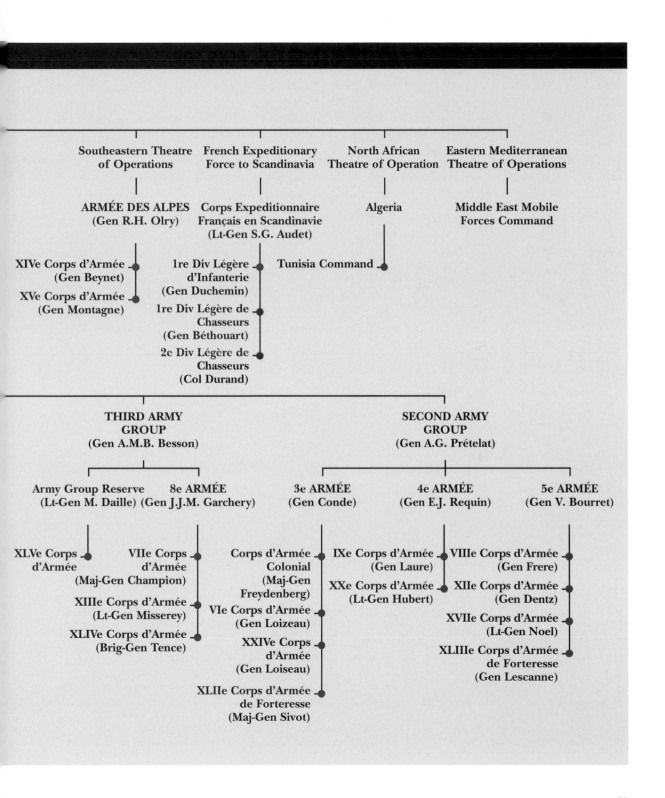

Southeastern Theatre
of Operations

French Expeditionary
Force to Scandinavia

North African
Theatre of Operation

Eastern Mediterranean
Theatre of Operations

ARMÉE DES ALPES
(Gen R.H. Olry)

Corps Expeditionnaire
Français en Scandinavie
(Lt-Gen S.G. Audet)

Algeria

Middle East Mobile
Forces Command

XIVe Corps d'Armée
(Gen Beynet)

XVe Corps d'Armée
(Gen Montagne)

1re Div Légère
d'Infanterie
(Gen Duchemin)

1re Div Légère de
Chasseurs
(Gen Béthouart)

2e Div Légère de
Chasseurs
(Col Durand)

Tunisia Command

THIRD ARMY
GROUP
(Gen A.M.B. Besson)

SECOND ARMY
GROUP
(Gen A.G. Prételat)

Army Group Reserve
(Lt-Gen M. Daille)

8e ARMÉE
(Gen J.J.M. Garchery)

3e ARMÉE
(Gen Conde)

4e ARMÉE
(Gen E.J. Requin)

5e ARMÉE
(Gen V. Bourret)

XLVe Corps
d'Armée
(Maj-Gen Champion)

VIIe Corps
d'Armée

XIIIe Corps d'Armée
(Lt-Gen Misserey)

XLIVe Corps d'Armée
(Brig-Gen Tence)

Corps d'Armée
Colonial
(Maj-Gen
Freydenberg)

VIe Corps d'Armée
(Gen Loizeau)

XXIVe Corps
d'Armée
(Gen Loiseau)

XLIIe Corps d'Armée
de Forteresse
(Maj-Gen Sivot)

IXe Corps d'Armée
(Gen Laure)

XXe Corps d'Armée
(Lt-Gen Hubert)

VIIIe Corps d'Armée
(Gen Frere)

XIIe Corps d'Armée
(Gen Dentz)

XVIIe Corps d'Armée
(Lt-Gen Noel)

XLIIIe Corps d'Armée
de Forteresse
(Gen Lescanne)

uniform. Commanders, both junior and senior, were often indifferent to a lack of discipline among the troops, who were frequently absent without leave. These issues were compounded by lengthy periods of inactivity, during which opportunities for training were squandered. Contrary to popular belief, the French Army was comparatively well equipped. Although half its 10,700 artillery pieces were produced during World War I, it still outgunned the Germans. Of 3254 tanks, 260 were the modern Somua S-35, equipped

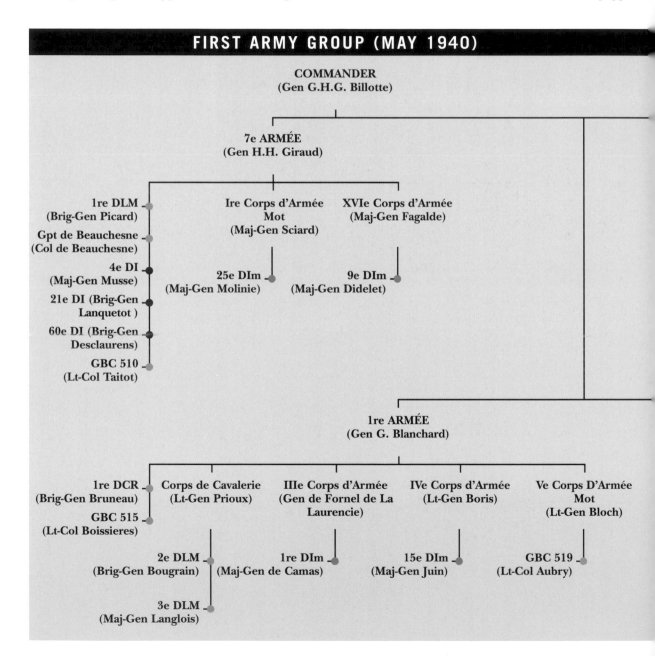

FIRST ARMY GROUP (MAY 1940)

COMMANDER
(Gen G.H.G. Billotte)

7e ARMÉE
(Gen H.H. Giraud)

1re DLM
(Brig-Gen Picard)

Gpt de Beauchesne
(Col de Beauchesne)

4e DI
(Maj-Gen Musse)

21e DI (Brig-Gen Lanquetot)

60e DI (Brig-Gen Desclaurens)

GBC 510
(Lt-Col Taitot)

Ire Corps d'Armée Mot
(Maj-Gen Sciard)

25e DIm
(Maj-Gen Molinie)

XVIe Corps d'Armée
(Maj-Gen Fagalde)

9e DIm
(Maj-Gen Didelet)

1re ARMÉE
(Gen G. Blanchard)

1re DCR
(Brig-Gen Bruneau)

GBC 515
(Lt-Col Boissieres)

Corps de Cavalerie
(Lt-Gen Prioux)

2e DLM
(Brig-Gen Bougrain)

3e DLM
(Maj-Gen Langlois)

IIIe Corps d'Armée
(Gen de Fornel de La Laurencie)

1re DIm
(Maj-Gen de Camas)

IVe Corps d'Armée
(Lt-Gen Boris)

15e DIm
(Maj-Gen Juin)

Ve Corps D'Armée Mot
(Lt-Gen Bloch)

GBC 519
(Lt-Col Aubry)

with a 47mm (1.8in) cannon and a 7.5mm (0.29in) machine gun. This was considered by many to be more than a match for any Allied or German tank then in production. Further, the French tank inventory outnumbered that of the Germans by nearly 800.

The failure of the French Army in 1940 lay in its defensive doctrine, communications reliant on couriers and pigeons, artillery and infantry formations that depended on horse-drawn transportation, and primarily in the employment of armour. 'Not even the most

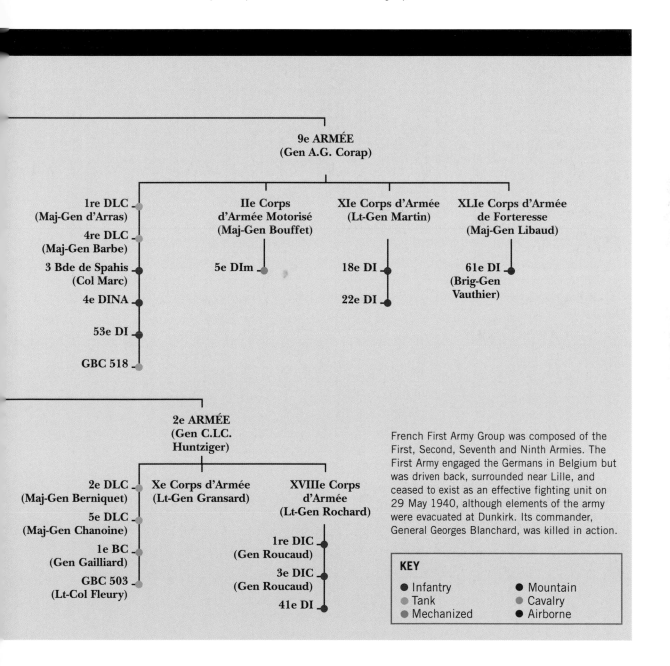

9e ARMÉE
(Gen A.G. Corap)

1re DLC
(Maj-Gen d'Arras)

4re DLC
(Maj-Gen Barbe)

3 Bde de Spahis
(Col Marc)

4e DINA

53e DI

GBC 518

IIe Corps
d'Armée Motorisé
(Maj-Gen Bouffet)

5e DIm

XIe Corps d'Armée
(Lt-Gen Martin)

18e DI

22e DI

XLIe Corps d'Armée
de Forteresse
(Maj-Gen Libaud)

61e DI
(Brig-Gen
Vauthier)

2e ARMÉE
**(Gen C.LC.
Huntziger)**

2e DLC
(Maj-Gen Berniquet)

5e DLC
(Maj-Gen Chanoine)

1e BC
(Gen Gailliard)

GBC 503
(Lt-Col Fleury)

Xe Corps d'Armée
(Lt-Gen Gransard)

XVIIIe Corps
d'Armée
(Lt-Gen Rochard)

1re DIC
(Gen Roucaud)

3e DIC
(Gen Roucaud)

41e DI

French First Army Group was composed of the First, Second, Seventh and Ninth Armies. The First Army engaged the Germans in Belgium but was driven back, surrounded near Lille, and ceased to exist as an effective fighting unit on 29 May 1940, although elements of the army were evacuated at Dunkirk. Its commander, General Georges Blanchard, was killed in action.

KEY

● Infantry ● Mountain
● Tank ● Cavalry
● Mechanized ● Airborne

DLM UNITS AND STRENGTHS (10 MAY 1940)			
Division	Regiment	Equipment	Strength
1re DLM	4e Cuirassiers	Somua S-35 Hotchkiss H-35	48 47
	18e Dragoons	Somua S-35 Hotchkiss H-35	48 47
	4e RDP	AMR	69
	6e Cuirassiers	AMD Panhard 178	48
	74e RATT	75mm Gun 105mm Howitzer	24 12
	10e BDAC	47mm AT Gun	8
	1020/405 Bie	25mm AA Gun	6
2e DLM	13e Dragoons	Somua S-35 Hotchkiss H-35	48 47
	29e Dragoons	Somua S-35 Hotchkiss H-35	48 47
	1e RDP	AMR	69
	8e Cuirassiers	AMD Panhard 178	48
	71e RATT	75mm Gun 105mm Howitzer	24 12
	10e BDAC	47mm AT Gun	8
	1018/405 Bie	25mm AA Gun	6
3e DLM	1e Cuirassiers	Somua S-35 Hotchkiss H-39	48 47
	2e Cuirassiers	Somua S-35 Hotchkiss H-39	48 47
	11e RDP	AMR	69
	12e Cuirassiers	AMD Panhard 178	48
	76e RATT	75mm Gun 105mm Howitzer	24 12
	10e BDAC	47mm AT Gun	8
	1023/404 Bie	25mm AA Gun	6
4e DLM	3e Cuirassiers	Somua S-35 Hotchkiss H-39	48 47
	7e Cuirassiers	Somua S-35 Hotchkiss H-39	48 47
	7e RDP	–	–
	10e Cuirassiers	AMD Panhard 178	48

DIm UNITS AND EQUIPMENT (10 MAY 1940)		
Division	Regiment	Equipment
1re DIm	7e GRDIm	Panhard 178 P-16
	1re RIm	–
	43e RIm	–
	110e RIm	–
3e DIm	6e GRDIm	Panhard 178 P-16
	51e RIm	–
	67e RIm	–
	91e RIm	–
5e DIm	1re GRDIm	Panhard 178 P-16
	8e RIm	–
	39e RIm	–
	129e RIm	–
9e DIm	2e GRDIm	Panhard 178 H-39
	13e RIm	–
	95e RIm	–
	131e RIm	–
12e DIm	3e GRDIm	Panhard 178 P-16
	8e RIm	–
	106e RIm	–
	150e RIm	–
15e DIm	4e GRDIm	Laffly P-16
	4e RIm	–
	27e RIm	–
	134e RIm	–
25e DIm	5e GRDIm	Panhard 178 H-35
	38e RIm	–
	92e RIm	–
	121e RIm	–

modern tanks can ever lead the fighting by themselves and for themselves,' said the December 1938 issue of *French Military Review*. Unlike the Germans, who used tanks as armoured spearheads, the French required their tanks to support infantry operations, thus restricting their speed and mobility.

BEF in France

The British Expeditionary Force (BEF) fought a valiant rearguard action against the Germans in Belgium and France before its encirclement along the coast of the English Channel at Dunkirk.

Within a week of the British declaration of war on 3 September 1939, four infantry divisions, elements of the British Expeditionary Force, were on the European continent to bolster defences. Led by General John Vereker, 6th Viscount Gort, these were the vanguard of an army that grew to 150,000 men and 21,000 vehicles prior to reaching a peak of 400,000 in the spring of 1940, its 10 divisions organized into three corps.

British preparations for movement to the Continent had been underway for some time, and on the day before the declaration of war the Royal Air Force had flown 49 officers and men of the British Army to France. During the following four weeks, the British Mercantile Marine delivered 32,600 tonnes (36,000 tons) of ammunition, 22,680 tonnes (25,000 tons) of petrol and 54,430 tonnes (60,000 tons) of frozen meat.

While the British Army was the most highly mechanized in the world, the only contiguous armoured units within the BEF were two battalions of the Royal Tank Regiment, assigned to the First Army Tank Brigade. The units included the Mk III Cruiser tank and the Matilda I and II. The Cruiser carried a 2-pounder cannon and a Vickers .303 (7.62mm) machine gun. Both Matilda variants were designed as infantry support tanks.

Continental deployment

The British were nominally under French command, but Gort was given the latitude to seek the approval of the British government before carrying out any order to which he objected. The initial disposition of BEF units in France was to the area of Bailleul and Maulde, northeast of the city of Douai. In May 1940, one of its 10 infantry divisions, the 51st Highland, had been diverted to the Saar to strengthen the Maginot Line. Located between the French First Army to the south and

JOHN VEREKER, 6TH VISCOUNT GORT (1886–1946)

Commander of the British Expeditionary Force in France and Belgium, John Standish Surtees Prendergast Vereker, 6th Viscount Gort (pictured right) was born in London in 1886. A graduate of the Royal Military Academy, Woolwich, he became an officer of the Grenadier Guards in 1905. Awarded the Victoria Cross for action at the Battle of Canal du Nord, on 27 September 1918, he was wounded twice during World War I.

• Gort was promoted to full general in 1937 and subsequently appointed Chief of the Imperial Staff.

• Appointed BEF commander in 1939, he arrived in France on 19 September and directed operations which ended with the evacuation at Dunkirk.

• He was appointed General Aide-de-Camp to King George VI on 25 June 1940.

• Gort later served as Governor of Gibraltar and then as Governor of Malta, where he was elevated to the rank of field marshal in June 1943. When the war ended, he was serving as High Commissioner for Palestine and Transjordan.

Gort died of cancer on 31 March 1946.

the Seventh Army to the north, the BEF was responsible in part for the defence of a 322km (200-mile) stretch of the French frontier. During the Phoney War, BEF troops engaged in training and continued to provision, but when the Germans launched *Fall Gelb,* or Case Yellow, and attacked France and the Low Countries many BEF troops were not fully equipped and a number of units were not adequately trained.

When the German attack began on 10 May 1940, French strategy played into the hands of the attackers. While tactically vital objectives were seized during strong feints against the Low Countries, the French and British advanced into Belgium, expecting to meet the main German thrust into France. Meanwhile, German tanks were dashing through the Ardennes and threatening to cut off the advancing Allies, splitting France in two.

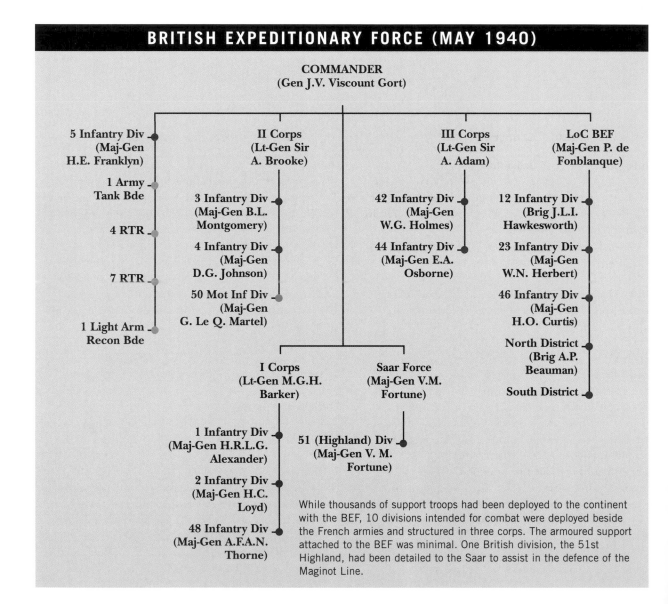

BRITISH EXPEDITIONARY FORCE (MAY 1940)

COMMANDER
(Gen J.V. Viscount Gort)

5 Infantry Div
(Maj-Gen H.E. Franklyn)

1 Army Tank Bde

4 RTR

7 RTR

1 Light Arm Recon Bde

II Corps
(Lt-Gen Sir A. Brooke)

3 Infantry Div
(Maj-Gen B.L. Montgomery)

4 Infantry Div
(Maj-Gen D.G. Johnson)

50 Mot Inf Div
(Maj-Gen G. Le Q. Martel)

III Corps
(Lt-Gen Sir A. Adam)

42 Infantry Div
(Maj-Gen W.G. Holmes)

44 Infantry Div
(Maj-Gen E.A. Osborne)

LoC BEF
(Maj-Gen P. de Fonblanque)

12 Infantry Div
(Brig J.L.I. Hawkesworth)

23 Infantry Div
(Maj-Gen W.N. Herbert)

46 Infantry Div
(Maj-Gen H.O. Curtis)

North District
(Brig A.P. Beauman)

South District

I Corps
(Lt-Gen M.G.H. Barker)

Saar Force
(Maj-Gen V.M. Fortune)

1 Infantry Div
(Maj-Gen H.R.L.G. Alexander)

51 (Highland) Div
(Maj-Gen V. M. Fortune)

2 Infantry Div
(Maj-Gen H.C. Loyd)

48 Infantry Div
(Maj-Gen A.F.A.N. Thorne)

While thousands of support troops had been deployed to the continent with the BEF, 10 divisions intended for combat were deployed beside the French armies and structured in three corps. The armoured support attached to the BEF was minimal. One British division, the 51st Highland, had been detailed to the Saar to assist in the defence of the Maginot Line.

Allied troops began moving into Belgium at 7.30 a.m. on 11 May, but the French ran into trouble when their troops were transported by rail to the border and no Belgian locomotives were available to complete the deployment to the Dyle River line. Belgian troops had also failed to remove roadblocks, and French engineers spent hours blowing them up to allow the troops to pass.

Early that morning, the British 3rd Infantry Division, led by Major-General Bernard Law Montgomery (who would later achieve fame in the North African desert), reached its assigned position in Belgium near the Dyle at Louvain. Three days later, the 3rd Division encountered the advancing Germans for the first time, beating back an armoured assault. In truth, this success was virtually meaningless due to the rapid deterioration of the French defences to the south. German spearheads had already broken through in the Ardennes, and the entire BEF was in danger of being outflanked.

Breakthrough at Sedan

The French defensive dispositions in the Ardennes contributed to their own defeat as German armour crossed the Meuse River and dashed to the English Channel.

In 1870, the village of Sedan had been the scene of the decisive battle of the Franco-Prussian War. For France, the defeat had led to humiliating surrender. History was now destined to repeat itself. In a coordinated offensive with artillery and air power, three German armoured divisions commanded by General Heinz Guderian, one of the architects of *Blitzkrieg*, crossed the Meuse River at Sedan on 13 May 1940. Anticipating the main German thrust through Belgium, the French had placed their weakest divisions directly in the path of the attack.

Bearing the brunt of the German onslaught was the French Second Army's 55th Division. Among the ranks of the unit were a number of aged reservists who panicked when artillery officers, unnerved by German dive bomber attacks, blew up their own guns and fled under fire. Without the cover of artillery, French infantrymen were extremely vulnerable, and their line began to collapse. Some French units did stand their ground. Half the German troops attempting to cross in rubber boats were killed or wounded by French machine-gun and artillery fire. By midnight, however, three of four crossing attempts were successful, and two bridges across the Ardennes Canal to the west were captured. Further north at Dinant, a dangerous gap now existed between the 5th Motorized Division and the 18th Infantry Division of the French Ninth Army. Probing tanks of the German 7th Panzer Division found the gap and poured through, brushing aside a counterattack and crossing the Meuse that evening.

The soldiers of the 42nd Colonial Demi Brigade held two German armoured divisions at the Meuse for two days. A pair of crossing attempts at Mezieres and Montherme were thrown back on 13 May before fire from German tanks destroyed bunkers and machine-gun nests in gathering darkness, finally allowing a tenuous bridgehead to be established. On the following day, French reinforcements continued to contest the crossing; however, by the morning of the 15th, German troops and tanks were transiting a pontoon bridge. An 80km (50-mile) wide breach had developed between the French Second and Ninth Armies.

Response to no avail
In the north, the BEF had not been heavily engaged on 13 May, and the French Seventh Army had fought the Germans in Holland but was still largely intact. Under orders from the French overall commander, General Maurice Gamelin, the Seventh Army was ordered south in an attempt to reinforce the collapsing Ninth Army, while seven divisions were ordered north from the Maginot Line. However, the speed of the German advance, which had extended more than 64km (40 miles) beyond the Meuse by the evening of 15 May, rendered these countermeasures ineffective.

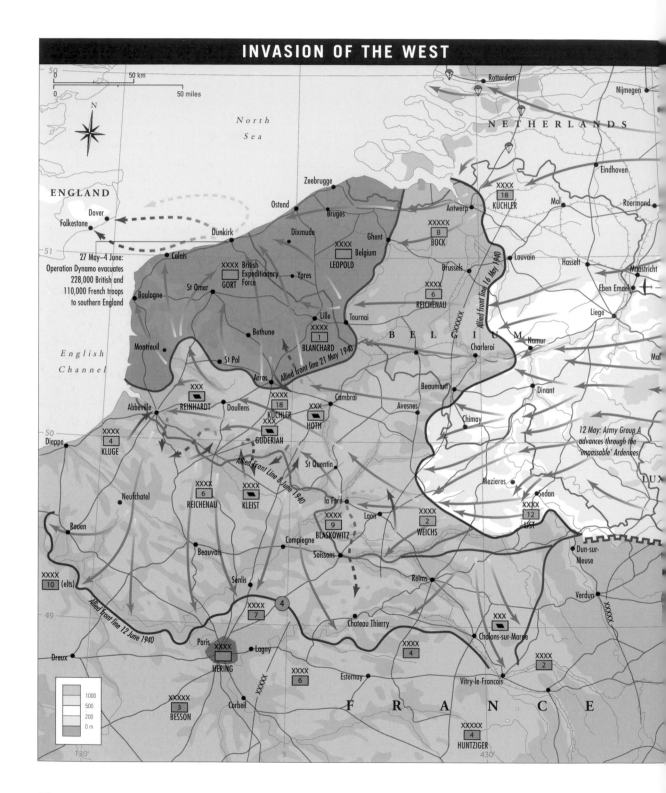

INVASION OF THE WEST

50 km

50 miles

N

North Sea

Rotterdam

Nijmegen

NETHERLANDS

Eindhoven

Roermond

XXXX | 18 | KÜCHLER

Mol

ENGLAND

Dover

Folkestone

27 May–4 June: Operation Dynamo evacuates 228,000 British and 110,000 French troops to southern England

Zeebrugge

Ostend

Bruges

Dixmude

Ghent

XXXX | Belgium | LEOPOLD

Antwerp

XXXXX | 8 | BOCK

Brussels

Louvain

Hasselt

Maastricht

Eben Emael

Liege

Dunkirk

Calais

Boulogne

St Omer

XXXX | British Expeditionary Force | GORT

Ypres

Lille

Tournai

XXXX | 6 | REICHENAU

B E L G I U M

Namur

Mal

English Channel

Montreuil

Bethune

St Pol

Arras

XXXX | 1 | BLANCHARD

Allied front line 21 May 1940

Allied front line 16 May 1940

Charleroi

Beaumont

Dinant

Abbeville

XXX | REINHARDT

Doullens

XXXX | 18 | KÜCHLER

XXX | HOTH

Cambrai

Avesnes

Chimay

12 May: Army Group A advances through the 'impassable' Ardennes

Dieppe

XXXX | 4 | KLUGE

XXX | GUDERIAN

Allied Front Line 8 June 1940

St Quentin

Mezieres

Sedan

LUX

Neufchatel

XXXX | 6 | REICHENAU

XXXX | KLEIST

la Fère

Laon

XXXX | 2 | WEICHS

XXXX | 12 | LIST

Roven

XXXX | 9 | BLASKOWITZ

Compiegne

Soissons

Dun-sur-Meuse

Beauvais

Reims

Verdun

XXXX | 10 | (elts)

Allied Front line 12 June 1940

Senlis

XXXX | 7

4

Chateau Thierry

XXX

Chalons-sur-Marne

Dreux

Paris

XXXX | HERING

Lagny

XXXX | 6

Esternay

XXXX | 4

Vitry-le-Francois

XXXX | 2

XXXXX | 3 | BESSON

Corbeil

F R A N C E

1000
500
200
0 m

XXXXX | 4 | HUNTZIGER

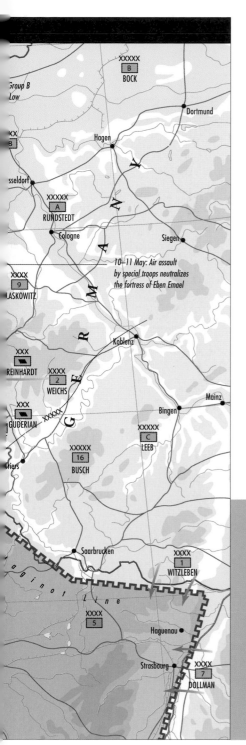

Two French counterattacks, both northeast of the town of Laon, were successful at first, but there were no reinforcements to exploit the gains.

Determined de Gaulle

Only three days prior to the German assault, Colonel Charles de Gaulle was given command of the newly formed French 4th Armoured Division. Before the war, de Gaulle had advocated the formation of four armoured divisions. Now, he was in command of one and facing a situation that was increasingly desperate. Adding to his difficulties was the fact that the division was still being formed, had never previously operated as a cohesive unit and was not present in full strength.

De Gaulle's orders near Laon on 17 May were to attack the Germans with the 80 tanks at his disposal and block the road to Paris. The French armour reached its objective of Moncornet in an attempt to cut the German lines of communication, but enemy fire and a lack of reinforcements compelled de Gaulle to withdraw. A second attack, this time with 150 tanks, was also successful before being forced to retire by German dive bombers and artillery.

On the north shoulder of the German advance, the BEF began an organized withdrawal to the Scheldt River. However, both of its flanks were in peril as the Germans captured the Belgian port city of Antwerp on 18 May while driving the Belgians to the outskirts of Ghent and the French First Army into an exposed position

Invasion of the West
May–June 1940

→	German attacks
→	Allied counterattacks
- →	Allied retreats
—	Allied front lines
⌐⌐	Allied defensive lines
▽	German paratroop drops
✝	German glider assault

May–June 1940

The lull of the Phoney War ended abruptly on 10 May 1940, when the German Army unleashed *Fall Gelb* (Case Yellow) and invaded the Low Countries and France.

While resistance in the Netherlands and Belgium was overcome within days, these German feints lured strong French and British forces northwards. German armour unexpectedly attacked through the lightly defended Ardennes, which the French had believed to be impassable.

The Allied response to the breakthrough at Sedan could not keep pace with the rapidly advancing Germans, who reached the English Channel in less than two weeks. A British counterattack was defeated at Arras on 21 May, and more than 300,000 Allied troops were later evacuated from the Continent at Dunkirk. France capitulated at Compiegne on 22 June.

southeast of Lille by the 21st. Meanwhile, the onrushing German armoured spearheads captured St Quentin on 18 May and reached Amiens and Doullens, a mere 64km (40 miles) from the coast, on the 19th. The following day, German panzers clattered into Abbeville. In an amazing feat, the Germans had traversed more than

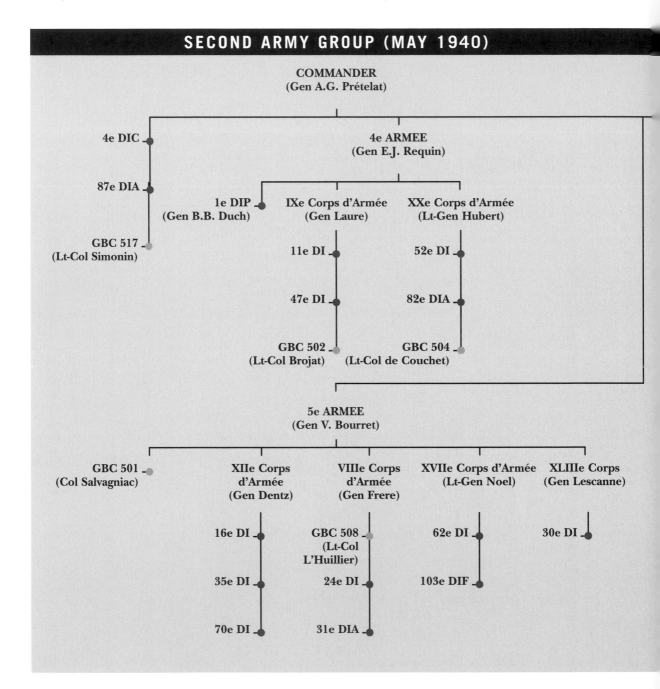

SECOND ARMY GROUP (MAY 1940)

COMMANDER
(Gen A.G. Prételat)

4e DIC

87e DIA

GBC 517
(Lt-Col Simonin)

4e ARMEE
(Gen E.J. Requin)

1e DIP
(Gen B.B. Duch)

IXe Corps d'Armée
(Gen Laure)

XXe Corps d'Armée
(Lt-Gen Hubert)

11e DI

52e DI

47e DI

82e DIA

GBC 502
(Lt-Col Brojat)

GBC 504
(Lt-Col de Couchet)

5e ARMEE
(Gen V. Bourret)

GBC 501
(Col Salvagniac)

**XIIe Corps
d'Armée**
(Gen Dentz)

**VIIIe Corps
d'Armée**
(Gen Frere)

XVIIe Corps d'Armée
(Lt-Gen Noel)

XLIIIe Corps
(Gen Lescanne)

16e DI

GBC 508
(Lt-Col
L'Huillier)

62e DI

30e DI

35e DI

24e DI

103e DIF

70e DI

31e DIA

386km (240 miles) of hostile territory in only 11 days. The position of the BEF was precarious. The collapse of the French Ninth Army left the British rear exposed.

Gort divided his command into two components of roughly brigade size and established the defensive Canal Line from Dunkirk to Arras.

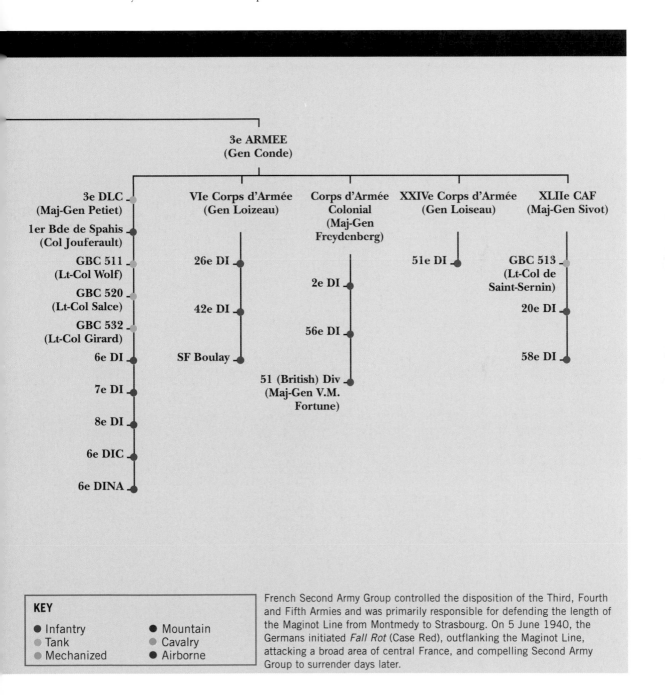

KEY

- ● Infantry
- ● Tank
- ● Mechanized
- ● Mountain
- ● Cavalry
- ● Airborne

French Second Army Group controlled the disposition of the Third, Fourth and Fifth Armies and was primarily responsible for defending the length of the Maginot Line from Montmedy to Strasbourg. On 5 June 1940, the Germans initiated *Fall Rot* (Case Red), outflanking the Maginot Line, attacking a broad area of central France, and compelling Second Army Group to surrender days later.

Counterattack at Arras

Desperate to stem the German tide, British and French forces attempted to stave off the seemingly inevitable with a strong and initially successful counterattack in northeastern France.

With German armour and infantry sweeping northwards towards the English Channel and threatening to cut off the BEF from its French allies, Gort and General Maxime Weygand (who had replaced the sacked Gamelin) ordered a counterattack near Arras to delay the Germans. The Allied counterstroke was to be delivered by two infantry divisions, the British 5th and 50th Northumbrian, supported by 74 British and 60 French tanks. Its objective was to close a gap between Peronne and Cambrai, through which the Germans might attack Boulogne and Calais and sever the BEF lines of communication. Under the command of Major-General Harold Franklyn, the Allied contingent, known as Frankforce, was simultaneously to attack southeast of Arras and hold a defensive line east of the city at the Scarpe River.

Attack begins

The largest attack by BEF forces during the Battle of France, the counterattack at Arras began on 21 May 1940, involving only a fraction of the originally allocated infantry and armour. Divided into two columns, the 6th and 8th Battalions of the Durham Light Infantry were accompanied by the 4th and 7th Royal Tank Regiments, altogether about 2000 soldiers and 58 Matilda I and 16 Matilda II tanks.

Both columns made good progress, the Germans unable to penetrate the armour of the British Matildas with their 37mm (1.45in) anti-tank weapons or the light firepower of their Panzer II and III tanks. Some German prisoners were taken, including SS troops of the Motorized Regiment *Totenkopf* (Death's Head).

Fearing that they had been attacked by a force of at least five divisions, the Germans improvised to stop the British tanks. General Erwin Rommel, commanding the German 7th Panzer Division, ordered that 88mm (3.46in) flak guns and 105mm (4.1in) field cannon be

DLM UNITS AND STRENGTHS (JUNE 1940)			
Division	**Regiment**	**Equipment**	**Strength**
1re DLM	4e Cuirassiers	Somua S-35 Hotchkiss H-39	10 10
	18e Dragoons	Somua S-35 Hotchkiss H-39	10 10
	4e RDP	–	–
	6e Cuirassiers	–	–
2e DLM	13e Dragoons	Somua S-35 Hotchkiss H-39	10 10
	29e Dragoons	Somua S-35 Hotchkiss H-39	10 10
	1st RDP	–	–
	8e Cuirassiers	–	–
3e DLM	1re Cuirassiers	Somua S-35	20
	2e Cuirassiers	Somua S-35	20
	11e RDP	–	–
	12e Cuirassiers	–	–
	Artillery	75mm Gun	12
4e DLM	De La Roche's Group	Somua S-35 Hotchkiss H-39	10 10
	1e Chasseurs	–	–
	5e RDP	–	–
	1re RAM	–	–
	Artillery	75mm Gun	8
7e DLM	8e Dragoons	Hotchkiss H-39 Hotchkiss H-35	20 20
	14e RDP	–	–
	31e Dragoons	–	–
	4e RAM	–	–
	Artillery	75mm Gun 105mm Howitzer 47mm AT Gun 25mm AA Gun	12 12 6 3

turned into anti-tank weapons. Finally, the attack ground to a halt. Rommel then launched a counterattack. However, the French 3rd Light Mechanized Division intervened, its heavier armour taking a toll on the German panzers. Two days later, a French counterattack was repulsed. Though the Allied attack at Arras ended in defeat, its ferocity concerned the German High

Command and may have contributed to their halting of offensive operations for a full day on 23 May and Hitler's decision to allow the *Luftwaffe* to finish off the Allies inside the Dunkirk perimeter. The brief respite was key to the eventual success of Operation Dynamo, the evacuation of the BEF and other Allied troops from the European continent.

Evacuation at Dunkirk

Pressed into a narrow perimeter around the French port city of Dunkirk, the British Expeditionary Force and thousands of French soldiers were transported to safety across the English Channel.

Their backs to the sea at Dunkirk, the remnants of the BEF and units of the French Army had only one hope: a miracle. It happened. From 27 May to 4 June 1940, a total of 338,226 Allied soldiers were evacuated by sea from the continent of Europe to safety in Great Britain. Under constant attack by German aircraft and artillery, a motley array of nearly 700 Royal Navy vessels, steamers, fishing boats, cabin cruisers, sailboats and other pleasure craft ran the gauntlet to bring the troops out.

The counterattack at Arras on 21 May had bought the BEF precious time, and the decision by Hitler to halt his ground attack in favour of the ability of the *Luftwaffe* to obliterate the beachhead has been criticized as one of the most significant blunders of the war. By the time he relented and German ground forces were again allowed to press the defences of Dunkirk, Operation Dynamo was well underway.

Unusable harbour
The port of Dunkirk was a shambles, and it was clear that the harbour facilities were unusable. Only the East Mole could be utilized by soldiers lining up to board smaller civilian craft that could ferry them out to larger vessels. Men would also be picked up directly from the beaches to the east and west.

On the first day of Operation Dynamo, fewer than 7700 men were evacuated; however, the pace quickened,

the smaller vessels repeatedly racing to and from the beaches. The waters of Dunkirk harbour became littered with the debris of war, while soldiers, many of them without food or weapons, continued to stream into the perimeter.

Heroic defence
A key component of the success of the 'Miracle of Dunkirk' was the heroism of the 2nd Battalion Irish Guards and a battalion of the Welsh Guards at Boulogne along with three battalions of the Rifle Brigade, the 3rd Royal Tank Regiment and about 800 French soldiers at Calais. Boulogne lay scarcely 65km (40 miles) from Dunkirk, and Calais about half that distance.

The grim task for these men was straightforward: to sacrifice themselves so that a defensive perimeter could be established at Dunkirk. Their ordeal began on 23 May, and in each locale the Allied troops fought heroically. At Calais, they arrived moments ahead of the Germans, and men of the non-combat 1st Searchlight Regiment took up arms to fend off the attackers. Three days of fighting in the streets of Calais ended when the city fell on the 27th. The Frenchmen who had decided to stand and fight are remembered as the 'Volunteers of Calais'.

At Boulogne, the defenders lost approximately 400 dead but held out against the Germans for two days.

DUNKIRK: OPERATION DYNAMO

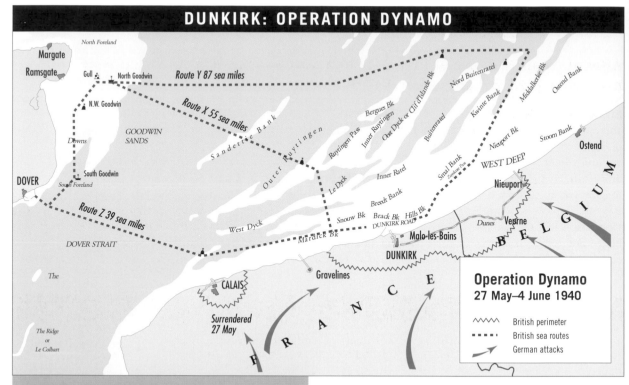

27 May – 4 June 1940

Nearly 340,000 British and French troops were evacuated from the beaches of Dunkirk on the coast of the English Channel during nine days of continuous attacks by German forces pressing southwards from the Low Countries and northeastwards from the Ardennes.

Startled by the suddenness of the German advance, the Allies were outflanked and squeezed into the narrow confines of the Dunkirk perimeter.

The epic of their evacuation has become known as the 'Miracle of Dunkirk'. A fierce counterattack at Arras, heroic delaying actions at Boulogne and Calais, the German halt to offensive operations for 24 hours on 23 May, and Hitler's ill-advised decision to allow the *Luftwaffe* to bomb the Allies into submission contributed to the success of one of history's largest wartime evacuation operations.

On 25 May, British destroyers entered the harbour, guns blazing away at German tanks, and took survivors aboard. Two companies of the Welsh Guards, cut off from the rest, continued to fight for another 48 hours.

Desperate Dynamo

As the perimeter around Dunkirk tightened, it became apparent that the evacuation of the BEF, remnants of the French First Army, and other Allied units was succeeding beyond expectations. However, time was running out.

The British Brigade of Guards and soldiers of the French XVI Corps manned the final defences. On three days (2–4 June), more than 50,000 troops were safely evacuated from the Dunkirk beaches. Of the nearly 340,000 rescued, 139,000 were French.

While virtually all of their equipment was destroyed or in German hands and they had been ejected from the European continent, the Dunkirk evacuees were hailed as heroes in Britain. Many of them would return to fight the Germans another day.

Capitulation

After the disaster in the north and the occupation of the Low Countries, the French Army attempted to regroup and defend the nation's honour.

An attitude of defeatism gripped the French military and political leadership following the lightning conquest of the Low Countries and the swift defeat of the BEF and the French Army in the north of the country. With only about 50 divisions remaining, Weygand was obliged to continue to garrison the Maginot Line and to patch together some cohesive defensive posture against the Germans, who were intent on bringing France to its knees. Following a brief respite, the Germans moved to complete their conquest of France, unleashing *Fall Rot*,

or Case Red. German attacks northwest of Paris on 5–6 June were followed by renewed assaults along the Aisne River on the 9th.

Weygand had correctly surmised the intent of the Germans to capture Paris and to deny the use of the remaining Channel ports, in order to prevent reinforcements and supplies from arriving from Britain. Weygand considered the defence of the ports and the plain of Champagne essential for the survival of France. Maintaining the lifeline to Britain and utilizing the flat

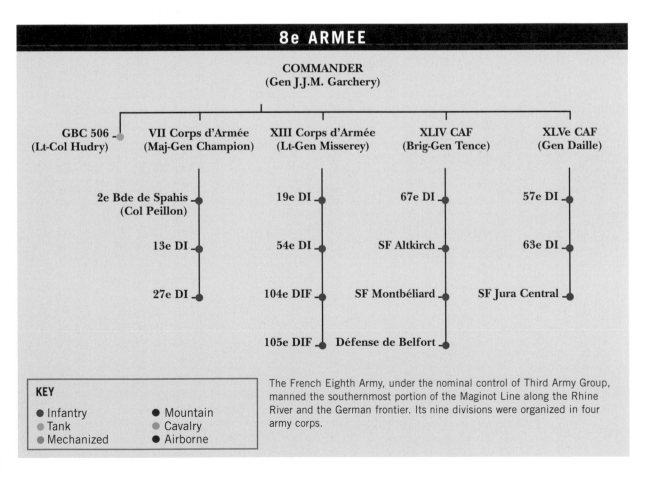

8e ARMEE

COMMANDER
(Gen J.J.M. Garchery)

GBC 506 (Lt-Col Hudry)	VII Corps d'Armée (Maj-Gen Champion)	XIII Corps d'Armée (Lt-Gen Misserey)	XLIV CAF (Brig-Gen Tence)	XLVe CAF (Gen Daille)
	2e Bde de Spahis (Col Peillon)	19e DI	67e DI	57e DI
	13e DI	54e DI	SF Altkirch	63e DI
	27e DI	104e DIF	SF Montbéliard	SF Jura Central
		105e DIF Défense de Belfort		

KEY
- Infantry
- Tank
- Mechanized
- Mountain
- Cavalry
- Airborne

The French Eighth Army, under the nominal control of Third Army Group, manned the southernmost portion of the Maginot Line along the Rhine River and the German frontier. Its nine divisions were organized in four army corps.

terrain of Champagne as good country for the remaining French tanks to manoeuvre, he established defensive positions along the Aisne and Somme rivers.

Defending the Somme

The French commander realized that the Somme portion of his line was considerably weaker from the outset, particularly due to German penetrations closer to the Channel coast. By 8 June, the attackers had secured bridgeheads across the Somme and achieved a

significant breakthrough northwest of Paris. The result was disastrous for Weygand as the troops withdrawing to the west uncovered the left flank of the previously strong positions along the Aisne.

Nevertheless, the French fought heroically on the banks of the Aisne when the Germans began their attacks on 9 June, holding the enemy at bay for three days. The 14th Infantry Division, under General Jean de Lattre de Tassigny, counterattacked at the town of Rethel, eliminating the bridgehead of the XXIII Corps

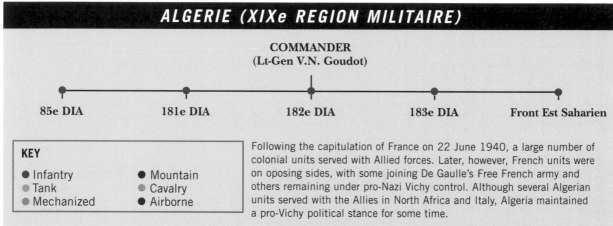

ALGERIE (XIXe REGION MILITAIRE)

COMMANDER
(Lt-Gen V.N. Goudot)

85e DIA   181e DIA   182e DIA   183e DIA   Front Est Saharien

KEY
- Infantry
- Tank
- Mechanized
- Mountain
- Cavalry
- Airborne

Following the capitulation of France on 22 June 1940, a large number of colonial units served with Allied forces. Later, however, French units were on oposing sides, with some joining De Gaulle's Free French army and others remaining under pro-Nazi Vichy control. Although several Algerian units served with the Allies in North Africa and Italy, Algeria maintained a pro-Vichy political stance for some time.

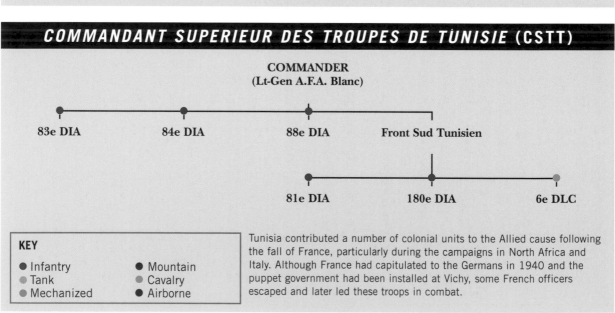

COMMANDANT SUPERIEUR DES TROUPES DE TUNISIE (CSTT)

COMMANDER
(Lt-Gen A.F.A. Blanc)

83e DIA   84e DIA   88e DIA   Front Sud Tunisien

81e DIA   180e DIA   6e DLC

KEY
- Infantry
- Tank
- Mechanized
- Mountain
- Cavalry
- Airborne

Tunisia contributed a number of colonial units to the Allied cause following the fall of France, particularly during the campaigns in North Africa and Italy. Although France had capitulated to the Germans in 1940 and the puppet government had been installed at Vichy, some French officers escaped and later led these troops in combat.

across the Aisne and taking 1000 German prisoners. By 11 June, however, the defenders were compelled to fall back behind the natural barrier of the Marne River, no longer able to defend their exposed flank. The following day, a strong German attack resulted in a breakthrough that was exploited by four armoured divisions. The race for Paris was on, and the end was growing near.

In the south, fascist Italy declared war on Britain and France and followed rapidly with an attack against the Army of the Alps, commanded by General Henri Olry. The French resisted valiantly against two full Italian armies and the nearby German XVI Panzer Corps, fighting them to a standstill.

A bond with Britain?

The withdrawal of the BEF from Dunkirk did not evacuate all British troops from France. A large number of British non-frontline soldiers, including engineers, medical personnel and communications troops, perhaps as many as 100,000, remained under the command of

Lieutenant-General Sir Alan Brooke, who had been ordered to the Continent in an attempt to reconstitute the BEF. General Archibald Beauman cobbled together the equivalent of nine infantry battalions, but their combat-worthiness was highly suspect.

The 51st Highland Division, detailed to support the Maginot Line defences, took up new positions near Rouen in May and engaged Rommel's 7th Panzer Division on 5 June. After Weygand had refused to allow them to withdraw across the Seine River, the Highlanders were trapped on the Havre peninsula and surrendered along with a large number of French troops. Fighting in the Seine Valley, the 1st Armoured Division had sustained tremendous losses trying to stem the German tide. Two fresh divisions, the 1st Canadian and the 52nd Lowland were offloaded at Cherbourg and Brest but were unable to bolster the rapidly disintegrating French Army.

In a desperate bid to keep France fighting, British Prime Minister Winston Churchill offered a formal

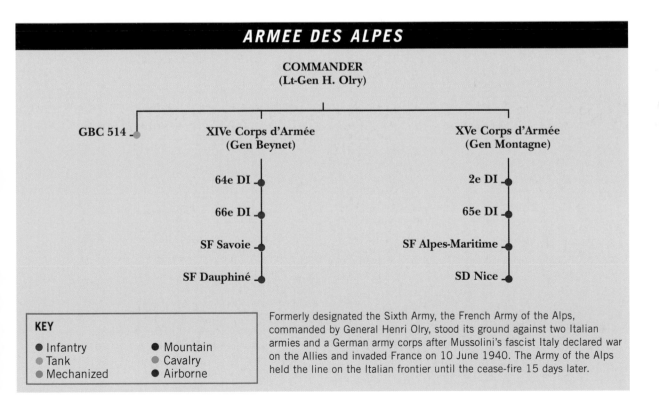

ARMEE DES ALPES

COMMANDER
(Lt-Gen H. Olry)

GBC 514

XIVe Corps d'Armée
(Gen Beynet)

- 64e DI
- 66e DI
- SF Savoie
- SF Dauphiné

XVe Corps d'Armée
(Gen Montagne)

- 2e DI
- 65e DI
- SF Alpes-Maritime
- SD Nice

KEY

- Infantry
- Tank
- Mechanized
- Mountain
- Cavalry
- Airborne

Formerly designated the Sixth Army, the French Army of the Alps, commanded by General Henri Olry, stood its ground against two Italian armies and a German army corps after Mussolini's fascist Italy declared war on the Allies and invaded France on 10 June 1940. The Army of the Alps held the line on the Italian frontier until the cease-fire 15 days later.

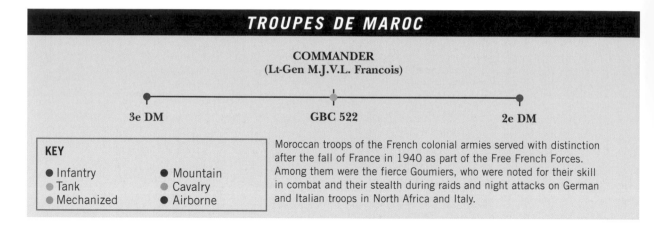

TROUPES DE MAROC

COMMANDER
(Lt-Gen M.J.V.L. Francois)

3e DM   GBC 522   2e DM

KEY
- Infantry
- Tank
- Mechanized
- Mountain
- Cavalry
- Airborne

Moroccan troops of the French colonial armies served with distinction after the fall of France in 1940 as part of the Free French Forces. Among them were the fierce Goumiers, who were noted for their skill in combat and their stealth during raids and night attacks on German and Italian troops in North Africa and Italy.

union with his country, declaring the union would '…concentrate its whole energy against the power of the enemy…' French Premier Paul Reynaud received the news with optimism; however, his government ministers voted to reject it, seemingly resigned to the fate of their nation. Reynaud was sacked and replaced with the elderly World War I hero Marshal Philippe Pétain.

A week prior to Churchill's offer of union, Paris lay undefended. Much of the French Army had ceased to exist as a cohesive military body. The government abandoned the capital on 10 June, fleeing to Tours, 210km (130 miles) to the southwest. On 14 June, German troops entered the City of Light and paraded through its streets. Parisians lined the avenues, many weeping openly or staring in disbelief.

Later, Hitler visited the city, riding in an open car through deserted streets and stopping at points of interest such as the Eiffel Tower and the tomb of Napoleon. It was the *Führer's* only visit to Paris.

An ignominious end

By 17 June, German tanks had rolled to the Swiss frontier, isolating half a million French troops manning the bypassed Maginot Line. France was prostrate, and on the 20th Marshal Pétain moved to initiate armistice negotiations. The surrender was a fait accompli.

Adding insult to injury, Hitler ordered the same rail car in which Germany had signed the armistice ending World War I to be towed from its museum and placed in the forest of Compiegne. When the French delegates arrived, they were astonished to find the Germans

already seated inside the car. There was no bargaining. The ultimatum was clear – sign or the fighting would be renewed. The humiliation was complete, and in the pre-dawn hours of 25 June 1940, the dazzling 42-day conquest of France had ended. France had lost nearly 324,000 casualties, Britain 68,000 and Germany 156,000.

Pétain was to lead a puppet regime from the town of Vichy and was later branded a collaborator. The remainder of French military power was contained largely in its colonial empire, but for the ordinary French citizen there was hardly a shred of honour. Their only glimmer of pride rested with de Gaulle, who fled the city of Bordeaux for London in a light aircraft.

June 1940

Following their swift conquest of the Low Countries and the north in May, the Germans resumed their offensive against the demoralized French during the first week of June 1940. Early in the campaign, the Germans had swept through the Ardennes and routed the Allies in northwestern France, leading to the evacuation of nearly 340,000 soldiers at Dunkirk.

Following a brief pause, German forces renewed assaults to the south and west, capturing the major port cities along the English Channel coast, bypassing the massive fortifications of the Maginot Line, rupturing French defences along the Aisne and Somme rivers, and marching into the undefended capital of Paris. In little more than a month, France had capitulated at Compiegne and Germany controlled all of Western Europe.

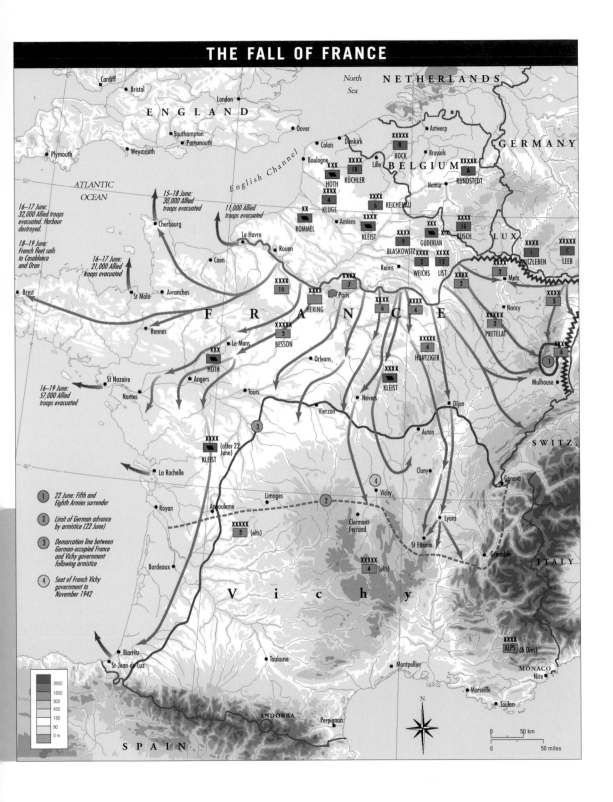

THE FALL OF FRANCE

16–17 June: 32,000 Allied troops evacuated. Harbour destroyed.

18–19 June: French fleet sails to Casablanca and Oran

16–17 June: 21,000 Allied troops evacuated

15–18 June: 30,000 Allied troops evacuated

11,000 Allied troops evacuated

16–19 June: 57,000 Allied troops evacuated

1 22 June: Fifth and Eighth Armies surrender

2 Limit of German advance by armistice (22 June)

3 Demarcation line between German-occupied France and Vichy government following armistice

4 Seat of French Vichy government to November 1942

Map labels: NETHERLANDS, GERMANY, BELGIUM, LUX, ENGLAND, FRANCE, Vichy, SWITZ., ITALY, SPAIN, ANDORRA

Cardiff, Bristol, London, Southampton, Portsmouth, Weymouth, Plymouth, Dover, Calais, Boulogne, Dunkirk, Antwerp, Brussels, Lille, Namur, Cherbourg, Le Havre, Rouen, Caen, Amiens, Reims, Brest, St Malo, Avranches, Rennes, Le Mans, Paris, Nancy, Metz, Mulhouse, Orleans, Nevers, Dijon, Auton, Cluny, Geneva, Angers, Tours, Vierzon, St Nazaire, Nantes, La Rochelle, Royan, Angouleme, Limoges, Vichy, Lyons, St Etienne, Grenoble, Bordeaux, Clermont-Ferrand, Biarritz, St-Jean-de-Luz, Toulouse, Montpellier, Marseille, Toulon, Nice, MONACO, Perpignan

North Sea, ATLANTIC OCEAN, English Channel

Unit labels: BOCK, KÜCHLER, HOTH, KLUGE, ROMMEL, REICHENAU, KLEIST, BLASKOWITZ, GUDERIAN, BUSCH, RUNDSTEDT, WITZLEBEN, LEEB, WEICHS, LIST, HERING, BESSON, HOTH, KLEIST, HUNTZIGER, PRETELAT, KLEIST, ALPS (6 Divs)

Scale bar: 3600, 1800, 900, 450, 180, 90, 0 m

0 50 km / 0 50 miles

North Africa: 1940–43

Forces of the British Commonwealth, later joined by the United States Army, fought the Italians and Germans for control of North Africa, which included domination of the Mediterranean as well as access to the Suez Canal and the oilfields of the Middle East.

British infantry with fixed bayonets run past a knocked-out German Panzer III during the campaign in the Western Desert.

In response to the imminent threat of invasion by the Italian Army in Libya and East Africa, the British Commonwealth committed defensive forces to Egypt during the 1930s. By the spring of 1940, however, there were some 300,000 Italian troops in Cyrenaica (a region of northwest Libya), and they outnumbered Commonwealth forces by 10 to one. Italian combat strength also included more than 1800 pieces of field artillery, 330 tanks and tankettes and 8000 motor vehicles.

War in the Western Desert
Allied military planners were keenly aware that a successful Italian thrust into Egypt would be a serious blow to British prestige and would also imperil the Royal Navy base at Alexandria and the Suez Canal, Britain's lifeline to its colonial empire, while the oilfields of the Middle East would lie open to attack. Further, Axis control of North Africa would close the Mediterranean, while also threatening the bastion of Gibraltar in the west and the fortress island of Malta.

The campaign in North Africa was characterized by numerous large-scale clashes of armour, swift movement, siege and prolonged defence. British forces often employed armoured brigades during the campaign, with these possessing approximately the same strength in tanks as a regular armoured division.

Divisional organization
Despite the logistical challenges of building troop strength and equipment stockpiles in North Africa, the British Army was one of the most highly mechanized in the world. In 1940, the standard British armoured division included approximately 10,750 soldiers and 342 tanks; however, by 1942 the number of troops had grown to 15,000 and tank strength, with the introduction of improved types, had been reduced to 290. The standard British infantry division numbered slightly less than 14,000 troops with 28 organic tanks, 140 tracked infantry carriers and more than 1700 vehicles in 1940. Two years later, troop strength had grown to 18,000, motor vehicles to 2158 and tanks to more than 200.

During 1940, Commonwealth troop strength in all of North and East Africa reached about 100,000, and these forces were obliged to defend not only Egypt but also the reaches of Palestine and of the Sudan to the south. Nevertheless, spectacular successes by the British, who, in contrast to their Italian enemy, were comparatively well trained and armed, liberated Ethiopia and British Somaliland, which the Italians had seized in 1935–36 and early 1940 respectively.

Rommel arrives
On 12 February 1941, two German divisions and Italian reinforcements landed at Tripoli, the Libyan capital. The Germans, designated the *Afrika Korps*, were led by General Erwin Rommel, who was to gain fame as the Desert Fox. British offensive actions launched during the spring and summer were thwarted. A series of thrusts and counterthrusts ensued, with the Germans driving to the Egyptian frontier before the Battle of Alam el Halfa stopped their advance.

In October 1942, the Battle of El Alamein signalled the beginning of the end for the Axis in North Africa. The British Eighth Army drove the enemy back across hundreds of kilometres of desert. Less than a week after El Alamein, Operation Torch, the invasion of North Africa in the west, landed 107,000 Allied troops, about three-quarters of them American, on the coast of Morocco and Algeria.

The Germans and Italians were forced to defend on two fronts, and Axis resistance in North Africa came to an end on 13 May 1943. It had been costly for the Allies: the British Commonwealth forces alone took 220,000 casualties.

7TH ARMOURED DIVISION (JUNE 1940)	
Personnel & Equipment	**Strength**
Troops	10,750
Automatic weapons	475
Artillery (greater than 75mm/3in)	16
Anti-tank weapons	254
Motor vehicles	1460
Trucked carriers	88
Tanks	342

East Africa

Commonwealth forces dealt a severe blow to the Italian Army in East Africa, liberating the first territory occupied by the Axis during World War II.

Following Italy's conquest of Ethiopia in the mid-1930s and the occupation of British Somaliland, along with frontier cities in both Kenya and the Sudan in the summer of 1940, Commonwealth forces in the Western Desert won surprising victories against the Italians. The respite earned by these victories allowed the British commander, General Sir Archibald Wavell, to relocate forces from the west in order to mount an offensive into the Horn of Africa.

British plans called for a thrust towards the port of Massawa on the Red Sea. In the process of liberating Massawa, the Commonwealth troops would also clear Eritrea, Somaliland and Ethiopia of Italian troops, offering the potential to restore Emperor Haile Selassie to the Ethiopian throne. In the event, the successful offensive became the first outright territorial victory of World War II for the British.

To the Horn

Among the Commonwealth forces diverted eastwards by Wavell were the 4th and 5th Indian Divisions, which joined approximately 4500 soldiers of the Sudan Defence Force, two East African brigades nearly 9000 strong and based in Kenya, a contingent of West African troops and a steadily growing number of South African soldiers. Commanded by British officers, the Indian divisions served with distinction in the Mediterranean and Middle East.

The 4th consisted of three infantry brigades (5th, 7th and 11th), along with attached units of the Royal Horse Artillery, engineers and other support formations, while in 1940 the 5th Indian Division included Indian infantry brigades 9, 10 and 29, expanding in 1942 with the addition of 123rd and 161st brigades. The 4th and 5th also included headquarters troops, which could be utilized as needed in combat situations.

The Sudan Defence Force, formed in 1925 in order to patrol the borders of the British Sudan, was expanded

from a peacetime strength of 4500 to 20,000 troops during the war. Its organization consisted of five battalion-sized formations, which were somewhat erroneously designated as corps: the Shendi Horse, the Equatorial Corps, the Eastern Arab Corps, the Western Arab Corps and the Sudan Camel Corps. Following the Italian declaration of war against Great Britain, the East Africa Force was quickly augmented. Troops from such West African countries as Gambia, Sierra Leone, Nigeria and the Gold Coast were mobilized.

Rapid gains

The first British attacks were launched on 19 January 1941, and within five weeks Commonwealth troops had marched into Mogadishu, the capital of Italian Somaliland. On 6 April, Addis Ababa, the Ethiopian capital, fell to the British. When the offensive commenced, the East Africa Force, commanded by General Alan Cunningham, numbered 77,000. During eight weeks of fighting, the force suffered only about 500 casualties and advanced 2735km (1700 miles).

June 1940–November 1941

Although British and Commonwealth forces in East Africa were outnumbered by the Italians in 1940-41, the Italians were poorly led and equipped.

While many Italian units disintegrated in the face of the British offensive, there was bitter fighting at Keren in the north as Commonwealth troops advanced towards the port of Massawa.

To the south, a rapid advance by the East Africa Force resulted in the capture of Mogadishu. Other British troops completed the three-pronged offensive, moving across the Gulf of Aden to Berbera in British Somaliland. Within weeks, the Ethiopian capital of Addis Ababa was liberated.

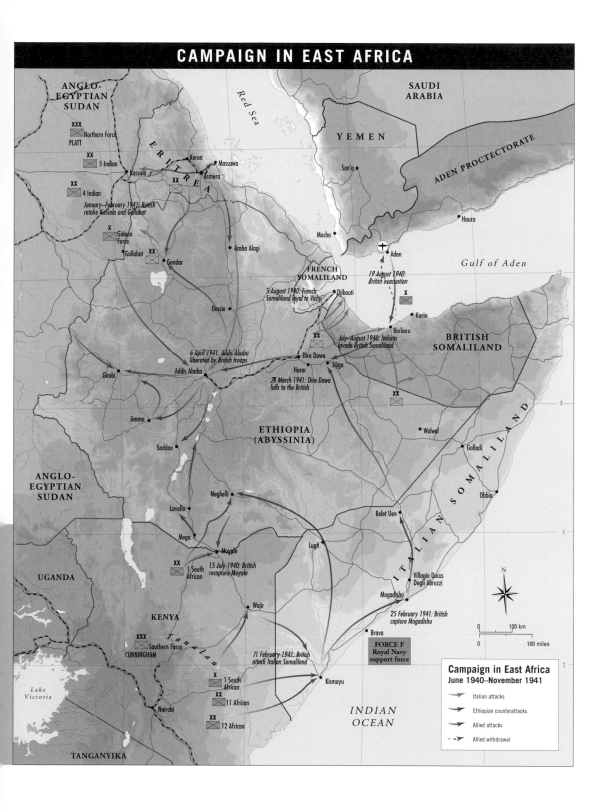

CAMPAIGN IN EAST AFRICA

ANGLO-EGYPTIAN SUDAN

SAUDI ARABIA

Red Sea

YEMEN

ADEN PROCTECTORATE

XXX Northern Force PLATT

XX 5 Indian

Keren

Massawa

ERITREA

Asmera

San'a

Kassala

XX 4 Indian

January–February 1941: British retake Kassala and Gallabat

Haura

X Gideon Force

Gallabat

XX Gondar

Amba Alagi

Mocha

Gulf of Aden

Aden

19 August 1940: British evacuation

FRENCH SOMALILAND

Dessie

5 August 1940: French Somaliland loyal to Vichy

Djibouti

X Karin

Berbera

BRITISH SOMALILAND

XX *July–August 1940: Italians invade British Somaliland*

6 April 1941: Addis Ababa liberated by British troops

Gimbi

Addis Ababa

XX Dire Dawa

Harar

Jijiga

28 March 1941: Dire Dawa falls to the British

Jimma

XX

ETHIOPIA (ABYSSINIA)

Soddou

Walwal

ITALIAN SOMALILAND

Galladi

ANGLO-EGYPTIAN SUDAN

Lavella

Neghelli

Obbia

UGANDA

Mega

XX 1/South African

Moyale

15 July 1940: British recapture Moyale

Lugh

Belet Uen

Villagio Duca Degli Abruzzi

Mogadishu

25 February 1941: British capture Mogadishu

Wajir

XXX Southern Force CUNNINGHAM

Tana River

11 February 1941: British attack Italian Somaliland

Brava

FORCE F Royal Navy support force

X 1 South African

Kismayu

Lake Victoria

XX 11 African

Nairobi

XX 12 African

INDIAN OCEAN

N

| 0 | | 100 km |
| 0 | | 100 miles |

TANGANYIKA

Campaign in East Africa
June 1940–November 1941

→ Italian attacks

→ Ethiopian counterattacks

→ Allied attacks

-▪-▶ Allied withdrawal

The Middle East

A nascent pro-German movement in the Middle East, particularly in Iraq, was of great concern to Allied commanders.

After the French capitulation in June 1940, the military governments of Syria and Lebanon, known as the Levant states, had remained loyal to the Vichy authorities. Subsequently, an Italian commission maintained control of the French presence and ultimately of the Vichy armed forces, which included four battalions of the French Foreign Legion and formations of colonial troops.

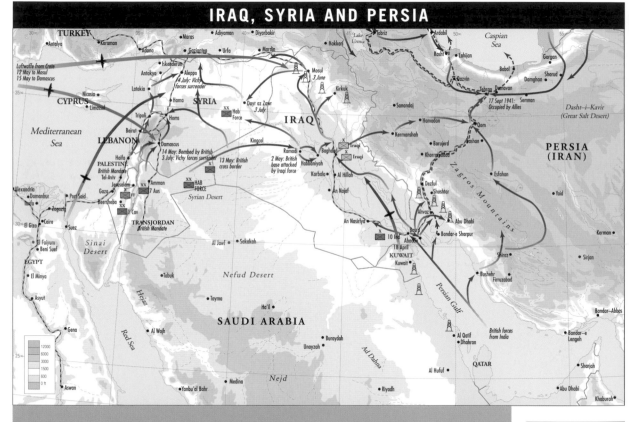

IRAQ, SYRIA AND PERSIA

April–September 1941

Concerns over pro-Nazi activities in the Middle East proved real when the British embassy in Baghdad was besieged by troops of the Iraqi Army. The British air base at Habbaniyah, 80km (50 miles) away, was also attacked, but Indian troops held the vital air link to India. The threat of greater unrest prompted an offensive by British, Free French, Indian and Australian troops through Transjordan and Palestine into Syria. On 21 June 1941, Damascus fell following heavy fighting against 30,000 Vichy French defenders. Within four weeks, Beirut had also surrendered. British and Soviet troops jointly occupied Iran to thwart any pro-German attempts to seize its oilfields.

Iraq, Syria and Persia
April–September 1941

- →→ Allied forces movements
- → Free French forces movements
- → Soviet forces movements
- ✛→ Allied bomber movements
- ✛→ German bomber movements
- ┅→ Allied supply routes
- 🛢 Oilfield

Meanwhile, pro-Axis nationalists took control of the Iraqi capital of Baghdad, compounding the threat of offensive action against Allied interests in the Middle East. General Sir Archibald Wavell, Commonwealth Commander-in-Chief Middle East, and General Sir Henry Maitland Wilson, commander of Commonwealth forces in Palestine and Transjordan, then began planning an offensive against the Levant states.

In the spring of 1941, the 10th Indian Division fought off attacks against Habbaniyah, while on 8 June, a combined force of British, Indian, Australian and Free French forces launched an ultimately successful offensive through Palestine and Transjordan into Syria, overcoming strong Vichy French resistance. British and Soviet troops later occupied Iran to protect its oilfields against the Germans.

Operation Compass

During little more than two months of combat against Italian forces, the first major British offensive of the desert war proved a spectacular success.

For several months during the summer and autumn of 1940, the small British and Commonwealth contingent

in North Africa was dwarfed by the Italian enemy. Reinforcements were few in the aftermath of the fall of

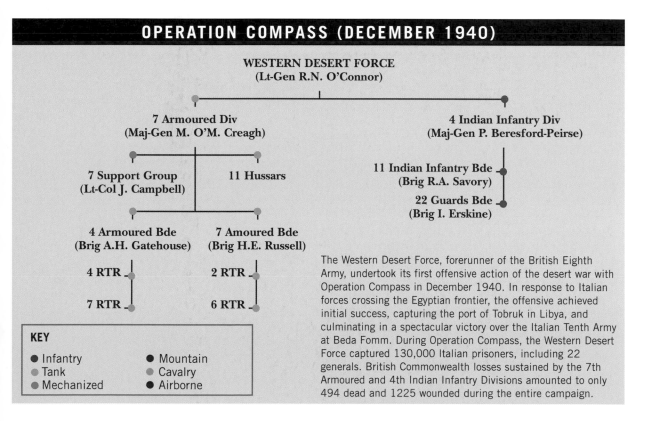

OPERATION COMPASS (DECEMBER 1940)

WESTERN DESERT FORCE
(Lt-Gen R.N. O'Connor)

7 Armoured Div
(Maj-Gen M. O'M. Creagh)

4 Indian Infantry Div
(Maj-Gen P. Beresford-Peirse)

7 Support Group
(Lt-Col J. Campbell)

11 Hussars

11 Indian Infantry Bde
(Brig R.A. Savory)

22 Guards Bde
(Brig I. Erskine)

4 Armoured Bde
(Brig A.H. Gatehouse)

7 Amoured Bde
(Brig H.E. Russell)

4 RTR

2 RTR

7 RTR

6 RTR

KEY
- Infantry
- Tank
- Mechanized
- Mountain
- Cavalry
- Airborne

The Western Desert Force, forerunner of the British Eighth Army, undertook its first offensive action of the desert war with Operation Compass in December 1940. In response to Italian forces crossing the Egyptian frontier, the offensive achieved initial success, capturing the port of Tobruk in Libya, and culminating in a spectacular victory over the Italian Tenth Army at Beda Fomm. During Operation Compass, the Western Desert Force captured 130,000 Italian prisoners, including 22 generals. British Commonwealth losses sustained by the 7th Armoured and 4th Indian Infantry Divisions amounted to only 494 dead and 1225 wounded during the entire campaign.

France and the evacuation of the BEF from the Continent. However, the threat of an invasion of Britain had subsided somewhat by November, and as a result nearly 130,000 troops were deployed to North Africa.

For a time, however, the Allied defenders were stretched woefully thin. Roughly 30,000 troops and only 65 tanks made up the sum of British strength in Egypt when Italy invaded in September 1940. These troops were designated the Western Desert Force and consisted of the 7th Armoured Division and the Indian 4th Division, under the command of Major-General Richard O'Connor. Despite their lack of numbers, the British had actually achieved some notable successes, including the capture of Fort Capuzzo, across the frontier in Italian Libya, on 17 June, only a week after the Italy's declaration of war.

On 1 January 1941, the Western Desert Force was redesignated as XIII Corps. By that time, Operation Compass was well underway. Intended originally as a five-day raid to slow the Italian advance into Egypt, Compass developed into a full-scale offensive after initial successes. Although the Italians had retaken Fort Capuzzo, XIII Corps, which later formed the nucleus of the famed Eighth Army, responded with a counterattack at Sidi Barrani on 9 December. Within three weeks, the British had crossed into Libya once again, defeating the Italians at Bardia. On 22 January, the port of Tobruk fell too, and by the first week of February the Italians were surrounded at Beda Fomm and surrendered.

Instrumental in the initial success of Operation Compass was the Support Group of the 7th Armoured

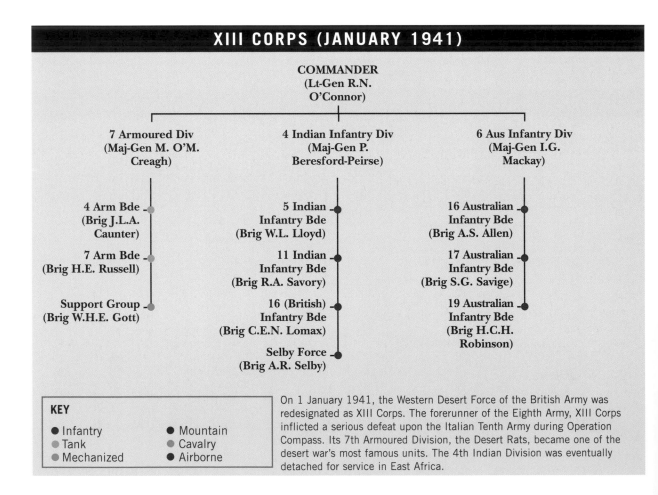

XIII CORPS (JANUARY 1941)

COMMANDER
(Lt-Gen R.N. O'Connor)

7 Armoured Div
(Maj-Gen M. O'M. Creagh)
- 4 Arm Bde (Brig J.L.A. Caunter)
- 7 Arm Bde (Brig H.E. Russell)
- Support Group (Brig W.H.E. Gott)

4 Indian Infantry Div
(Maj-Gen P. Beresford-Peirse)
- 5 Indian Infantry Bde (Brig W.L. Lloyd)
- 11 Indian Infantry Bde (Brig R.A. Savory)
- 16 (British) Infantry Bde (Brig C.E.N. Lomax)
- Selby Force (Brig A.R. Selby)

6 Aus Infantry Div
(Maj-Gen I.G. Mackay)
- 16 Australian Infantry Bde (Brig A.S. Allen)
- 17 Australian Infantry Bde (Brig S.G. Savige)
- 19 Australian Infantry Bde (Brig H.C.H. Robinson)

KEY
- Infantry
- Tank
- Mechanized
- Mountain
- Cavalry
- Airborne

On 1 January 1941, the Western Desert Force of the British Army was redesignated as XIII Corps. The forerunner of the Eighth Army, XIII Corps inflicted a serious defeat upon the Italian Tenth Army during Operation Compass. Its 7th Armoured Division, the Desert Rats, became one of the desert war's most famous units. The 4th Indian Division was eventually detached for service in East Africa.

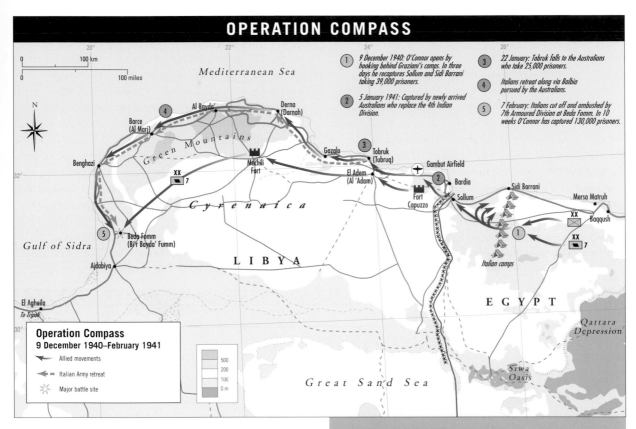

OPERATION COMPASS

1. 9 December 1940: O'Connor opens by hooking behind Graziani's camps. In three days he recaptures Sollum and Sidi Barrani taking 39,000 prisoners.

2. 5 January 1941: Captured by newly arrived Australians who replace the 4th Indian Division.

3. 22 January: Tobruk falls to the Australians who take 25,000 prisoners.

4. Italians retreat along via Balbia pursued by the Australians.

5. 7 February: Italians cut off and ambushed by 7th Armoured Division at Beda Fomm. In 10 weeks O'Connor has captured 130,000 prisoners.

Operation Compass
9 December 1940–February 1941

→ Allied movements
←‑ Italian Army retreat
✳ Major battle site

Division, which consisted of the 2nd Rifle Brigade, Coldstream Guards, 11th Hussars and the 3rd and 4th Royal Horse Artillery. Commanded by Lieutenant-Colonel John 'Jock' Campbell, the 7th Armoured Support Group – the 'Jock Columns' – managed to contain the Italian advance into Egypt. The Jock Columns consisted of ad hoc units of armoured cars, the Royal Horse Artillery, plus supporting infantry. Always outnumbered and lightly armed, they employed about 120 truck-transported infantrymen and a few 25-pounder field guns and armoured cars to great effect.

Reinforced offensive

Significant reinforcements contributed to the success of Operation Compass. Among these were three armoured regiments, the 3rd Hussars, the 2nd Royal Tank Regiment and the 7th Royal Tank Regiment, which arrived at Port Said in Egypt on 24 September 1940 and trained rigorously prior to the December offensive. The

9 December 1940 –February 1941

The bold stroke of the British XIII Corps, dubbed Operation Compass, succeeded well beyond the expectations of its planners. Not only did the Commonwealth forces eject the Italians from Egypt, they destroyed Mussolini's Tenth Army, capturing 130,000 prisoners. In the process, they won victories at Sidi Barrani, Bardia, the great port of Tobruk and Beda Fomm. During two months of fighting, the Italians had been driven back 800km (500 miles), their morale shattered. Hitler was later required to send German troops to support the Italians in North Africa. On 12 February 1941, two German divisions under General Erwin Rommel arrived in Tripoli.

2nd Royal Tank Regiment fielded three variants of the Cruiser tank (the A13, A9 and A10) while the 3rd Hussars operated the functionally obsolescent Mk IV Light Tank. The 7th Royal Tank Regiment included

48 heavily armoured Matilda tanks. The Matilda's thick armour plating made it impervious to small-arms fire. However, it quickly became apparent to the British that even their smaller calibre bullets were capable of penetrating the thin skins of Italian armoured vehicles.

Italian collapse

During the early hours of Operation Compass, approximately 20,000 prisoners were captured, and the demoralized Italian Tenth Army was in headlong retreat. Birk Force, commanded by Lieutenant H. Birk, and Combe Force, led by Lieutenant-Colonel John Combe, dogged the retreating Italians. These fast-moving composite forces were designed for rapid pursuit and operated with only limited armoured support due to the necessity of the tanks to refuel. Combe Force included a

few Light and Cruiser tanks, elements of the 11th Hussars, a squadron of the King's Dragoon Guards, a squadron of Royal Air Force armoured cars, the 2nd Rifle Brigade of the 7th Armoured Support Group, the 25-pounder guns of C Battery, Royal Horse Artillery, and nine 37mm (1.45in) anti-tank guns of the 106th Battery, Royal Horse Artillery, portee-mounted on trucks. Its total strength was about 2000 men.

When Operation Compass concluded, the victory was astounding. Ten Italian divisions had ceased to exist and 400 tanks and 1300 artillery pieces had been destroyed or captured. More than 130,000 Italian soldiers had been taken prisoner and hundreds killed or wounded. A British force of only about two divisions had rolled 800km (500 miles) in roughly eight weeks, suffering fewer than 500 dead and 1225 wounded.

Operation Crusader

While German and Italian forces under General Erwin Rommel, 'the Desert Fox', besieged the port of Tobruk, the British mounted a drive to rescue the port city's fighting garrison.

For seven months, Tobruk had been under siege by the German *Afrika Korps*. By November 1941, the British were aware of Rommel's intention to take the Libyan port city. Designed as a preemptive strike to raise the siege of Tobruk and destroy German armour in a decisive battle, Operation Crusader was launched on 18 November.

Manoeuvring into position during two days of heavy rain, a rare occurrence in the desert, the veteran 7th Armoured Division clashed with two German panzer divisions, the 15th and 21st, at Sidi Rezegh to open the battle. The British plan was for the two corps of the recently formed Eighth Army, commanded by General Sir Alan Cunningham, to attack in cooperation. The XIII Corps with the 1st Army Tank Brigade was to advance to Halfaya Pass and occupy the German defenders along the coast of the Mediterranean while the concentrated armour of XXX Corps swept southwest

around the German flank to Gabr Saleh, to defeat the German panzers and link up with the Tobruk garrison.

Operation Crusader was the first engagement for the Eighth Army, which originally included a strength equal to seven divisions of Commonwealth troops. Before the conclusion of the campaign in North Africa, its strength would grow to more than 220,000 soldiers.

Along with the British, Cunningham commanded troops from South Africa, New Zealand, India and Poland during Operation Crusader. The combined armoured strength of XXX Corps totalled 453 tanks, including 287 Crusaders and 166 Stuarts. Early versions of the Crusader, the Mk I and Mk II, mounted a 2-pounder cannon while the Mk III was upgunned to a 6-pounder. This was one of the primary tanks of the British Army in North Africa, and more than 5300 were built from a design by Nuffield Mechanisation and Aero. Its secondary armament consisted of a either a single

BRITISH EIGHTH ARMY (NOVEMBER 1941)

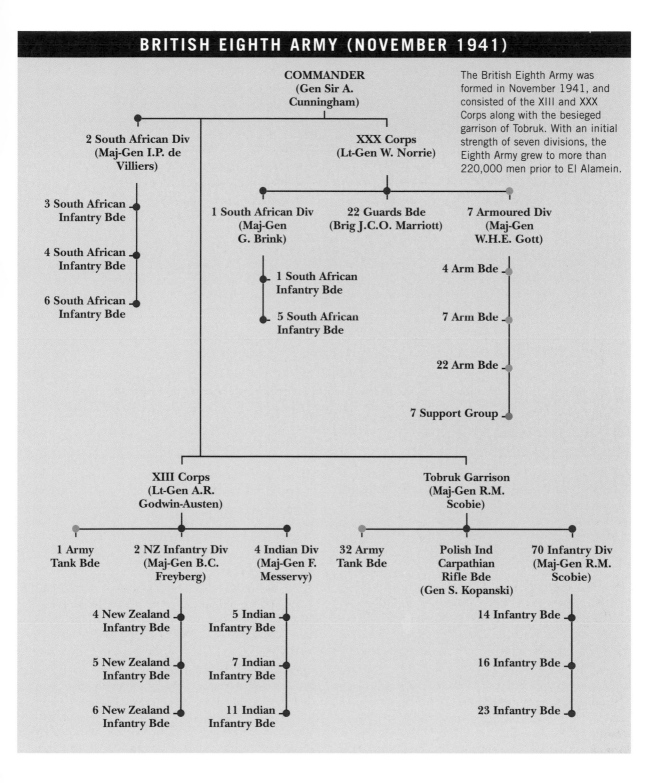

COMMANDER
(Gen Sir A. Cunningham)

The British Eighth Army was formed in November 1941, and consisted of the XIII and XXX Corps along with the besieged garrison of Tobruk. With an initial strength of seven divisions, the Eighth Army grew to more than 220,000 men prior to El Alamein.

2 South African Div
(Maj-Gen I.P. de Villiers)

3 South African Infantry Bde

4 South African Infantry Bde

6 South African Infantry Bde

XXX Corps
(Lt-Gen W. Norrie)

1 South African Div
(Maj-Gen G. Brink)

1 South African Infantry Bde

5 South African Infantry Bde

22 Guards Bde
(Brig J.C.O. Marriott)

7 Armoured Div
(Maj-Gen W.H.E. Gott)

4 Arm Bde

7 Arm Bde

22 Arm Bde

7 Support Group

XIII Corps
(Lt-Gen A.R. Godwin-Austen)

1 Army Tank Bde

2 NZ Infantry Div
(Maj-Gen B.C. Freyberg)

4 New Zealand Infantry Bde

5 New Zealand Infantry Bde

6 New Zealand Infantry Bde

4 Indian Div
(Maj-Gen F. Messervy)

5 Indian Infantry Bde

7 Indian Infantry Bde

11 Indian Infantry Bde

Tobruk Garrison
(Maj-Gen R.M. Scobie)

32 Army Tank Bde

Polish Ind Carpathian Rifle Bde
(Gen S. Kopanski)

70 Infantry Div
(Maj-Gen R.M. Scobie)

14 Infantry Bde

16 Infantry Bde

23 Infantry Bde

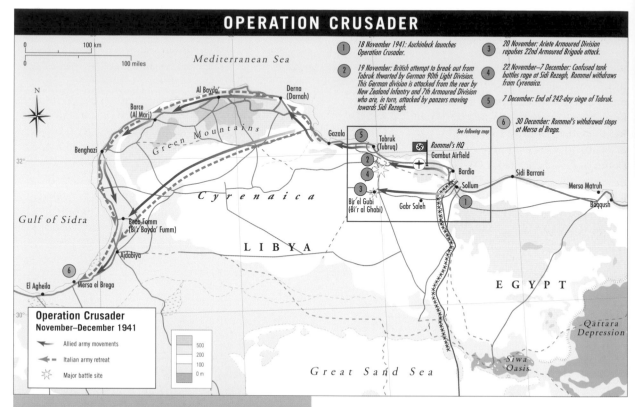

OPERATION CRUSADER

1. 18 November 1941: Auchinleck launches Operation Crusader.
2. 19 November: British attempt to break out from Tobruk thwarted by German 90th Light Division. This German division is attacked from the rear by New Zealand Infantry and 7th Armoured Division who are, in turn, attacked by panzers moving towards Sidi Rezegh.
3. 20 November: Ariete Armoured Division repulses 22nd Armoured Brigade attack.
4. 22 November–7 December: Confused tank battles rage at Sidi Rezegh, Rommel withdraws from Cyrenaica.
5. 7 December: End of 242-day siege of Tobruk.
6. 30 December: Rommel's withdrawal stops at Mersa el Brega.

Operation Crusader
November–December 1941

⬅ Allied army movements
⬅ Italian army retreat
✳ Major battle site

500
200
100
0 m

November–December 1941

In a major effort to relieve the besieged garrison of the Libyan port city of Tobruk, the British Eighth Army launched Operation Crusader on 18 November 1941. With XIII Corps advancing towards Halfaya Pass in the north and XXX Corps attacking through Sidi Rezegh to the southwest, large tank battles erupted during the first week of Operation Crusader. Although German forces appeared to gain the upper hand and General Sir Alan Cunningham was relieved of command in favour of General Neil Ritchie, German attempts to encircle the Eighth Army failed, and the siege of Tobruk was lifted. The British had won a victory, but they had no armoured reserves or reinforcements with which to exploit their hard-won gains.

Besa machine gun or a pair. The Stuart light tank was of US manufacture and provided to the British through arms sales and Lend-Lease. Its primary armament was a 37mm (1.45in) cannon. Three .30-calibre (7.62mm) Browning machine guns provided supporting fire. The

1st Army Tank Brigade attached to the XIII Corps included some 135 Matilda and Valentine tanks, both of which were relatively new designs with improved armour protection but lacking somewhat in firepower. While the Matilda was armed with a machine gun, the Valentine was equipped with the 2-pounder cannon, later upgunned to a 6-pounder cannon.

Furious tank battles

On 19 November, heavy fighting took place along the coast and to the south. The 7th Armoured Division's recently formed 22nd Armoured Brigade engaged the Italian *Ariete* Division at Bir el Gubi and destroyed 34 enemy tanks. However, this was the first time under fire for the 22nd Brigade, and its regiments lost 25 Crusaders to enemy artillery and mines while another 30 experienced mechanical failure. Half its armoured strength was lost in one action. The 4th Armoured Brigade lost 23 Stuart tanks during the desert war's first major tank battle at Gabr Saleh. The Germans withdrew after the engagement, but it was the British who took the worst of the exchange.

Reversal of fortune

By 22 November, Rommel had cancelled an offensive of his own and ordered a counterattack against Sidi Rezegh, defended by only the 7th Armoured Brigade. Reinforcements hurried to the area, but the 7th was mauled and reduced to only 10 battleworthy tanks as the Germans retook the town. The following day, while driving towards Bir el Gubi, the Germans took a beating, losing 70 tanks. During their advance, they had encountered a brigade of South African infantry which fought to the last man, leaving 3400 dead and wounded. Cunningham, convinced that his attacks were futile,

now advocated a halt. General Sir Claude Auchinleck, the successor to Wavell, replaced him swiftly with General Neil Ritchie. Rommel expected the British to retreat, but the battered Eighth Army instead stood its ground, allowing the armoured spearheads to pass through before pummelling the German supply lines. Eventually, Rommel's gamble to drive around the British flank and relieve the pressure on his northern troops near Halfaya Pass proved unsuccessful. The British 70th Division, which included the 14th, 16th and 23rd Infantry Brigades, broke out of Tobruk and linked up with New Zealand troops by December. The leading regiments of the 70th, the 2nd York and Lancaster Regiment and the 2nd Black Watch, suffered tremendous casualties.

Loss of Tobruk

In the spring of 1942, British Commonwealth fortunes in North Africa turned sharply for the worse as a German offensive pushed the overextended Eighth Army steadily eastwards.

Although Operation Crusader had succeeded in its goal of relieving Tobruk, the Eighth Army had sustained serious losses and actually overextended itself. Rommel and Panzer Army Africa, however, received sorely needed reinforcements and supplies during late December 1941. The following month, he was ready to counterattack, driving the British back some 480km (300 miles) to the Gazala Line.

Lull in the fighting

A four-month lull ensued as both sides licked their wounds and continued to grow in strength. The Eighth Army defences on the Gazala Line included six strongholds, or boxes, manned by XIII Corps in the north and XXX Corps to the south. Eighth Army tank strength neared 850, most of which were the Matilda, Valentine and Stuart light models. However, nearly 70 of these were the newly arrived American-built Grant tanks armed with a 37mm (1.45in) cannon in a traversing

7TH ARMOURED DIVISION (APRIL 1942)	
Brigade	**Units**
4th Armoured Brigade	1st RHA 8th Hussars 3rd Royal Tank Regiment 5th Royal Tank Regiment 1st King's Royal Rifle Corps
7th Motor Brigade	4th RHA 2nd Rifle Brigade 9th Rifle Brigade 9th King's Royal Rifle Corps
Divisional units	102nd RHA King's Dragoon Guards

turret and a 75mm (2.95in) hull-mounted gun capable of holding its own in a slugfest with German panzers. Unfortunately, Ritchie committed a tactical error in widely dispersing his armoured strength. When Rommel launched his offensive against the Gazala Line on 26

May 1942, two of the boxes, defended by Indian troops, were quickly overrun. The 4th Armoured Brigade was again thrown into the breach and fought a bitter tank battle, blunting the German thrust and forcing Rommel to assume the defensive temporarily.

Establishing a cordon of artillery and tanks, which the British dubbed the 'Cauldron', the Germans could not hold out forever as their ammunition and provisions depleted. Further, the fight had not gone out of the Allied troops on the Gazala Line.

In the midst of the Cauldron stood the box of the 150th Brigade Group at Sidi Muftah, which held out for three days against six German armoured assaults and repeated attacks by German dive bombers. The 25-pounder field guns of the defenders fired continually on German supply lines, and the 150th fought to the last man. Company B, 5th Green Howard Regiment offered the last resistance at Sidi Muftah. Along with the 150th,

the 10th Indian Brigade and the 22nd Armoured Brigade sustained heavy losses.

Bir Hacheim

The most vital of the fortified positions was at Bir Hacheim in the south. Defended by the 3600 troops of the Free French Brigade, the box had been bypassed early in the German offensive, and the French had repulsed attacks by the Italian *Trieste* Division. Commanded by Major-General Pierre Koenig, the defenders held out until 10 June, and nearly 2700 were able to evade capture. During the 16-day siege, 600 French soldiers died.

The defenders of Bir Hecheim included the 2nd and 3rd Battalions of the 13th Foreign Legion Demi-Brigade, two colonial battalions from French possessions in the Pacific, a battalion of *Fusiliers Marins* (naval troops specifically trained for defensive fighting), a battalion of

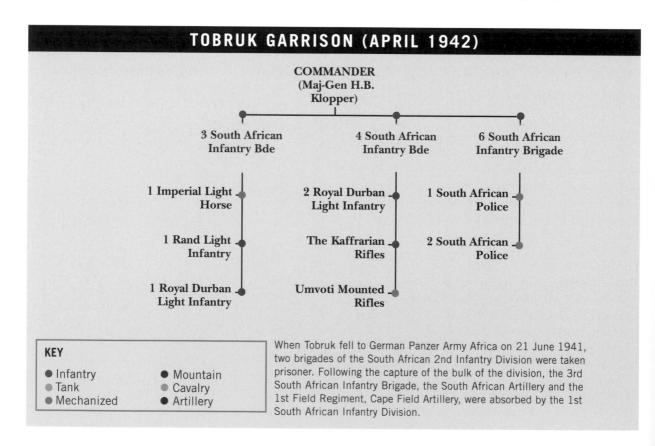

TOBRUK GARRISON (APRIL 1942)

COMMANDER
(Maj-Gen H.B. Klopper)

3 South African Infantry Bde	4 South African Infantry Bde	6 South African Infantry Brigade
1 Imperial Light Horse	2 Royal Durban Light Infantry	1 South African Police
1 Rand Light Infantry	The Kaffrarian Rifles	2 South African Police
1 Royal Durban Light Infantry	Umvoti Mounted Rifles	

KEY

- Infantry
- Tank
- Mechanized
- Mountain
- Cavalry
- Artillery

When Tobruk fell to German Panzer Army Africa on 21 June 1941, two brigades of the South African 2nd Infantry Division were taken prisoner. Following the capture of the bulk of the division, the 3rd South African Infantry Brigade, the South African Artillery and the 1st Field Regiment, Cape Field Artillery, were absorbed by the 1st South African Infantry Division.

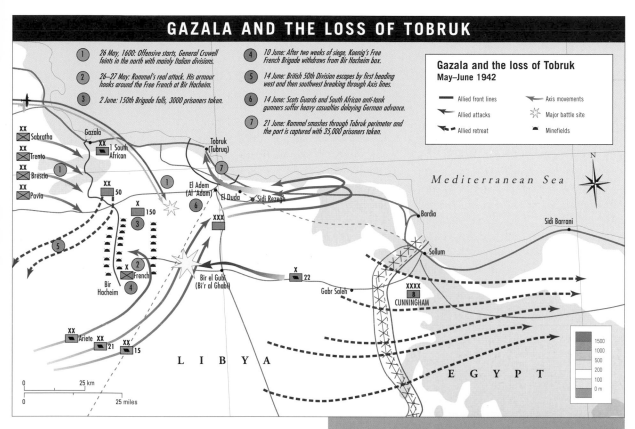

GAZALA AND THE LOSS OF TOBRUK

1. 26 May, 1600: Offensive starts, General Cruwell feints in the north with mainly Italian divisions.

2. 26–27 May: Rommel's real attack. His armour hooks around the Free French at Bir Hacheim.

3. 2 June: 150th Brigade falls, 3000 prisoners taken.

4. 10 June: After two weeks of siege, Koenig's Free French Brigade withdraws from Bir Hacheim box.

5. 14 June: British 50th Division escapes by first heading west and then southwest breaking through Axis lines.

6. 14 June: Scots Guards and South African anti-tank gunners suffer heavy casualties delaying German advance.

7. 21 June: Rommel smashes through Tobruk perimeter and the port is captured with 35,000 prisoners taken.

Gazala and the loss of Tobruk
May–June 1942

- Allied front lines
- Allied attacks
- Allied retreat
- Axis movements
- Major battle site
- Minefields

Marines, and other smaller units. Outgunned, the French artillery consisted mainly of obsolete 75mm (2.95in) cannon. Foodstuffs were originally estimated to last for about 10 days. General Koenig rejected several German surrender overtures. Under cover of darkness, he led the daring escape through German lines to a rendezvous with British trucks.

Fall of Tobruk

For the British, the situation in the Cauldron rapidly deteriorated. During Rommel's breakout, the Eighth Army lost 6000 casualties and 150 tanks in a single day. By mid-June, defeat appeared imminent for the British. At the Knightsbridge Box, the 201st Guards Motor Brigade, originally the 22nd Infantry Brigade and consisting of the 3rd Battalion, Coldstream Guards, 2nd Battalion, Scots Guards, 1st Battalion, The Worcestershire Regiment, 9th Battalion, The Rifle Brigade, and 1st Battalion, Durham Light Infantry,

May–June 1942

Pushed back by the Germans in January 1942, the Eighth Army established the Gazala Line, 480km (300 miles) from its furthest penetration into Libya, while the port city of Tobruk was taken under siege by Rommel and Panzer Army Africa. The Gazala Line consisted of six fortified positions, or boxes, which Rommel attacked with the resumption of his offensive on 26 May, following a four-month lull in the fighting. The most important of the Gazala boxes was at Bir Hacheim in the south. Defended by the Free French Brigade, Bir Hacheim was taken on 11 June. Meanwhile, the Germans assumed the offensive in the embattled Cauldron and inflicted heavy losses on the British. On 21 June, Tobruk fell.

offered a spirited defence but was forced out of its positions. Rommel fended off a series of British counterattacks, and on 21 June, Tobruk fell, yielding a horde of much-needed supplies to the Germans.

El Alamein

Recognized as the turning point of the war in the desert, the Battle of El Alamein was the beginning of the end for Axis forces in North Africa.

Even before the fall of Tobruk, the Eighth Army was in retreat across the frontier of Egypt. Rommel, flush with victory, attacked British positions 160km (100 miles) inside Egypt at Mersa Matruh. With but 60 tanks, the Germans defeated four British divisions during three days of combat that began on 26 June. After another in a rapid succession of defeats, the Eighth Army fell back 190km (120 miles) to the east. Its last stand, just 240km (150 miles) from the Egyptian capital of Cairo, would be

made at El Alamein. This was perhaps the strongest defensive position in North Africa, its right flank closed by the sea and its left by a steep, virtually impassible area of loose sand known as the Qattara Depression. Auchinleck, relieving Ritchie, took personal command of the Eighth Army and mounted a flexible defence.

A strident stand

Auchinleck employed defensive boxes, and among the

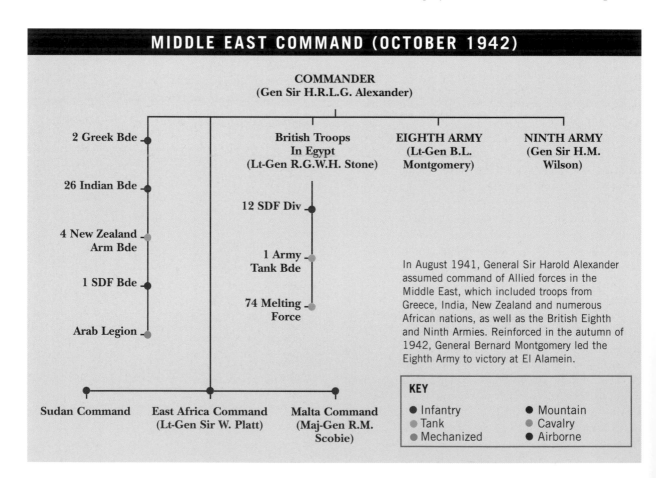

MIDDLE EAST COMMAND (OCTOBER 1942)

COMMANDER
(Gen Sir H.R.L.G. Alexander)

2 Greek Bde

26 Indian Bde

4 New Zealand Arm Bde

1 SDF Bde

Arab Legion

British Troops In Egypt
(Lt-Gen R.G.W.H. Stone)

12 SDF Div

1 Army Tank Bde

74 Melting Force

EIGHTH ARMY
(Lt-Gen B.L. Montgomery)

NINTH ARMY
(Gen Sir H.M. Wilson)

Sudan Command

East Africa Command
(Lt-Gen Sir W. Platt)

Malta Command
(Maj-Gen R.M. Scobie)

In August 1941, General Sir Harold Alexander assumed command of Allied forces in the Middle East, which included troops from Greece, India, New Zealand and numerous African nations, as well as the British Eighth and Ninth Armies. Reinforced in the autumn of 1942, General Bernard Montgomery led the Eighth Army to victory at El Alamein.

KEY
- Infantry
- Tank
- Mechanized
- Mountain
- Cavalry
- Airborne

7TH ARMOURED DIVISION (OCTOBER 1942)	
Brigade	**Regiments**
4th Light Armoured Bde	3rd RHA 8th Hussars 4th Hussars Royal Scots Greys 2nd Derbyshire Yeomanry 1st King's Royal Rifle Corps
22nd Armoured Brigade	1st Royal Tank Regiment 5th Royal Tank Regiment 4th County of London Ymn 4th Field Regiment RA 97th Field Regiment RA 1st Rifle Brigade
131st Queens Brigade	1/5th Queens Royal Rgt 1/6th Queens Royal Rgt 1/7th Queens Royal Rgt
	11th Hussars
8th Armoured Brigade	3rd Royal Tank Regiment

troops involved were the 3rd South African Infantry Brigade, the 9th and 18th Indian Infantry Brigades and the 6th New Zealand Brigade. The 1st and 7th Armoured Divisions mustered 155 tanks between them. During three weeks in July, British forces managed to parry German thrusts, counterattacking wherever an opportunity presented itself. On the 21st and 22nd, the Battle of Ruweisat Ridge, also known as the First Battle of El Alamein, was fought to a standstill.

Although Auchinleck had stopped the Germans, at least temporarily, British Prime Minister Winston Churchill replaced him in August with General Sir Harold Alexander as commander of Allied forces in the Middle East. At the same time, General Bernard Law Montgomery ascended to command of the Eighth Army.

El Alamein victory

Rommel shot his offensive bolt in early September, when the Eighth Army's 44th Infantry Division, newly arrived in Egypt, and the 7th and 10th Armoured Divisions, with a combined strength of 400 tanks, halted the Germans at Alam el Halfa Ridge.

Time had now become an ally of the British. Immediately after the fall of Tobruk, US President Franklin D. Roosevelt had promised 300 American M4

BERNARD LAW MONTGOMERY (1887–1976)

The hero of the Battle of El Alamein in North Africa, Bernard Montgomery, 1st Viscount Montgomery of Alamein, was born in Kennington, London, and attended the Royal Military Academy, Sandhurst. During World War I, he was seriously wounded at Bailleul in 1914 and nearly died. He became one of the most famous commanders in the history of the British Army during World War II.

• Montgomery commanded the 3rd Infantry Division and later the II Corps of the BEF during operations on the European continent in 1940.

• He was appointed to command of the Eighth Army in August 1942 and defeated the Germans at El Alamein in October.

• Montgomery commanded the Eighth Army during much of the Italian Campaign in 1943–44 prior to being recalled to England.

• He commanded 21st Army Group during Operation Overlord, the invasion of Western Europe, which began on 6 June 1944.

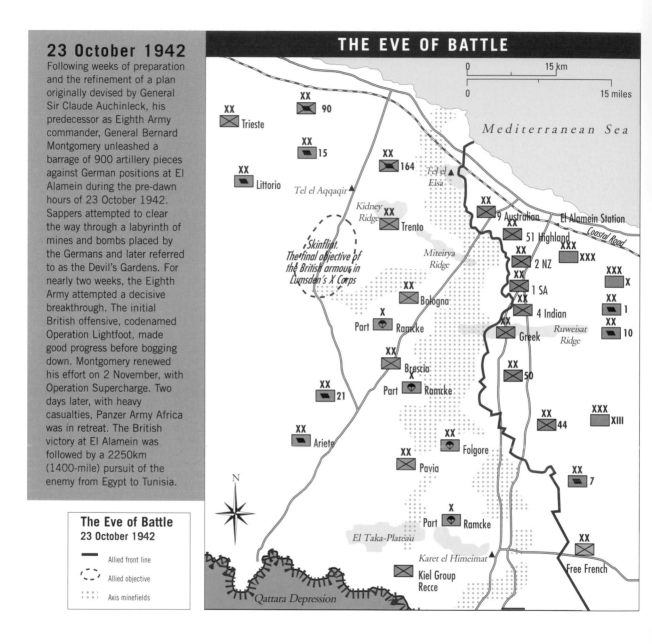

23 October 1942

Following weeks of preparation and the refinement of a plan originally devised by General Sir Claude Auchinleck, his predecessor as Eighth Army commander, General Bernard Montgomery unleashed a barrage of 900 artillery pieces against German positions at El Alamein during the pre-dawn hours of 23 October 1942. Sappers attempted to clear the way through a labyrinth of mines and bombs placed by the Germans and later referred to as the Devil's Gardens. For nearly two weeks, the Eighth Army attempted a decisive breakthrough. The initial British offensive, codenamed Operation Lightfoot, made good progress before bogging down. Montgomery renewed his effort on 2 November, with Operation Supercharge. Two days later, with heavy casualties, Panzer Army Africa was in retreat. The British victory at El Alamein was followed by a 2250km (1400-mile) pursuit of the enemy from Egypt to Tunisia.

THE EVE OF BATTLE

The Eve of Battle
23 October 1942

— Allied front line
- - - Allied objective
···· Axis minefields

Sherman tanks, mounting 75mm (2.95in) cannon, along with 100 self-propelled guns, to the British.

During the weeks that followed the defensive success at Alam el Halfa Ridge, Montgomery refined a plan of attack formulated by Auchinleck and increased his forces to an advantage of nearly three to one over the Germans. By the time that the decisive Battle of El

Alamein began, the Eighth Army numbered more than 200,000 men, equipped with more than 1000 tanks and 2300 artillery pieces.

On 23 October 1942, the 51st Highland Division, 9th Australian Division, the 2nd New Zealand Division and the 1st South African Division advanced through the Devil's Gardens, sown with mines and barbed wire by

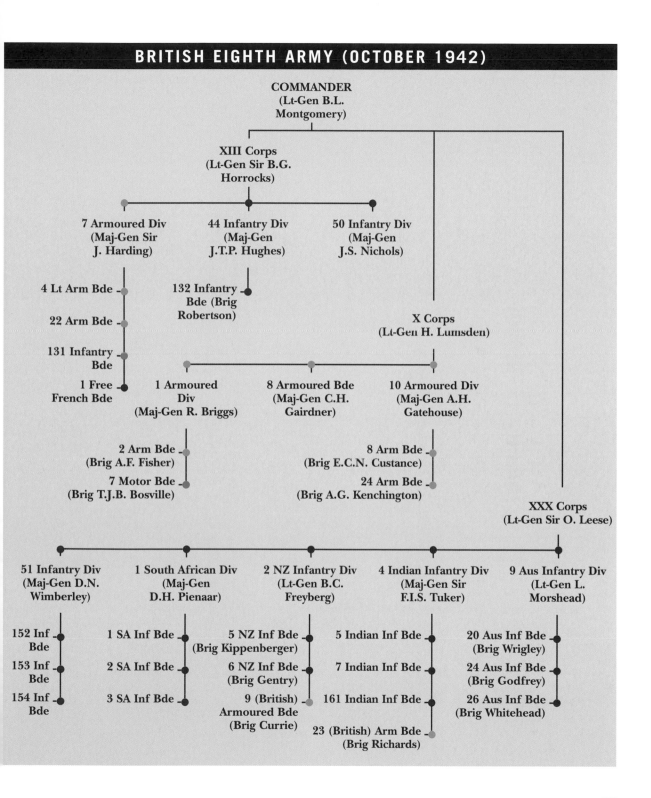

BRITISH EIGHTH ARMY (OCTOBER 1942)

COMMANDER
(Lt-Gen B.L. Montgomery)

XIII Corps
(Lt-Gen Sir B.G. Horrocks)

7 Armoured Div
(Maj-Gen Sir J. Harding)

44 Infantry Div
(Maj-Gen J.T.P. Hughes)

50 Infantry Div
(Maj-Gen J.S. Nichols)

4 Lt Arm Bde

22 Arm Bde

131 Infantry Bde

1 Free French Bde

132 Infantry Bde (Brig Robertson)

X Corps
(Lt-Gen H. Lumsden)

1 Armoured Div
(Maj-Gen R. Briggs)

8 Armoured Bde
(Maj-Gen C.H. Gairdner)

10 Armoured Div
(Maj-Gen A.H. Gatehouse)

2 Arm Bde
(Brig A.F. Fisher)

7 Motor Bde
(Brig T.J.B. Bosville)

8 Arm Bde
(Brig E.C.N. Custance)

24 Arm Bde
(Brig A.G. Kenchington)

XXX Corps
(Lt-Gen Sir O. Leese)

51 Infantry Div
(Maj-Gen D.N. Wimberley)

1 South African Div
(Maj-Gen D.H. Pienaar)

2 NZ Infantry Div
(Lt-Gen B.C. Freyberg)

4 Indian Infantry Div
(Maj-Gen Sir F.I.S. Tuker)

9 Aus Infantry Div
(Lt-Gen L. Morshead)

152 Inf Bde

153 Inf Bde

154 Inf Bde

1 SA Inf Bde

2 SA Inf Bde

3 SA Inf Bde

5 NZ Inf Bde
(Brig Kippenberger)

6 NZ Inf Bde
(Brig Gentry)

9 (British) Armoured Bde
(Brig Currie)

23 (British) Arm Bde
(Brig Richards)

5 Indian Inf Bde

7 Indian Inf Bde

161 Indian Inf Bde

20 Aus Inf Bde
(Brig Wrigley)

24 Aus Inf Bde
(Brig Godfrey)

26 Aus Inf Bde
(Brig Whitehead)

OPERATION LIGHTFOOT

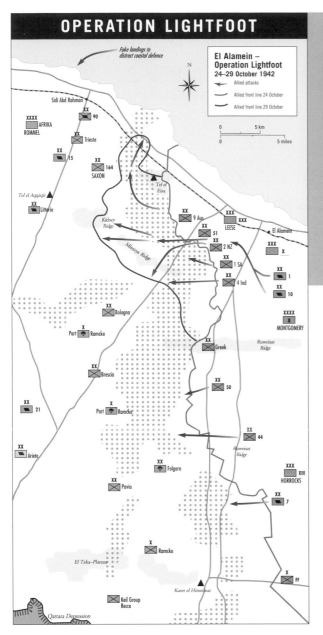

El Alamein – Operation Lightfoot
24–29 October 1942

→ Allied attacks
— Allied front line 24 October
— Allied front line 29 October

0   5 km
0   5 miles

N

Fake landings to distract coastal defence

24–29 October 1942

Operation Lightfoot, the opening offensive of the Battle of El Alamein, made good progress during its first hours, particularly as the 2nd New Zealand Division captured portions of Miteirya Ridge.

However, extensive minefields slowed the advance of much of the British armour, which had been meant to exploit any breaches in the German defences and to consolidate gains. Stiff resistance from a well-entrenched enemy took its toll, and the 10th Armoured Division, having cleared the minefields at long last, then became bogged down along Miteirya Ridge, sustaining heavy casualties. Fighting raged as the Germans attempted to dislodge Allied troops from nearby Kidney Ridge. Montgomery had expected the heavy fighting to last more than 10 days, and although his timetable had been disrupted he refused to relinquish an offensive posture.

1st FREE FRENCH BRIGADE (OCTOBER 1942)	
Brigade	**Units**
1st Fighting Free French Brigade HQ	1st Fighting French Flying Cln
	2nd Btn French Foreign Legion
	3rd Btn Infantry Marine Pacifique
	1st Fighting French Tank Coy
	1st Moroccan Spahis

2–4 November 1942

Operation Supercharge, an even more powerful offensive than its predecessor, began with the 7th Battalion, Argyll and Sutherland Highlanders, rapidly advancing on 2 November, while more than 200 tanks and armoured vehicles of the 1st Armoured Division spearheaded a drive toward Tel el Aqqaqir. Finally, XXX Corps had driven more than 3km (2 miles) into the German lines.

The 7th and 10th Armoured Divisions, along with the 9th Armoured Brigade and New Zealand infantry units, rapidly exploited the breakthrough. Sledgehammer attacks the following day finally succeeded in clearing German positions between Kidney Ridge and the Mediterranean Sea. During the fighting at El Alamein, German armoured strength was reduced to only 35 tanks, while casualties were estimated at 50,000. The British lost about 14,000 dead and wounded.

the Germans. As paths were cleared, the 1st and 10th Armoured Divisions followed.

The Eighth Army attacked the German defensive line for 11 days before Rommel, his fuel and ammunition depleted, undertook the 2250km (1400-mile) retreat to Tunisia.

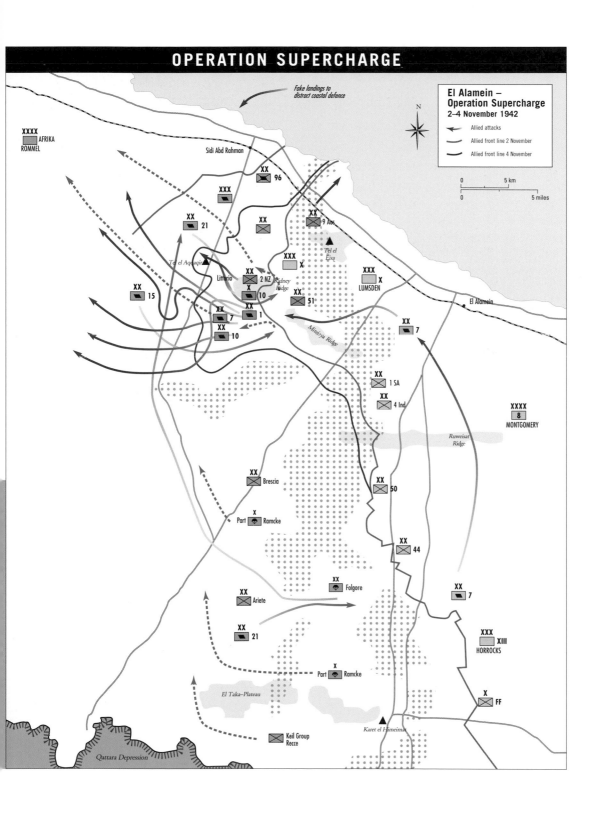

OPERATION SUPERCHARGE

Fake landings to
distract coastal defence

**El Alamein –
Operation Supercharge
2–4 November 1942**

N

Allied attacks

Allied front line 2 November

Allied front line 4 November

0   5 km

0   5 miles

XXXX
AFRIKA
ROMMEL

Sidi Abd Rahman

XX
96

XXX

XX
21

XX

XX
9 Aus

Tel el Aqqaqir

Littorio

XXX
X

Tel el
Eisa

XX
X   2 NZ
10   Kidney
Ridge

XXX
X
LUMSDEN

XX
15

XX
51

XX
X   1

XX
X   7

XX
X   10

Miteirya Ridge

XX
7

El Alamein

XX
1 SA

XX
4 Ind

XXXX
8
MONTGOMERY

Ruweisat
Ridge

XX
Brescia

XX
50

X
Part   Ramcke

XX
44

XX
Folgore

XX
7

XX
Ariete

XXX
XIII
HORROCKS

XX
21

X
Part   Ramcke

X
FF

El Taka–Plateau

Karet el Himeimat

XX
Keil Group
Recce

Qattara Depression

US Forces, 1942

With only two active divisions in 1940, the United States Army underwent a tremendous expansion and modernization prior to facing the enemy in North Africa at the end of 1942.

Less than two years before its entry into World War II, the United States Army consisted only of the 1st Cavalry and the 2nd Infantry Divisions. Influenced by the isolationist movement and constricted by the Great Depression during the 1930s, its post-World War I strength had dwindled to fewer than 200,000 soldiers by the end of the decade. Two officers were chiefly responsible for the reorganization and transformation of the US Army into a modern fighting force of more than eight million: General George C. Marshall, Army Chief of Staff, and General Lesley J. McNair, commander of Army Ground Forces.

US ARMORED DIVISIONS (APRIL 1942)		
Division	Armored Regiments	Armored Infantry Regiments
1 Armored	1, 13	6
2 Armored	66, 67	41
3 Armored	32, 33	36
4 Armored	35, 37	51
5 Armored	34, 81	46
6 Armored	68, 69	50
7 Armored	31, 40	48
8 Armored	36, 80	49
9 Armored	2, 14	52
10 Armored	3, 11	54
11 Armored	41, 42	55
12 Armored	43, 44	56
13 Armored	45, 46	59
14 Armored	47, 48	62
16 Armored	5, 16	476
20 Armored	9, 20	480

By the end of 1941, the US Army had grown to include 30 infantry, one cavalry and five armoured divisions. In 1945, a total of 89 divisions, 66 of these infantry, 16 armoured and five airborne, were fielded, while 70 of them were deployed to Europe.

Doctrine versus reality

While McNair worked to develop a modern army characterized by speed and mobility, the prevailing doctrine in the US armed forces establishment was to close with the main force of the enemy and defeat it in direct combat. McNair, however, favoured a structure and weaponry that facilitated movement. For example, the tank was considered an infantry support weapon, its best employment being against enemy infantry rather than in tank-versus-tank combat. Therefore, the US armoured division was developed within the concept of a modern-day cavalry force that would exploit breakthroughs via mobility.

When the United States entered the war in December 1941, the army had organized 36 divisions numbering more than 1.5 million soldiers. Prior to Pearl Harbor, McNair also reshaped the standard infantry division from a 'square' configuration numbering 22,000 troops to a 'triangular' format with three standard regiments and other personnel totalling 15,514. As the war progressed, further refinements took place.

Firepower and mobility

In keeping with the doctrine of rapid movement, weapons were also designed for mobility. Despite growing concern from some quarters as the Nazi *Blitzkrieg* raged in Europe, an American tank design that incorporated a 75mm (2.95in) gun was not approved for production until 1940. Tanks were generally armed only with machine guns or light 37mm (1.45in) cannon. Anti-tank weapons were also light and ineffective against

US INFANTRY DIVISIONS (APRIL 1942)	
Division	**Regiments**
1 Infantry	16, 18, 26 Infantry
2 Infantry	9, 23, 38 Infantry
3 Infantry	7, 15, 30 Infantry
5 Infantry	2, 10, 11 Infantry
6 Infantry	1, 20, 63 Infantry
7 Infantry	17, 32, 159 Infantry
8 Infantry	13, 28, 121 Infantry
9 Infantry	39, 47, 60 Infantry
24 Infantry	19, 21, 34, 299 Infantry
25 Infantry	27, 35, 298 Infantry
26 Infantry	101, 104, 181 Infantry
27 Infantry	105, 106, 165 Infantry
28 Infantry	109, 110, 112 Infantry
29 Infantry	115, 116, 175 Infantry
30 Infantry	117, 118, 119 Infantry
31 Infantry	154, 155, 156, 167 Infantry
32 Infantry	126, 127, 128 Infantry
33 Infantry	129, 130, 136 Infantry
34 Infantry	133, 135, 268 Infantry
35 Infantry	134, 137, 140 Infantry
36 Infantry	141, 143 Infantry
37 Infantry	145, 148, 147 Infantry
38 Infantry	149, 151, 152 Infantry
40 Infantry	160, 184, 185 Infantry
41 Infantry	162, 163, 186 Infantry
43 Infantry	103, 169, 172 Infantry
44 Infantry	71, 114, 174 Infantry
45 Infantry	157, 179, 180 Infantry
63 Infantry	253, 354, 355 Infantry
66 Infantry	262, 263, 264 Infantry
69 Infantry	271, 272, 273 Infantry
70 Infantry	274, 275, 276 Infantry
75 Infantry	289, 290, 291 Infantry
76 Infantry	304, 385, 417 Infantry
77 Infantry	305, 306, 307 Infantry
78 Infantry	309, 310, 311 Infantry

US INFANTRY DIVISIONS (APRIL 1942)	
Division	**Regiments**
79 Infantry	313, 314, 315 Infantry
80 Infantry	317, 318, 319 Infantry
81 Infantry	321, 322, 323 Infantry
82 Infantry	325, 326, 327 Infantry
83 Infantry	329, 330, 331 Infantry
84 Infantry	333, 334, 335 Infantry
85 Infantry	337, 338, 339 Infantry
86 Infantry	341, 342, 343 Infantry
87 Infantry	345, 346, 347 Infantry
88 Infantry	349, 350, 351 Infantry
90 Infantry	357, 358, 359 Infantry
91 Infantry	361, 362, 363 Infantry
92 Infantry	365, 370, 371 Infantry
93 Infantry	25, 368, 369 Infantry
94 Infantry	301, 302, 376 Infantry
95 Infantry	377, 378, 379 Infantry
96 Infantry	381, 382, 383 Infantry
97 Infantry	303, 386, 387 Infantry
98 Infantry	389, 390, 391 Infantry
99 Infantry	393, 394, 395 Infantry
100 Infantry	397, 398, 399 Infantry
102 Infantry	405, 406, 407 Infantry
103 Infantry	409, 410, 411 Infantry
104 Infantry	413, 414, 415 Infantry
106 Infantry	422, 423, 424 Infantry
American (23 Inf)	132, 164, 182 Infantry

thick armour, limited to 37mm (1.45in) until midway through the war. The development of self-propelled artillery lagged, while the standard field gun of World War II was the towed 105mm (4.1in) howitzer.

In 1942, Marshall reduced the command structure of the army to three components: ground forces under McNair; air, commanded by General Henry 'Hap' Arnold; and supply, directed by General Brehon Somervell. A War Plans division was created to provide strategic direction for forces deployed during wartime.

Torch Landings

In their first large-scale joint operation of World War II, on 8 November 1942, Allied forces landed on the coast of northwest Africa, compelling the enemy to fight on two fronts.

The largest amphibious force assembled up to that time successfully landed Allied troops at three key locations during Operation Torch. The 25,000-man Western Task Force, under General George S. Patton, Jr., came ashore at Casablanca; the Central Task Force, commanded by General Lloyd Fredendall and composed of 39,000 troops, hit the beach at Oran; and the Eastern Task Force, led by General Charles Ryder, landed at Algiers with 20,000 American troops and later 23,000 British soldiers. The Americans had trained extensively; however, they had no combat experience.

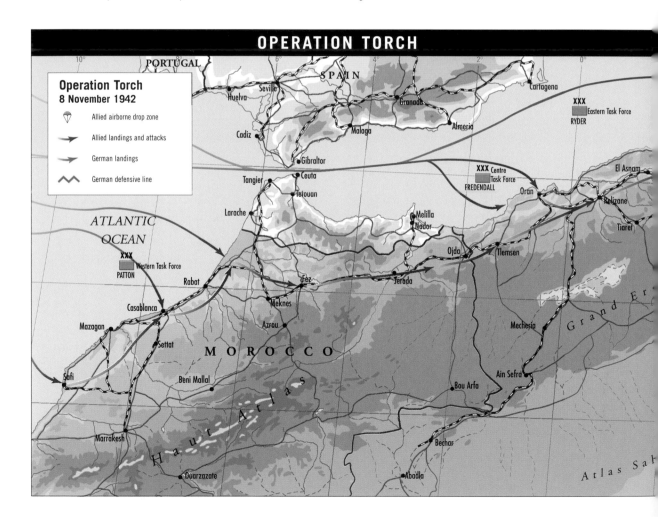

US ARMED FORCES COMMAND, MIDDLE EAST (OCTOBER 1942)

US ARMED FORCES, MIDDLE EAST
(Maj-Gen R.L. Maxwell)

- **Air Force (Maj-Gen L.H. Brereton)**
- **Services of Supply (Cairo, Egypt)**
  - **Eritrea Service Command**
  - **Delta Service Command**
  - **Levant Service Command**
  - **Persian Gulf Service Command (Maj-Gen D.H. Connolly)**

Commanded by Major-General R.L. Maxwell, the US Armed Forces Command, Middle East, maintained liaison and logistic structure in East Africa, Palestine and the territories of the Eastern Mediterranean.

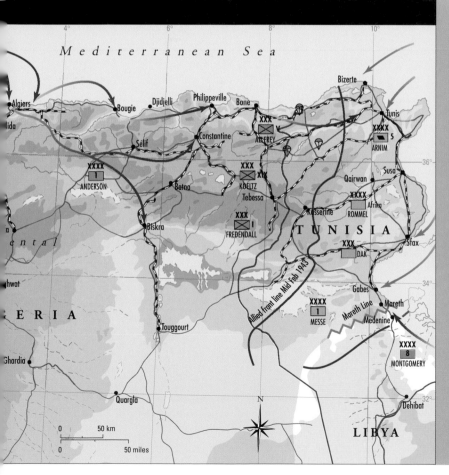

8 November 1942

Operation Torch, the Allied landings on the coast of northwest Africa at Casablanca, Oran and Algiers, was launched on 8 November 1942, and opened a second front against the Axis, placing American troops in combat for the first time against the Germans and Italians.

Torch was the largest amphibious undertaking in history up to that time. Vichy French forces resisted stubbornly at all three landing sites, while Vichy Deputy Premier Admiral Jean Francois Darlan was reluctant to sign an armistice until three days after the landings took place.

The objectives of Operation Torch included the seizure of key ports and airfields to prevent the reinforcement or evacuation of Axis troops from the continent of Africa and to squeeze the enemy between the landing forces and the British Eighth Army, which was pursuing the enemy westwards after El Alamein.

TORCH INVASION FORCE (NOVEMBER 1942)

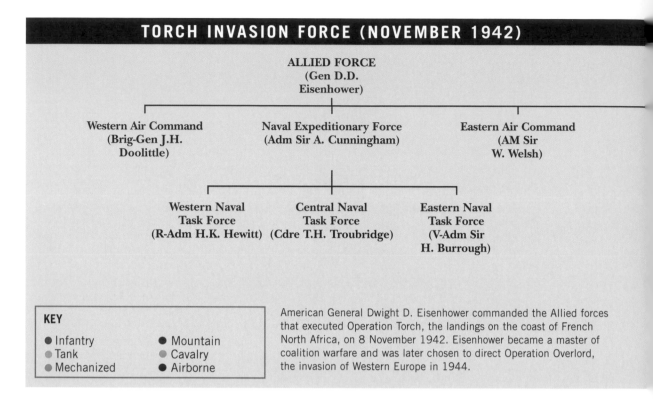

ALLIED FORCE
(Gen D.D. Eisenhower)

Western Air Command
(Brig-Gen J.H. Doolittle)

Naval Expeditionary Force
(Adm Sir A. Cunningham)

Eastern Air Command
(AM Sir W. Welsh)

Western Naval Task Force
(R-Adm H.K. Hewitt)

Central Naval Task Force
(Cdre T.H. Troubridge)

Eastern Naval Task Force
(V-Adm Sir H. Burrough)

KEY
- Infantry
- Tank
- Mechanized
- Mountain
- Cavalry
- Airborne

American General Dwight D. Eisenhower commanded the Allied forces that executed Operation Torch, the landings on the coast of French North Africa, on 8 November 1942. Eisenhower became a master of coalition warfare and was later chosen to direct Operation Overlord, the invasion of Western Europe in 1944.

Intent on seizing port facilities and airfields, the Allied forces would eventually grip the Germans and Italians in North Africa in a vice and force them to evacuate what men and equipment they could by sea. Seizing control of Tunis and Bizerte also offered the possibility of preventing the reinforcement or escape of any Axis troops. The Germans responded to the Torch landings by transferring troops to Africa from Sicily and occupying Vichy France.

Vichy resistance

For the Allies, a troubling question could not be answered until the moment the Torch landings commenced. Would the Vichy French troops in North Africa fight? The answer was not long in coming. Allied troops came under attack at all three landing points.

Resistance at Casablanca was the most stubborn as Vichy French naval units attacked the landing force and aircraft strafed the beaches. Patton's threat to unleash naval and air bombardment on the city finally brought about an armistice, signed by Admiral Jean

Francois Darlan, deputy of Vichy Premier Philippe Pétain, on 11 November. At Algiers, two British warships had been hit by artillery fire and were able to land only 250 of a 600-man contingent which was to secure port facilities in concert with beach landings. Oran had fallen within 48 hours, but not before one 600-man unit lost 300 dead and the rest captured.

Assault on Port Lyautey

One key element of the Western Task Force plan was the seizure of Port Lyautey near Casablanca. 'Sub Task Force Goalpost' was formed for the operation, under the command of General Lucian Truscott. The bulk of the force consisted of the 1st, 2nd and 3rd Battalions of the 9th Infantry Division's 60th Regiment, as well as the 66th Armoured Landing Team, 1st Battalion, 66th Armoured Regiment. The ground troops numbered more than 5000, and their training had been extensive.

Sub Task Force Goalpost was to occupy the village of Mehdiya on the coast, secure a defending fortress

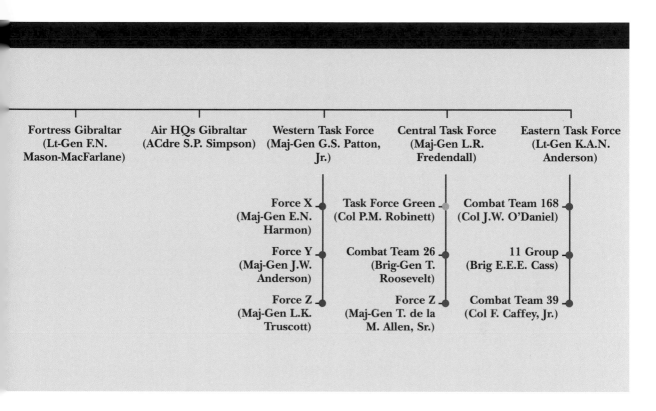

Fortress Gibraltar (Lt-Gen F.N. Mason-MacFarlane)	Air HQs Gibraltar (ACdre S.P. Simpson)	Western Task Force (Maj-Gen G.S. Patton, Jr.)	Central Task Force (Maj-Gen L.R. Fredendall)	Eastern Task Force (Lt-Gen K.A.N. Anderson)
		Force X (Maj-Gen E.N. Harmon)	Task Force Green (Col P.M. Robinett)	Combat Team 168 (Col J.W. O'Daniel)
		Force Y (Maj-Gen J.W. Anderson)	Combat Team 26 (Brig-Gen T. Roosevelt)	11 Group (Brig E.E.E. Cass)
		Force Z (Maj-Gen L.K. Truscott)	Force Z (Maj-Gen T. de la M. Allen, Sr.)	Combat Team 39 (Col F. Caffey, Jr.)

that commanded the approaches to the mouth of the Sebou River, and capture a nearby airfield. The defenders of Port Lyautey included French Foreign Legionnaires, the 8th Tabor Battalion of Moroccan Goums and the 1st Moroccan Infantry Regiment.

Typical of the confusion that reigned at numerous locations was the ordeal of two American officers who attempted to negotiate with the Vichy authorities before the Port Lyautey landings. One of them was killed by machine-gun fire, while the other was told that the authorities sympathized with the Allies but that they would lay down their arms only in response to a direct order.

Thrown off schedule, the first and second waves of troops became intermingled. Although the landings should have taken place under cover of darkness, the event occurred at 6 a.m. – in daylight. The Americans were able to secure their beachhead on the first day but were unable to take the airfield or Port Lyautey itself, which lay further inland, until 10 November. It had cost them 225 dead and wounded.

Regimental Combat Team and Combat Command
The US force at Port Lyautey has also been referred to as the 60th Regimental Combat Team (RCT). The RCT was a concept whose roots lay in tactics of the American Revolution. In World War II, such a team consisted of combat units with attached support such as an artillery battalion or anti-aircraft battery, along with engineers, a medical company and a signal detachment combined to achieve a specific mission.

Comparable in size to a brigade or a regiment, the Combat Command (CC) was utilized by American armoured forces from 1942. The CC was similar to a Regimental Combat Team in that it brought together combat elements such as tanks, armoured infantry, field artillery, tank destroyer battalions, engineers and other support troops.

However, the CC achieved flexibility in battle conditions at the expense of unit cohesion since battalions were not always kept together as in traditional regiments. The RCT did maintain infantry regiments with permanently assigned battalions.

Advance into Tunisia

While the Eighth Army pursued retreating Panzer Army Africa, the German Fifth Panzer Army was also assailed by Allied forces that had come ashore during Operation Torch.

While Axis forces in northern Tunisia retained control of Tunis, their only avenue of supply or escape, Allied forces that had come ashore during Operation Torch were organized into the British First Army, commanded by General Sir Kenneth Anderson. The three corps of First Army – the II US, V British and XIX French – were to drive for the Tunisian coast and the capital city, eventually linking up with Montgomery's Eighth Army moving westwards.

Although Rommel and Fifth Panzer Army commander General Jurgen von Arnim disliked one another, they recognized the need to work together and to strike the Allied forces in the west before Montgomery could hem them in. When Rommel reached Tunisia, his troops, reduced to only 78,000 with fewer than 130 tanks, occupied the old French fortifications of the Mareth Line. Meanwhile, the Americans were to experience combat against the veteran Germans.

Kasserine Pass

In mid-February, the Germans launched an offensive aimed at the untried Americans, with Rommel attacking towards Gafsa, and Arnim making for Sidi Bou Zid. Tanks and supporting infantry of the 21st Panzer Division trapped about 2500 American soldiers in the hills surrounding Sidi Bou Zid, and an abortive rescue attempt by a battalion of the American 1st Armoured Division was shredded by German artillery, tanks and dive bombers the following day. The rescue force lost 46 tanks and more than 300 men, while only 300 of the trapped soldiers, attempting to fight their way out, reached safety.

The Germans now threatened a large Allied supply base at Tebessa, 64km (40 miles) to the west. The narrowest point for a stand by the disorganized Americans was Kasserine Pass. While the green US troops were to learn bitter lessons in combat in North Africa, Kasserine proved to be the bitterest of them all.

On 19 February, the Germans attacked but were held off by American artillery. The next day, a heavy assault broke the defensive line, sending the Americans in headlong retreat. Rommel, however, hesitated, allowing the Allies to patch together a new line. By 22 February,

7TH ARMOURED DIVISION (FEBRUARY 1943)	
Brigade	**Units**
4th Light Arm Brigade	3rd RHA Royal Dragoons King's Dragoons Guards 2nd King's Royal Rifle Corps
22nd Arm Brigade	1st Royal Tank Regiment 5th Royal Tank Regiment 4th County of London Yeomanry 5th Field Regiment RHA 1st Rifle Brigade
131st Queens Brigade	1/5th Queens Royal Regiment 1/6th Queens Royal Regiment 1/7th Queens Royal Regiment 11th Field Company RE
Divisional units	11th Hussars

Nov 1942–Feb 1943

After the Torch landings, Allied armies closed in on the Axis forces in Tunisia. However, plenty of fight remained in the veteran troops of Rommel and Arnim. The Germans bought time with an offensive in the west before the First and Eighth Armies could link up. Three days of attacks against untried American forces inflicted the stinging defeat at Kasserine Pass and cost the US forces dearly: there were more than 6300 casualties. Rommel, expecting a counterattack, halted his advance for a full day, long enough for the Allies to reorganize. A new defensive line, protecting the town of Thala and the supply base at Tebessa, finally stopped the German tanks. General George S. Patton, Jr. assumed command of the US II Corps, restoring discipline and fighting spirit.

the imminent danger had passed, but the II Corps had been bloodied with 300 dead, 3000 wounded and another 3000 missing or taken prisoner.

Battle for the Mareth Line

On 6 March, Rommel turned his attention to Montgomery, attacking southeast towards Medenine. The Desert Rats of the 7th Armoured Division and the 51st Highland Division were waiting. The Germans lost more than 50 tanks and 700 killed and wounded. Rommel became convinced that North Africa was lost.

Two weeks later, the 2nd New Zealand Division, commanded by General Bernard Freyberg, attacked the Mareth Line defences but were bogged down by bad weather. Throwing the 1st Armoured Division in, Montgomery termed the intensified attack his 'left hook'. When the rear of the Mareth Line was threatened, he sent the 4th Indian Division to dislodge Italian defenders at Wadi Akarit. These were followed by the hard-driving 50th Infantry and 51st Highland Divisions. The Axis forces began a general retreat towards the coast of the Mediterranean Sea.

Victory in North Africa

Following the compromise of the Mareth Line defences, the endgame for the Axis in North Africa followed swiftly.

With the Germans and Italians in retreat, elements of the First Army's II Corps and the Eighth Army's 12th Lancers finally linked up near the town of Sfax on 7 April 1943, five months after the Torch landings and nearly three years since the first shots of the desert war

had been fired in 1940. Arnim prepared the last stand of his forces, which now numbered about 175,000, in the northeast corner of Tunisia. Rommel, weary and in ill-health, had been recalled to Germany in March. The overwhelming superiority of the Allies in troops

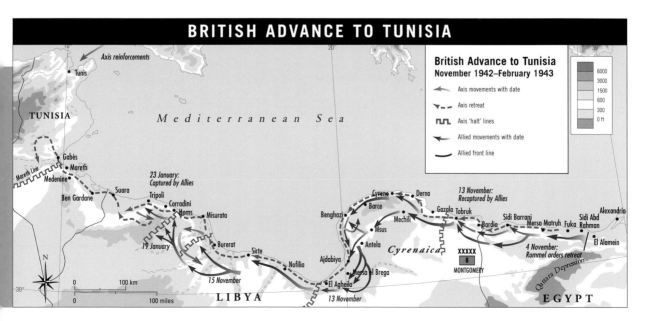

BRITISH ADVANCE TO TUNISIA

and equipment began to tell. With 380,000 soldiers, 1200 tanks and 1500 artillery pieces, they prepared for the final push.

As Arnim attempted to defend a front extending 200km (125 miles), the Allies assaulted surrounding high ground. On 22 April, the British 36th Infantry Brigade was repulsed at Longstop Hill west of Bizerte, but the next day the 8th Battalion, Argyll and Sutherland Highlanders, succeeded, although at heavy cost. Elements of the US II Corps used 17 Sherman tanks to destroy German defensive positions on Hill 609 to the north.

On 6 May, a barrage of 600 Allied guns launched the decisive attack against Arnim. Temporarily detached from the Eighth to the First Army, the 4th Indian Division and the 7th Armoured Division pierced defences at the Merjerda Gap. Rapidly, the remnants of the Fifth Panzer Army and Panzer Army Africa fell back towards Enfidaville. On the afternoon of 7 May, the 11th Hussars led the 7th Armoured into Tunis. The same day, US forces captured Bizerte. Pockets of resistance lingered, between Bizerte and Tunis, and at Cape Bon.

The Allies doggedly pursued Arnim, whose few remaining tanks ran out of petrol. Evacuation attempts

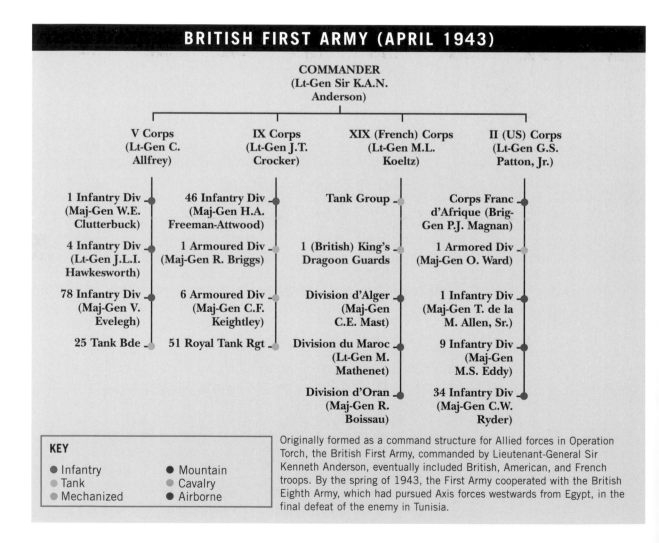

BRITISH FIRST ARMY (APRIL 1943)

COMMANDER
(Lt-Gen Sir K.A.N. Anderson)

V Corps (Lt-Gen C. Allfrey)	IX Corps (Lt-Gen J.T. Crocker)	XIX (French) Corps (Lt-Gen M.L. Koeltz)	II (US) Corps (Lt-Gen G.S. Patton, Jr.)
1 Infantry Div (Maj-Gen W.E. Clutterbuck)	46 Infantry Div (Maj-Gen H.A. Freeman-Attwood)	Tank Group	Corps Franc d'Afrique (Brig-Gen P.J. Magnan)
4 Infantry Div (Lt-Gen J.L.I. Hawkesworth)	1 Armoured Div (Maj-Gen R. Briggs)	1 (British) King's Dragoon Guards	1 Armored Div (Maj-Gen O. Ward)
78 Infantry Div (Maj-Gen V. Evelegh)	6 Armoured Div (Maj-Gen C.F. Keightley)	Division d'Alger (Maj-Gen C.E. Mast)	1 Infantry Div (Maj-Gen T. de la M. Allen, Sr.)
25 Tank Bde	51 Royal Tank Rgt	Division du Maroc (Lt-Gen M. Mathenet)	9 Infantry Div (Maj-Gen M.S. Eddy)
		Division d'Oran (Maj-Gen R. Boissau)	34 Infantry Div (Maj-Gen C.W. Ryder)

KEY
- Infantry
- Tank
- Mechanized
- Mountain
- Cavalry
- Airborne

Originally formed as a command structure for Allied forces in Operation Torch, the British First Army, commanded by Lieutenant-General Sir Kenneth Anderson, eventually included British, American, and French troops. By the spring of 1943, the First Army cooperated with the British Eighth Army, which had pursued Axis forces westwards from Egypt, in the final defeat of the enemy in Tunisia.

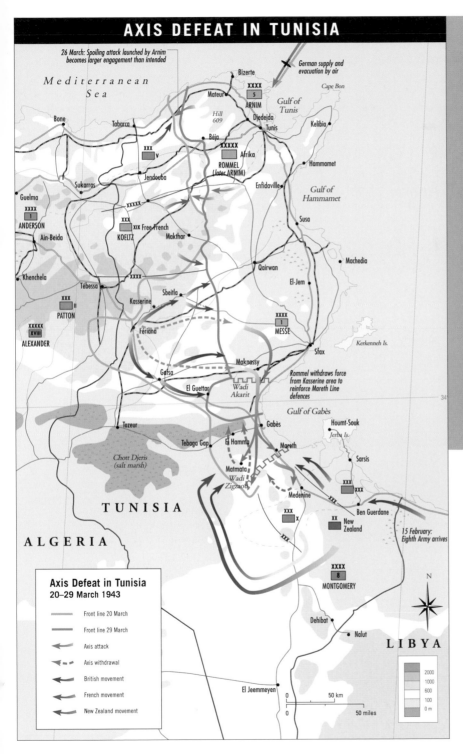

AXIS DEFEAT IN TUNISIA

26 March: Spoiling attack launched by Arnim becomes larger engagement than intended

German supply and evacuation by air

Mediterranean Sea

Bone
Tabarca
Bizerte
Mateur
Hill 609
XXXX 5 ARNIM
Djedejda
Tunis
Cape Bon
Gulf of Tunis
Kelibia

XXX V
Béja
XXXXX Afrika
ROMMEL (later ARNIM)
Hammamet

Sukarras
Jendouba
Enfidaville
Gulf of Hammamet

Guelma
XXXX 1 ANDERSON
XXXXX
Susa

Ain-Beida
XXX XIX Free-French KOELTZ
Makthar
Machedia

Khenchela
XXXX
Qairwan

Tébessa
Sbeitla
El-Jem
Kerkenneh Is.

XXX II PATTON
Kasserine
XXXX 1 MESSE

XXXXX XVIII ALEXANDER
Feriana
Sfax

Maknassy
Rommel withdraws force from Kasserine area to reinforce Mareth Line defences

Gafsa
El Guettar
Wadi Akarit
Gulf of Gabès

Tozeur
Gabès
Houmt-Souk
Jerba Is.

Chott Djeris (salt marsh)
Tebaga Gap
El Hamma
Mareth
Sarsis

Matmata
Wadi Zigzaou
XXX XXX

TUNISIA
Medenine
Ben Guerdane

ALGERIA
XXX X
XX New Zealand
15 February: Eighth Army arrives

XXXX 8 MONTGOMERY

Dehibat
Nalut
LIBYA

N

Axis Defeat in Tunisia 20–29 March 1943

Front line 20 March
Front line 29 March
Axis attack
Axis withdrawal
British movement
French movement
New Zealand movement

El Jeemmeyen
0 50 km
0 50 miles

2000 1000 600 100 0 m

March 1943

Elements of the British Eighth Army, under General Bernard Law Montgomery, repulsed counterattacks by Rommel at Medenine in early March, convincing the Desert Fox that the war in North Africa was lost. Montgomery followed with an offensive against Rommel's fixed defences at the Mareth Line, succeeding in unhinging Italian troops along its flank and rear.

On 7 April, the First and Eighth British Armies linked up at Sfax. During the first week of May, the Tunisian capital of Tunis and the city of Bizerte, with its vital airfield, fell to the Allies, and the Axis forces in North Africa were reduced to two defensive pockets, one between Bizerte and Tunis, and the other at Cape Bon. Organized resistance ended on 12 May, and the Axis surrender came the following day.

were largely unsuccessful, and on 12 May the final Axis resistance in North Africa ended. The following day, the Germans and Italians formally surrendered. Combat in Tunisia had cost the Axis 40,000 killed and more than 260,000 taken prisoner along with the loss of 250 tanks. Indeed, their losses during the North African campaign in terms of killed, wounded and captured were 620,000. Allied casualties in Tunisia exceeded 50,000. The British had lost 220,000 men in the desert war.

The Balkans: 1941–45

Conquest by Axis forces, vicious Partisan warfare, liberation and revolutionary ideology marked four years of struggle for supremacy in Greece, Yugoslavia and other nations of the peninsula.

Great Partisan leader Josip Broz Tito (centre, left) and other Yugoslav fighters pose for a photographer somewhere in Bosnia.

For Great Britain and the Commonwealth, the defence of the Balkans was problematic from the beginning. Although the Royal Navy held sway in the Eastern Mediterranean, the logistical challenges of inserting a formidable fighting force in support of the Greek and Yugoslav armies, battling first the Italians and then the combined forces of Mussolini, Nazi Germany, Hungary and Bulgaria, proved daunting.

Less than a week after Italian troops occupied Albania in April 1939, Britain and France guaranteed the sovereignty of Greece and Romania. On 23 October 1940, Italy invaded Greece. The following spring, Axis forces subdued the Royal Yugoslav Army in 11 days.

Resolute resistance

Although Mussolini had envisioned a spectacular military success when his forces invaded Greece, it soon became apparent that the small Greek Army was full of fight. In fact, a counter-offensive dislodged the Italians from Greek soil and pushed them rapidly back into Albania. The intervention of Hitler on behalf of his fascist ally set the Balkans fully ablaze.

While some British commanders argued that the transfer of troops from North Africa to Greece was ill-advised, the 62,000 British, Australian and New Zealand soldiers of W Force were deployed at the end of March 1941, only to be withdrawn scarcely a month later when the prospects for victory, or even for holding the line against the Axis, had waned.

This evacuation was followed by a heroic but futile defence of the island of Crete and the organization of resistance movements in Albania, Yugoslavia and Greece. Resistance activities inflicted losses on the German and Italian occupiers, who were unable to maintain permanent control of areas outside major cities and population centres.

By 1945, with the Soviet Red Army's surge westwards, the collapse of pro-Axis regimes in Romania, Hungary and Bulgaria, and the growing resistance movement, Germany was compelled to withdraw the bulk of its forces from the Balkans, although thousands were cut off. The Western Allies were involved in the liberation of the Balkans on a limited basis, with covert operations supporting Partisan activities and some British ground troops reintroduced into Greece.

BERNARD CYRIL FREYBERG, 1ST BARON FREYBERG (1889–1963)

Freyberg was born in London and relocated to New Zealand with his parents at the age of two. He commanded Commonwealth forces, primarily those of New Zealand, in the Balkans, North Africa and the Italian campaign. Serving with the British Army in World War I, he was wounded and received the Victoria Cross for valour. A heart condition forced his retirement in 1937.

• In 1939, Freyberg returned to active duty with the rank of major-general.

• Later that year, he was appointed commander of the 2nd New Zealand Expeditionary Force.

• As commander of Commonwealth forces on Crete, he was responsible for evacuating troops from the island.

• Freyberg played a key role in the planning and execution of the pivotal Eighth Army offensive, which began with the Battle of El Alamein.

• During the Italian campaign, he was instrumental in the controversial decision to bomb the abbey of Monte Cassino.

After the war, Freyberg served as Governor General of New Zealand. He was raised to the peerage with a barony in 1951.

Yugoslav Army: 1941

Internal ethnic tensions and external border threats from neighbouring countries required Yugoslavia to field a large army prior to the outbreak of war.

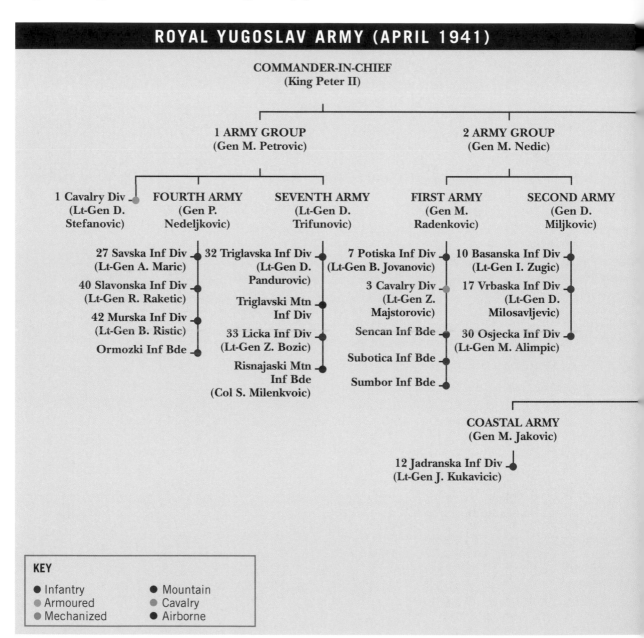

ROYAL YUGOSLAV ARMY (APRIL 1941)

COMMANDER-IN-CHIEF
(King Peter II)

1 ARMY GROUP
(Gen M. Petrovic)

2 ARMY GROUP
(Gen M. Nedic)

1 Cavalry Div
(Lt-Gen D. Stefanovic)

FOURTH ARMY
(Gen P. Nedeljkovic)

SEVENTH ARMY
(Lt-Gen D. Trifunovic)

FIRST ARMY
(Gen M. Radenkovic)

SECOND ARMY
(Gen D. Miljkovic)

27 Savska Inf Div
(Lt-Gen A. Maric)

40 Slavonska Inf Div
(Lt-Gen R. Raketic)

42 Murska Inf Div
(Lt-Gen B. Ristic)

Ormozki Inf Bde

32 Triglavska Inf Div
(Lt-Gen D. Pandurovic)

Triglavski Mtn
Inf Div

33 Licka Inf Div
(Lt-Gen Z. Bozic)

Risnajaski Mtn
Inf Bde
(Col S. Milenkvoic)

7 Potiska Inf Div
(Lt-Gen B. Jovanovic)

3 Cavalry Div
(Lt-Gen Z. Majstorovic)

Sencan Inf Bde

Subotica Inf Bde

Sumbor Inf Bde

10 Basanska Inf Div
(Lt-Gen I. Zugic)

17 Vrbaska Inf Div
(Lt-Gen D. Milosavljevic)

30 Osjecka Inf Div
(Lt-Gen M. Alimpic)

COASTAL ARMY
(Gen M. Jakovic)

12 Jadranska Inf Div
(Lt-Gen J. Kukavicic)

KEY

- Infantry
- Armoured
- Mechanized
- Mountain
- Cavalry
- Airborne

Yugoslavia's entry into World War II was precipitated by a coup d'état in the spring of 1941. When the government headed by the regent, Prince Paul, signed an alliance with the Axis, Serbian elements within the army executed the coup and installed 17-year-old King Peter II, who promptly renounced the previous government's policy.

In turn, the German Army, accompanied by Italian and Hungarian forces, invaded Yugoslavia with 52 divisions on 6 April 1941. In less than two weeks, the

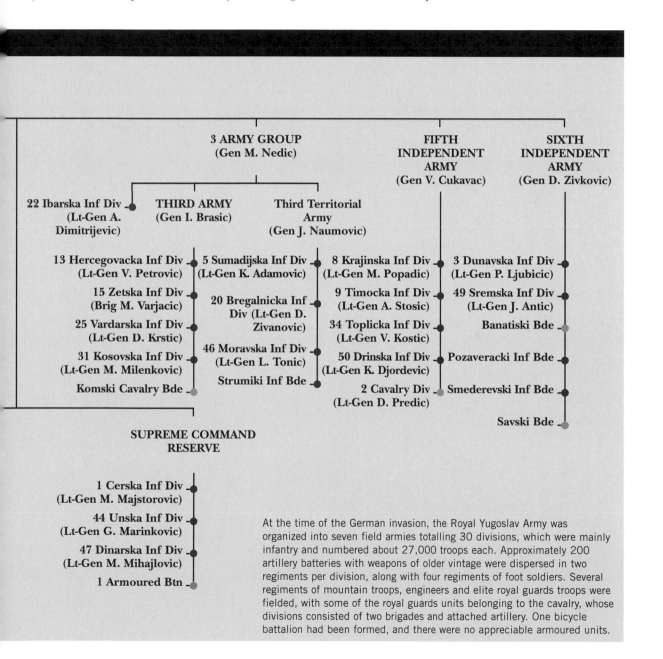

3 ARMY GROUP
(Gen M. Nedic)

FIFTH INDEPENDENT ARMY
(Gen V. Cukavac)

SIXTH INDEPENDENT ARMY
(Gen D. Zivkovic)

22 Ibarska Inf Div
(Lt-Gen A. Dimitrijevic)

THIRD ARMY
(Gen I. Brasic)

Third Territorial Army
(Gen J. Naumovic)

13 Hercegovacka Inf Div
(Lt-Gen V. Petrovic)

5 Sumadijska Inf Div
(Lt-Gen K. Adamovic)

8 Krajinska Inf Div
(Lt-Gen M. Popadic)

3 Dunavska Inf Div
(Lt-Gen P. Ljubicic)

15 Zetska Inf Div
(Brig M. Varjacic)

20 Bregalnicka Inf Div (Lt-Gen D. Zivanovic)

9 Timocka Inf Div
(Lt-Gen A. Stosic)

49 Sremska Inf Div
(Lt-Gen J. Antic)

25 Vardarska Inf Div
(Lt-Gen D. Krstic)

34 Toplicka Inf Div
(Lt-Gen V. Kostic)

Banatiski Bde

31 Kosovska Inf Div
(Lt-Gen M. Milenkovic)

46 Moravska Inf Div
(Lt-Gen L. Tonic)

50 Drinska Inf Div
(Lt-Gen K. Djordevic)

Pozaveracki Inf Bde

Komski Cavalry Bde

Strumiki Inf Bde

2 Cavalry Div
(Lt-Gen D. Predic)

Smederevski Inf Bde

Savski Bde

SUPREME COMMAND RESERVE

1 Cerska Inf Div
(Lt-Gen M. Majstorovic)

44 Unska Inf Div
(Lt-Gen G. Marinkovic)

47 Dinarska Inf Div
(Lt-Gen M. Mihajlovic)

1 Armoured Btn

At the time of the German invasion, the Royal Yugoslav Army was organized into seven field armies totalling 30 divisions, which were mainly infantry and numbered about 27,000 troops each. Approximately 200 artillery batteries with weapons of older vintage were dispersed in two regiments per division, along with four regiments of foot soldiers. Several regiments of mountain troops, engineers and elite royal guards troops were fielded, with some of the royal guards units belonging to the cavalry, whose divisions consisted of two brigades and attached artillery. One bicycle battalion had been formed, and there were no appreciable armoured units.

command structure of the Royal Yugoslav Army had failed, due partly to its inability to coordinate defences on several fronts, including the south, where Greece was succumbing to German offensive pressure. When a counter-offensive against Axis forces in Albania failed to make appreciable gains, most of the Yugoslav Army was trapped in a pocket in Bosnia. On 17 April, the Yugoslav government surrendered and 340,000 prisoners were taken by the Germans.

Yugoslav arms

With all able-bodied men required to serve 18-month enlistments, the Royal Yugoslav Army was impressive on paper in 1939, having more than 150,000 soldiers. An extensive reserve also enabled the military to call up 700,000 troops as the threat of war grew by 1941. Nevertheless, the Yugoslav Army encountered serious challenges: mobility depended on the horse; armament was generally obsolete, although some modern equipment had been obtained from Czechoslovakia; and some of the army's rank and file had received as little as a month of training when war came.

The Royal Yugoslav Army surrendered, but thousands of soldiers refused to lay down their arms and fled into the countryside. Large resistance groups were organized and plagued the occupiers for the duration.

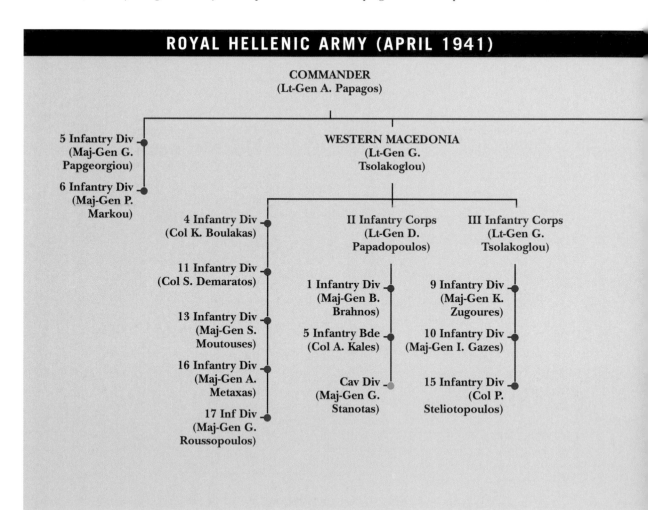

ROYAL HELLENIC ARMY (APRIL 1941)

COMMANDER
(Lt-Gen A. Papagos)

5 Infantry Div
(Maj-Gen G. Papgeorgiou)

6 Infantry Div
(Maj-Gen P. Markou)

WESTERN MACEDONIA
(Lt-Gen G. Tsolakoglou)

4 Infantry Div
(Col K. Boulakas)

11 Infantry Div
(Col S. Demaratos)

13 Infantry Div
(Maj-Gen S. Moutouses)

16 Infantry Div
(Maj-Gen A. Metaxas)

17 Inf Div
(Maj-Gen G. Roussopoulos)

II Infantry Corps
(Lt-Gen D. Papadopoulos)

1 Infantry Div
(Maj-Gen B. Brahnos)

5 Infantry Bde
(Col A. Kales)

Cav Div
(Maj-Gen G. Stanotas)

III Infantry Corps
(Lt-Gen G. Tsolakoglou)

9 Infantry Div
(Maj-Gen K. Zugoures)

10 Infantry Div
(Maj-Gen I. Gazes)

15 Infantry Div
(Col P. Steliotopoulos)

Greek Army, 1941

Experienced and taking full advantage of its mountainous frontier, the Greek Army proved a difficult adversary for the Italians until Hitler intervened with the might of the German *Wehrmacht*.

When the army of fascist Italy invaded Greece on 23 October 1940, Mussolini's grand vision of a stirring victory was quickly shattered. The Greek Army had mobilized weeks earlier and prepared to defend the difficult terrain stubbornly. Many Greek officers and soldiers had experienced combat during minor border disputes and during a brief but decisive reversal of fortune against the Turkish Army during the 1920s.

The large Greek Army was, however, deficient in modern equipment and transportation, continuing to

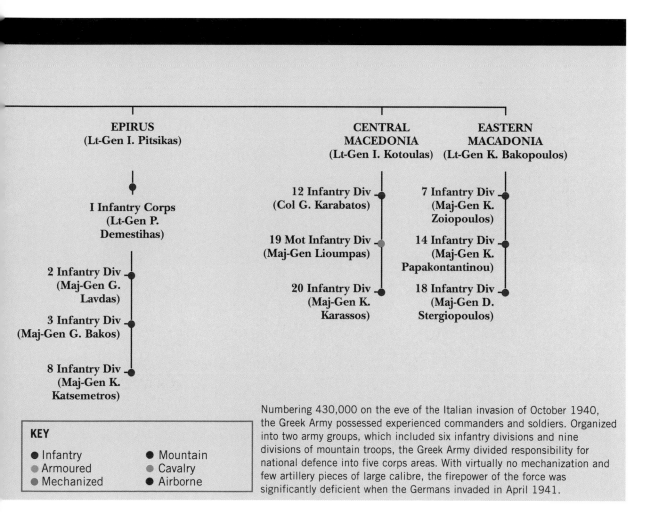

EPIRUS
(Lt-Gen I. Pitsikas)

I Infantry Corps
(Lt-Gen P. Demestihas)

2 Infantry Div
(Maj-Gen G. Lavdas)

3 Infantry Div
(Maj-Gen G. Bakos)

8 Infantry Div
(Maj-Gen K. Katsemetros)

CENTRAL MACEDONIA
(Lt-Gen I. Kotoulas)

12 Infantry Div
(Col G. Karabatos)

19 Mot Infantry Div
(Maj-Gen Lioumpas)

20 Infantry Div
(Maj-Gen K. Karassos)

EASTERN MACADONIA
(Lt-Gen K. Bakopoulos)

7 Infantry Div
(Maj-Gen K. Zoiopoulos)

14 Infantry Div
(Maj-Gen K. Papakontantinou)

18 Infantry Div
(Maj-Gen D. Stergiopoulos)

KEY

- ● Infantry
- ● Armoured
- ● Mechanized
- ● Mountain
- ● Cavalry
- ● Airborne

Numbering 430,000 on the eve of the Italian invasion of October 1940, the Greek Army possessed experienced commanders and soldiers. Organized into two army groups, which included six infantry divisions and nine divisions of mountain troops, the Greek Army divided responsibility for national defence into five corps areas. With virtually no mechanization and few artillery pieces of large calibre, the firepower of the force was significantly deficient when the Germans invaded in April 1941.

rely on horses and pack mules to carry provisions. Infantry shoulder arms and support weapons consisted mainly of bolt action rifles of pre-World War I vintage and French Hotchkiss and St Etienne machine guns. Few artillery pieces were heavier than 75mm (2.95in), since guns of greater calibre were impractical to deploy in mountainous terrain. A few smaller artillery pieces were specifically designed for use as mountain guns.

Greek Army organization

With 430,000 soldiers, the Greek Army of 1940 was organized into two army groups with five territorial corps areas to be defended. Each army group included six headquarters organizations, six infantry divisions, nine divisions of mountain troops, a cavalry division and four additional mountain brigades.

The mountain divisions, the core strength of the Greek Army, each included an artillery regiment and

6–28 April 1941

In response to a coup d'état in the Yugoslav capital of Belgrade, German forces invaded that nation on 6 April 1941. Swiftly, the Germans launched an invasion of northern Greece in support of the abortive attempt of the Italian Army to conquer the Peloponnese.

Greek forces resisted from behind the fortifications of the Metaxas Line, but the Germans, attacking from Yugoslavia and Bulgaria, steadily advanced in the eastern part of the country, capturing Salonika, Greece's second largest city, and trapping 70,000 soldiers.

On 20 April, the Greek First Army capitulated at Ionnena, and the Germans brushed aside delaying actions to capture Athens a week later. Sent to assist the Greeks, troops of the British and Commonwealth W Force were withdrawn by the end of the month.

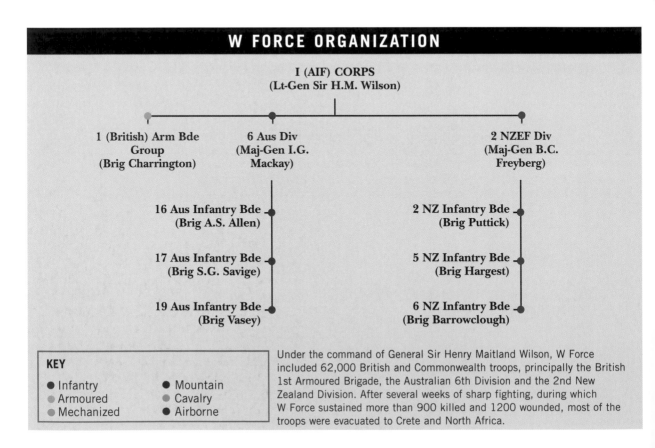

W FORCE ORGANIZATION

I (AIF) CORPS
(Lt-Gen Sir H.M. Wilson)

1 (British) Arm Bde Group
(Brig Charrington)

6 Aus Div
(Maj-Gen I.G. Mackay)

2 NZEF Div
(Maj-Gen B.C. Freyberg)

16 Aus Infantry Bde
(Brig A.S. Allen)

17 Aus Infantry Bde
(Brig S.G. Savige)

19 Aus Infantry Bde
(Brig Vasey)

2 NZ Infantry Bde
(Brig Puttick)

5 NZ Infantry Bde
(Brig Hargest)

6 NZ Infantry Bde
(Brig Barrowclough)

KEY
- Infantry
- Armoured
- Mechanized
- Mountain
- Cavalry
- Airborne

Under the command of General Sir Henry Maitland Wilson, W Force included 62,000 British and Commonwealth troops, principally the British 1st Armoured Brigade, the Australian 6th Division and the 2nd New Zealand Division. After several weeks of sharp fighting, during which W Force sustained more than 900 killed and 1200 wounded, most of the troops were evacuated to Crete and North Africa.

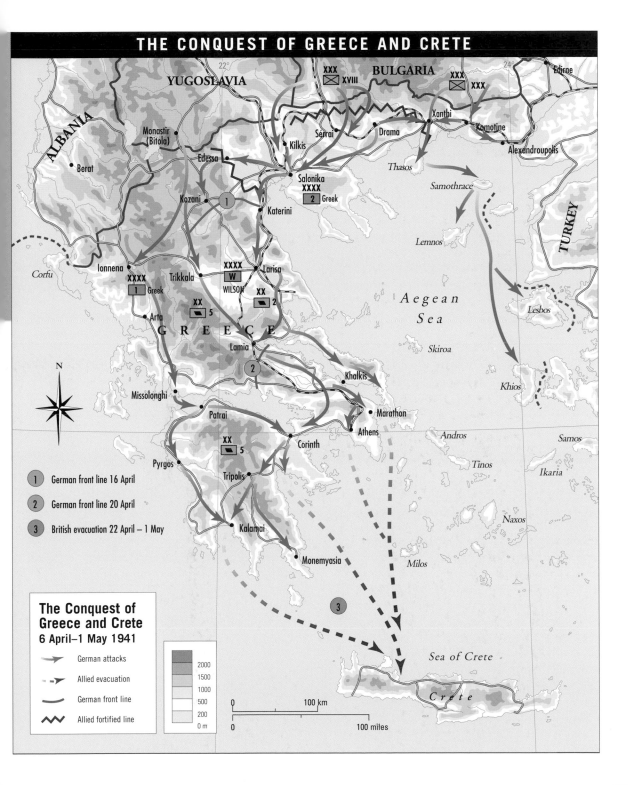

THE CONQUEST OF GREECE AND CRETE

YUGOSLAVIA

BULGARIA

ALBANIA

Berat

Monastir
(Bitola)

Edessa

Kozani

Katerini

Kilkis

Serrai

Drama

Xanthi

Komotine

Alexandroupolis

Edirne

Salonika

Greek

Thasos

Samothrace

Lemnos

TURKEY

Ionnena

Trikkala

Larisa

WILSON

Greek

5

2

G R E E C E

Lamia

*Aegean
Sea*

Skiroa

Missolonghi

Khalkis

Lesbos

Khios

Patrai

Marathon

Athens

Corinth

5

Andros

Samos

Pyrgos

Tripolis

Tinos

Ikaria

Naxos

Kalamai

Monemyasia

Milos

N

1 German front line 16 April

2 German front line 20 April

3 British evacuation 22 April – 1 May

**The Conquest of
Greece and Crete
6 April–1 May 1941**

German attacks

Allied evacuation

German front line

Allied fortified line

2000
1500
1000
500
200
0 m

0   100 km

0   100 miles

Sea of Crete

C r e t e

three infantry regiments. The Royal Guard, or *Evzones*, were the elite of the Greek armed forces and had been formed during the war for independence from the Ottoman Empire during the early nineteenth century.

When the Italians invaded, the Greeks had no tanks and few heavy weapons with which to oppose them. However, temperatures that dipped well below –17°C (0°F) and strong prepared positions in the mountains allowed the Greeks to stun the attackers. Prior to unleashing their own offensive, Greek troops trapped an Italian alpine division in the Pindus Mountains and killed 13,000 enemy soldiers. Later, the Greeks fought the Germans from behind the fortifications of the Metaxas Line, which was stubbornly defended. While they battled heroically with British assistance, the Greeks were finally compelled to accept defeat, surrendering on 1 June 1941.

British W Force

Under the command of British General Sir Henry Maitland Wilson, a contingent of British, Australian and New Zealand troops, 62,000 strong, was committed to the defence of Greece in February 1941. Consisting of the Australian 6th Division, the 2nd New Zealand Division and the British 1st Armoured Brigade, these troops became known collectively as W Force.

At Monastir Gap, elements of W Force held the advancing Germans at bay for three days in mid-April, with the Royal Horse Artillery firing its 25-pounder guns at the enemy until German tanks had closed to within 365m (400 yards). A week later, W Force conceded the defences around Mount Olympus and fell back towards the Greek capital of Athens. By 20 April, it was determined that the majority of the Commonwealth troops should be evacuated. From 24 April to 1 May, more than 50,000 W Force soldiers were safely extracted from the Greek mainland. The force had suffered about 2100 casualties. Greek Prime Minister Alexandros Koryzis, in a fit of despair, committed suicide.

On 27 April, the Germans marched into Athens. By this time, troops of the Greek First Army, who had previously driven the Italians out of their country, had been forced to capitulate. The Greeks had lost 70,000 dead and wounded.

Defence of Crete

Allied forces on the island of Crete made its conquest a pyrrhic victory for the German airborne troops participating in Operation Mercury.

Defeat on the Balkan mainland had been almost a foregone conclusion for the Allies. Once again, the odds were long that the island of Crete could be held against a concerted German effort to capture it. Continued Allied resistance was organized under General Bernard Freyberg, a British-born New Zealander. The German assault on Crete, codenamed Operation Mercury, was conceived as the first airborne invasion in military history. General Kurt Student, chief of the German airborne forces, had advocated such an operation with 22,000 troops and, despite significant misgivings, the *Führer* allowed it to proceed.

To oppose the Germans, Freyberg had at his disposal 31,000 Allied troops, including a significant number that had been evacuated from the Greek mainland. Known as Creforce, Freyberg's command included the British 14th Brigade, the Australian 19th Brigade, the New Zealand Division and 12,000 Greek soldiers. The 14th Brigade, which would prove itself a worthy adversary during the fighting at Heraklion airfield, consisted of the 2nd Battalion, Queen's Own Regiment; 1st Battalion, Argyll and Sutherland Highlanders; 2nd Battalion, The Rifle Brigade; 1st Battalion, Bedfordshire and Hertfordshire Regiment; 2nd Battalion, York and Lancaster Regiment; 2nd Battalion, Black Watch; and 7th Battalion, The Royal Leicestershire Regiment.

While the defenders did have the advantage of prepared positions, Freyberg had been appointed to

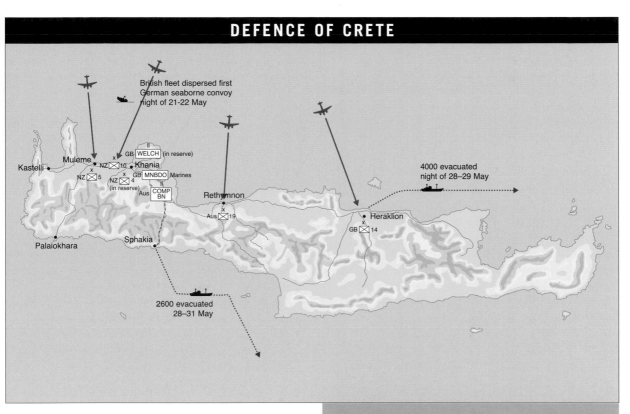

DEFENCE OF CRETE

British fleet dispersed first German seaborne convoy night of 21-22 May

4000 evacuated night of 28–29 May

Kastelli

Muleme

GB WELCH (in reserve)

NZ 10 Khania

NZ 5

NZ 4 GB MNBDO Marines
(in reserve)

Aus COMP BN

Rethymnon

Aus 19

Heraklion

GB 14

Sphakia

Palaiokhara

2600 evacuated 28–31 May

---

command only three weeks before Operation Mercury commenced on 20 May 1941. Creforce was also relatively lightly armed, its few tanks having seen a great deal of action in North Africa and being badly in need of repairs. A portion of the available artillery included guns captured from the Italians in North Africa and transported to Crete. A number of these weapons were in disrepair and virtually inoperable.

Communications were unreliable, with few working radios; therefore, the defenders relied heavily on runners and field telephones. Moreover, the *Luftwaffe* dominated the air, and the few fighter planes based on Crete were removed to North Africa on the day before the invasion.

Fighting like tigers

The Germans had seriously underestimated the number of defending troops on Crete, and when the day of the airborne invasion arrived, the reception was hot. British Intelligence had warned Freyberg of the basic plan for

21–31 May 1941

The 31,000 British and Commonwealth soldiers comprising Creforce offered a spirited initial defence of the island of Crete. On the opening day of Operation Mercury, German airborne and glider troops attacked airfields at Maleme, Rethymnon and Heraklion.

Warned by British Intelligence of the coming airborne invasion, Freyberg's troops shot down a number of German transport planes and inflicted heavy casualties on the invaders during the opening hours of Operation Mercury. The confused withdrawal of the 22nd New Zealand Battalion from Hill 107 near the airfield at Maleme facilitated German control of the facility and the landing of reinforcing mountain troops, which turned the tide in favour of the Germans and compelled Freyberg to order the evacuation of British and Commonwealth troops from the island.

the attack. Paratroopers and glider-borne infantry assaulted vital airfields at Maleme, Rethymnon and Heraklion, from west to east along the northern coast of the island. Anti-aircraft fire took a heavy toll in transport aircraft, some of which went down in flames before their cargoes of paratroopers could jump. Gliders flew so low that infantrymen riddled them with rifle and machine-gun bullets before they skidded to a stop.

The morning assaults had gone badly for the Germans, and the afternoon was no better. The 1500 attackers at Heraklion were reduced by one-third in short order. By the end of the day, 40 per cent of the German troops had been killed, wounded or captured. At Maleme, the New Zealand 5th Brigade defended Hill 107 bravely, but during the night the 22nd Battalion of New Zealanders lost its communication link and withdrew, fearing that it had been cut off. German forces gained control of the airfield and were then able to land reinforcing mountain troops.

With the unhinging of the western defences at Maleme, the situation deteriorated rapidly for Creforce. On 26 May, the coastal town of Khania was abandoned and Freyberg came to the painful conclusion that Crete must be evacuated. The troops on the western end of the island began to make their way towards the small harbour at Sphakia in the south. The evacuation,

harassed by constant German air raids, was conducted from 28–31 May. Some 4000 soldiers at Heraklion in the northeast were also pulled out. The remnants of the embattled Australian 19th Brigade, surrounded at Rethymnon, surrendered to the Germans on 30 May.

Defeat and withdrawal

By 1 June, the fighting on Crete was over. Operation Mercury had ended in a German victory; however, the price could hardly justify the gain. Nearly 2000 German soldiers had died on the island, while several hundred others were killed in the air or when their transport planes crashed at sea. Over 2500 Germans were wounded and 1800 captured or missing. Two hundred German aircraft, which could not easily be replaced, were lost. Never again would the German airborne arm launch such an ambitious attack.

For the British, the loss of Crete was another devastating defeat. More than 12,000 Commonwealth troops had been captured, while 1750 were killed and 1740 wounded. About 19,000 men were evacuated successfully, although 3000 soldiers drowned when their rescue vessels were sunk by German planes.

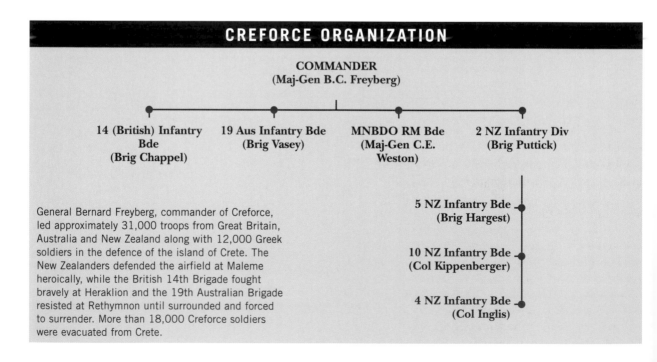

CREFORCE ORGANIZATION

COMMANDER
(Maj-Gen B.C. Freyberg)

14 (British) Infantry Bde
(Brig Chappel)

19 Aus Infantry Bde
(Brig Vasey)

MNBDO RM Bde
(Maj-Gen C.E. Weston)

2 NZ Infantry Div
(Brig Puttick)

5 NZ Infantry Bde
(Brig Hargest)

10 NZ Infantry Bde
(Col Kippenberger)

4 NZ Infantry Bde
(Col Inglis)

General Bernard Freyberg, commander of Creforce, led approximately 31,000 troops from Great Britain, Australia and New Zealand along with 12,000 Greek soldiers in the defence of the island of Crete. The New Zealanders defended the airfield at Maleme heroically, while the British 14th Brigade fought bravely at Heraklion and the 19th Australian Brigade resisted at Rethymnon until surrounded and forced to surrender. More than 18,000 Creforce soldiers were evacuated from Crete.

Partisan War: 1942–45

Communist irregular forces called Partisans took their toll and kept the Germans in the Balkans off-balance, while the Serbian nationalist Chetniks fought both for and against the Axis.

From the time that Axis forces set foot in Yugoslavia, the efforts of Partisan fighters to eject the invaders from their land had begun to build. The Germans were required to divert combat troops from the front lines, both east and later west, in order to combat the communist National Liberation Army, led by Josip Broz, known to his comrades as Tito.

Tito and the Chetniks
A rival grouping to the communists, the Chetniks, also emerged under the leadership of Draza Mihailovic. The Chetniks were initially organized to fight for the restoration of the monarchy but became increasingly more aligned with Serbian nationalism.

While the Partisans and Chetniks attempted to cooperate with one another, it became readily apparent that this could not take place. While the British declined to support the communists, they did, in fact, supply aid to the Chetniks in the beginning, unaware that Mihailovic was also accepting arms from the Germans and had begun participating in attacks against Tito's National Liberation Army.

Tito tackles the Axis
Once it became clear to them, through operatives within the Chetnik organization, that they were being double-crossed by Mihailovic, the British began to provide arms and supplies to Tito, who was industriously building an army to take on all-comers. At the end of 1942, the communist leader could count up to 150,000 soldiers organized into 23 brigades. Early Partisan activities centred around sabotage, disruption

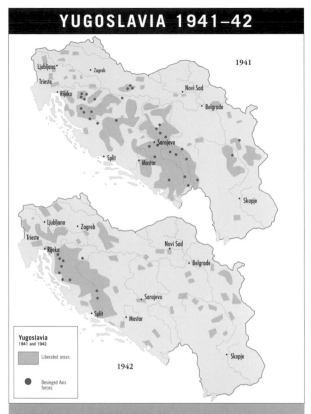

YUGOSLAVIA 1941–42

1941

Ljubljana · Zagreb
Trieste
· Rijeka
Novi Sad
Belgrade
· Sarajevo
· Split
· Mostar
· Skopje

Ljubljana · Zagreb
Trieste
· Rijeka
Novi Sad
Belgrade
Sarajevo
· Split
· Mostar
· Skopje

1942

Yugoslavia
1941 and 1942
   Liberated areas
● Besieged Axis forces

Partisan control
While the occupying Axis forces may have controlled the major cities and population centres, the Yugoslav countryside was the domain of the Partisans. Communist insurgents led by the capable commander Josip Broz, known as Tito, trained continually at camps in the mountains and as early as 1941 were carrying on irregular warfare against the Germans. Superb organizational skills allowed Tito to train and equip large numbers of guerrilla soldiers, particularly in western Serbia, where his forces occupied the town of Uzice, 64km (40 miles) south of Ravna Gora, a stronghold of the rival Chetniks.

The continuing threat of Partisan attacks compelled the Germans to maintain strong anti-guerrilla forces in Yugoslavia, troops that might otherwise have fought the Soviet Red Army on the Eastern Front. From 1943 until the end of the war, the Germans did launch five major offensive efforts to eliminate the Partisans. On several occasions, these came close to succeeding, and Tito himself was nearly killed.

of enemy communications and hit-and-run attacks against convoys and troops. As his strength grew, however, Tito boldly attacked in force, inflicting serious casualties on Italian occupation troops and taking control of significant areas in Serbia, including the town of Uzice. As Tito grew stronger, the threat of open revolt demanded action on the part of the Axis forces, which mounted five major offensive operations involving German, Italian and Bulgarian troops along with the collaborationist Chetniks.

Fall Weiss and beyond

As the Allies considered an invasion of Yugoslavia, the Germans had also become aware of the potential for an Allied invasion of the Balkans. To eliminate the

PARTISAN DETACHMENTS (1941–45)	
Area	Numbers
Bosnia and Herzegovina	59
Croatia	72
Macedonia	20
Montenegro	14
Slovenia	29
Serbia	41
Kosovo	6
Vojvodina	36

YUGOSLAVIA 1943

Yugoslavia
1941–1943

Liberated
areas

Besieged
Axis forces

1943

Large numbers of Axis troops were employed to suppress Partisan operations in Yugoslavia. Early in 1943, despite German efforts to decisively defeat the Partisans, Tito and the National Liberation Army effectively controlled significant areas of the country.

Tito extended his influence during the final years of World War II, seizing control of the Dalmatian coast when fascist Italy surrendered and eventually cooperating with the Soviet Red Army during the drive to liberate Belgrade.

threat of Partisan support for such an event, the Germans determined to eliminate the Partisans.

The first full-scale offensive against the Partisans, from January to April 1943, was termed *Fall Weiss* and included a force of 20,000 Chetniks. German and Italian forces encircled Tito and the Partisans on the banks of the Neretva River. Caught between the Germans to the west of the river and the Chetniks blocking their escape route to the east, the Partisans fought their way across the only bridge available to them, defeated the Chetniks and survived as an intact fighting force. Tito lost 8000 troops in the event.

The fifth and final offensive launched against the Partisans culminated with the Battle of the Sutjeska, an encounter lasting from 15 May to 16 June 1943. More than 125,000 Axis troops attacked 16 brigades of Tito's army, numbering about 18,000 soldiers, encircling the Partisans in the Durmitor Mountains of Montenegro.

Three Partisan divisions managed to break out of the trap, but nearly 6400 Partisans were killed, wounded or captured. Of these, three brigades and more than 2000 wounded Partisans surrounded at a field hospital were executed.

Britain rebuffed

In spite of Britain's continuing aid to Tito and the National Liberation Army, overtures of cooperation on the ground by Prime Minister Winston Churchill were flatly declined by the Partisans. Tito went as far as to warn Churchill that he would resist Allied troops if he

PARTISAN DIVISIONS (1941–45)
Division
1st Proletarian Division
2nd Proletarian Division
3rd Assault Division
4th Krajina Division
5th Krajina Division
6th Lika Proletarian Division 'Nikola Tesla'
7th Banija Division
8th Division
9th Dalmatian Division
10th Krajina Division
11th Krajina Division
12th Slavonian Division
13th Primorsko-Goranska Division
14th Slovenian Division
15th Slovenian Division
16th Vojvodina Division
17th Eastern Bosnian Division
18th Slovenian Division
19th Dalmatian Division
20th Dalmatian Division
21st Serbian Division
22nd Serbian Division
23rd Serbian Division
24th Serbian Division
25th Serbian Division
26th Dalmatian Division
27th Eastern Bosnian Division
28th Slavonian Division
29th Herzegovina Division

PARTISAN DIVISIONS (1941–45)
Division
30th Slovenian Division
31st Slovenian Division
Trieste Division
32nd Zagorie Division
33rd Croatian Division
34th Croatian Division
35th Lika Division
36th Vojvodina Division
37th Sandzak Division
38th Bosnian Division
39th Bosnian Division
40th Slavonian Division
41st Macedonian Division
42nd Macedonian Division
43rd Istrian Division
45th Serbian Division
46th Serbian Division
47th Serbian Division
48th Macedonian Division
49th Macedonian Division
50th Macedonian Division
51st Vojvodina Division
52nd Kosmet Division
53rd Central Bosnian Division
Garibaldi Division
Garibaldi Fontanot Division
Garibaldi Natisone Division
Venetia Division

believed such measures necessary. Later, even though the Soviet Union provided virtually no aid to the Partisans, Tito met with Soviet Premier Josef Stalin in Moscow and cooperated with the Red Army to achieve the liberation of Belgrade, the Yugoslav capital.

When Italy exited the war in 1943, Tito exploited the power vacuum by taking control of the Dalmatian coast, extending his influence even among non-communist Yugoslavs. Forming a provisional government in 1944, he became Yugoslavia's prime minister two years later and ordered Mihailovic executed. By war's end, Tito dominated Yugoslavia. In 1953, he proclaimed the Yugoslav Communist Republic.

Allied Liberation of Greece

A civil war was already raging in Greece as British troops returned to the Balkans in 1944. The German occupation of Greece ended in the autumn of 1944 as thousands of *Wehrmacht* troops began the long trek northwards through hostile country.

More than 20,000 Germans on garrison duty on islands in the Aegean Sea were left to surrender to Allied forces. On 1 October 1944, British commandos landed on the island of Poros, and this was followed by a contingent of British troops, which arrived on the 12th. By the time the British landed, the Greek Civil War was well underway. As early as 1943, the communist National Popular Liberation Army (ELAS) and the republican EDES were fighting one another, having cooperated against the Germans in only one major operation to destroy a viaduct and railroad line. This operation occurred while both armed forces were under British control.

With the Italian surrender in 1943, ELAS seized the abandoned weapons of the Italian Army and began fighting the EDES guerrillas rather than the Germans. While the Greek government in exile still functioned in Great Britain, the political arm of ELAS, known as EAM, established an alternative communist government. Meanwhile, the British contingent that had landed in Greece included more administrative troops than combat formations. This was due to the

October–November 1944

British troops returned to Greece in October 1944 and quickly became embroiled in the lingering Greek Civil War in support of the country's government in exile, which functioned in London. The communist ELAS and republican EDES factions had been fighting for some time, and the British Army was required to divert thousands of combat troops from Italy to restore order.

German Army Group E, however, managed to avoid a prolonged struggle with the Partisans or the advancing Soviet Red Army in Yugoslavia during its withdrawal from Greece. The Germans were harried by communist insurgents in Albania, eventually occupying a defensive line they maintained until the end of the war, stretching along the Danube River.

fact that a negotiated settlement reached several months earlier indicated that the rival Greek factions would recognize the government in exile when liberation was achieved. They would also allow their military forces to function under British control. While the communists received little support from Moscow,

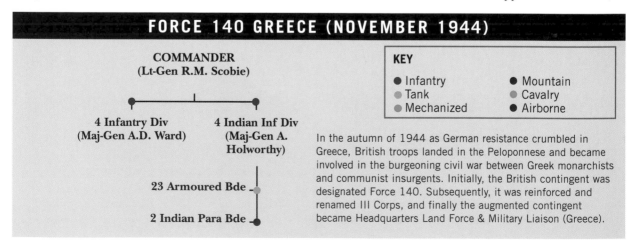

FORCE 140 GREECE (NOVEMBER 1944)

COMMANDER
(Lt-Gen R.M. Scobie)

KEY

- Infantry
- Tank
- Mechanized
- Mountain
- Cavalry
- Airborne

4 Infantry Div
(Maj-Gen A.D. Ward)

4 Indian Inf Div
(Maj-Gen A. Holworthy)

23 Armoured Bde

2 Indian Para Bde

In the autumn of 1944 as German resistance crumbled in Greece, British troops landed in the Peloponnese and became involved in the burgeoning civil war between Greek monarchists and communist insurgents. Initially, the British contingent was designated Force 140. Subsequently, it was reinforced and renamed III Corps, and finally the augmented contingent became Headquarters Land Force & Military Liaison (Greece).

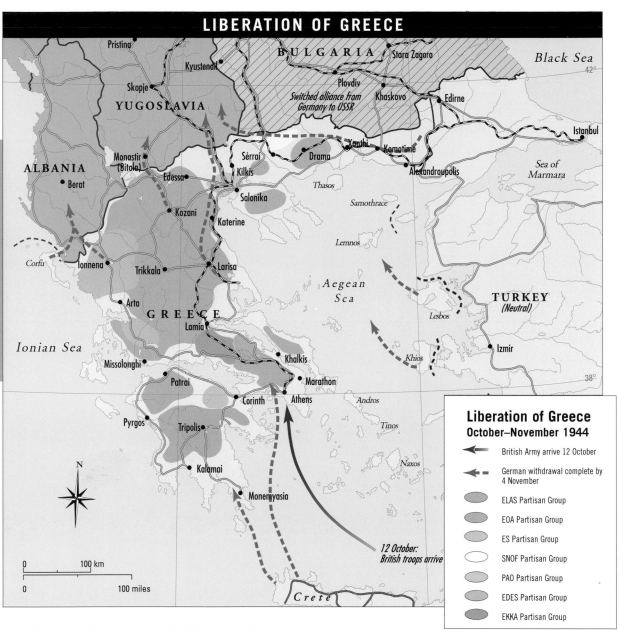

LIBERATION OF GREECE

Liberation of Greece
October–November 1944

→ British Army arrive 12 October

⇢ German withdrawal complete by 4 November

ELAS Partisan Group

EOA Partisan Group

ES Partisan Group

SNOF Partisan Group

PAO Partisan Group

EDES Partisan Group

EKKA Partisan Group

12 October: British troops arrive

they did eventually engage the British in armed conflict. The fighting grew so intense that by December the British held only 2.5sq km (1 sq mile) of the capital city of Athens and its vital airport facilities. Britain was forced to divert troops from Italy to quell the communist uprising. By February 1945, the ELAS forces were beaten and a cease-fire had been implemented. During the final months of World War II, Britain deployed 75,000 troops to Greece and suffered more than 2300 casualties. Following the plebiscite that validated the return of the Greek government in exile, the civil war erupted once more, lasting until 1949.

Sicily and Italy: 1943–45

With victory in North Africa complete with the capture of Tunis in May 1943, Allied military planners continued the second front strategy with assaults against fascist Italy.

A US M10 tank destroyer passes watching crowds as the US Fifth Army drives victoriously through liberated Rome.

Following the Allied victory in North Africa, discussions concerning future operations against Axis forces involved several options. Some strategists, primarily British, advocated an invasion of the Balkans, while others, many of them American, suggested that a cross-Channel assault on Northwest Europe should take place in 1943. Still others believed that a strike against the Italian islands of Sicily or Sardinia would be preferable.

Logistical challenges, including the continuing build-up of men and war materiel for the invasion of Normandy and the sheer distances necessary for an offensive in the Balkans, discounted two of these options. An amphibious invasion of Sicily appeared to be the most favourable course of action: the plan, codenamed Operation Husky, was formulated amid some wrangling between Allied leaders and was eventually executed in July 1943. Within weeks, the island was secured. Landings at Salerno and in the Taranto area on the Italian mainland took place in September. The subsequent Allied offensive up the boot of Italy proved to be a bitter two-year struggle.

Allied forces

General Dwight D. Eisenhower, commander of Allied forces in the Mediterranean, was to lead the Allied operations in Sicily and Italy until the end of 1943, when he transferred to England to command the Allied invasion of Normandy the following spring. Allied ground forces in the Mediterranean theatre were organized into the 15th Army Group, commanded by British General Sir Harold Alexander, and consisted initially of the US Seventh Army, under General George S. Patton, Jr., and the British Eighth Army, commanded by General Sir Bernard Law Montgomery.

The six divisions of the Seventh Army were divided into two corps, General Omar N. Bradley's II Corps and the Provisional Corps commanded by General Geoffrey Keyes. Montgomery's Eighth Army consisted of six divisions, two armoured brigades and an infantry brigade organized into XXX Corps under General Sir Oliver Leese and XIII Corps commanded by General Miles Dempsey.

As the war progressed, the British Army made a concerted effort to improve firepower at the battalion level, adding a support company, which included a motorized mortar platoon with six weapons, a platoon of anti-tank 6-pounder guns, which were towed by carriers, and an additional four carriers for the movement of troops and ammunition. In 1944, in the midst of the Italian campaign, flamethrowers mounted on carriers, nicknamed Wasps, were added.

Operation Husky

The invasion of Sicily on 10 July 1943 was the largest amphibious operation undertaken in modern warfare to that time. The assembled Allied invasion force consisted of 160,000 troops delivered and screened by a force of 2590 ships, and supported by 600 tanks, 1800 artillery pieces and 14,000 other vehicles.

Montgomery's Eighth Army came ashore at Syracuse on the southeastern tip of the island, while Patton's Seventh Army landed in the vicinity of Gela to the west.

The plan, upon which Montgomery had insisted, was for the Seventh Army to screen his left flank, while the Eighth Army made the main thrust against the 315,000 German and Italian soldiers on Sicily, capturing the port of Messina and trapping them on the island. Montgomery's progress, however, was slower than hoped. Meanwhile, Patton pushed the Seventh Army westwards and, with the approval of Alexander, captured the city of Palermo in the northwest. The Seventh Army then turned eastwards and outflanked Axis positions with a series of amphibious operations along the coast.

OPERATION HUSKY (9 JULY 1943)

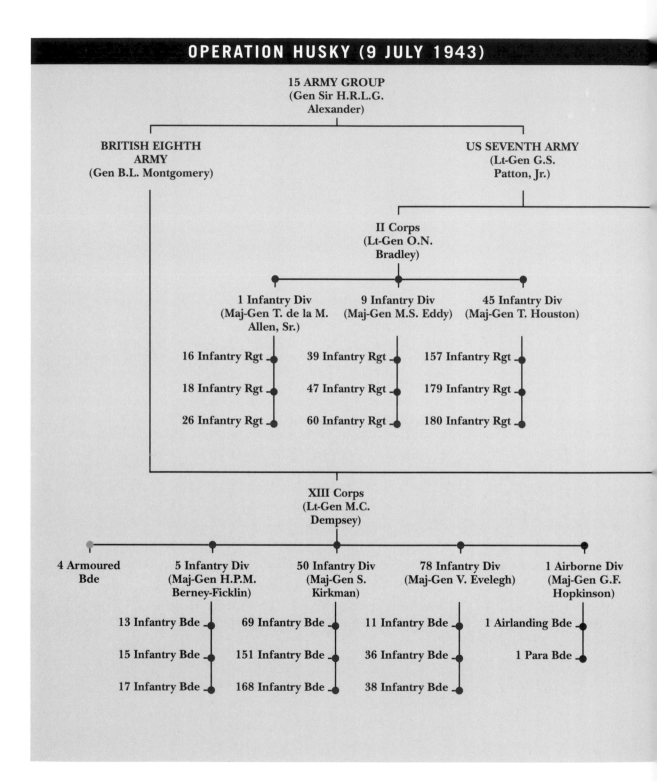

15 ARMY GROUP
(Gen Sir H.R.L.G.
Alexander)

**BRITISH EIGHTH
ARMY**
(Gen B.L. Montgomery)

US SEVENTH ARMY
(Lt-Gen G.S.
Patton, Jr.)

II Corps
(Lt-Gen O.N.
Bradley)

1 Infantry Div
(Maj-Gen T. de la M.
Allen, Sr.)

9 Infantry Div
(Maj-Gen M.S. Eddy)

45 Infantry Div
(Maj-Gen T. Houston)

16 Infantry Rgt

18 Infantry Rgt

26 Infantry Rgt

39 Infantry Rgt

47 Infantry Rgt

60 Infantry Rgt

157 Infantry Rgt

179 Infantry Rgt

180 Infantry Rgt

XIII Corps
(Lt-Gen M.C.
Dempsey)

**4 Armoured
Bde**

5 Infantry Div
(Maj-Gen H.P.M.
Berney-Ficklin)

50 Infantry Div
(Maj-Gen S.
Kirkman)

78 Infantry Div
(Maj-Gen V. Evelegh)

1 Airborne Div
(Maj-Gen G.F.
Hopkinson)

13 Infantry Bde

15 Infantry Bde

17 Infantry Bde

69 Infantry Bde

151 Infantry Bde

168 Infantry Bde

11 Infantry Bde

36 Infantry Bde

38 Infantry Bde

1 Airlanding Bde

1 Para Bde

KEY

- Infantry
- Tank
- Mechanized
- Mountain
- Cavalry
- Airborne

The Allied command structure in the Mediterranean included General Dwight D. Eisenhower, an American, as theatre commander, while General Sir Harold Alexander, a Briton, commanded the 15th Army Group, which bore the brunt of the fighting during the Italian campaign. In the Mediterranean, Eisenhower began to rapidly display his ability to overcome the personality conflicts and rivalries which characterize coalition warfare.

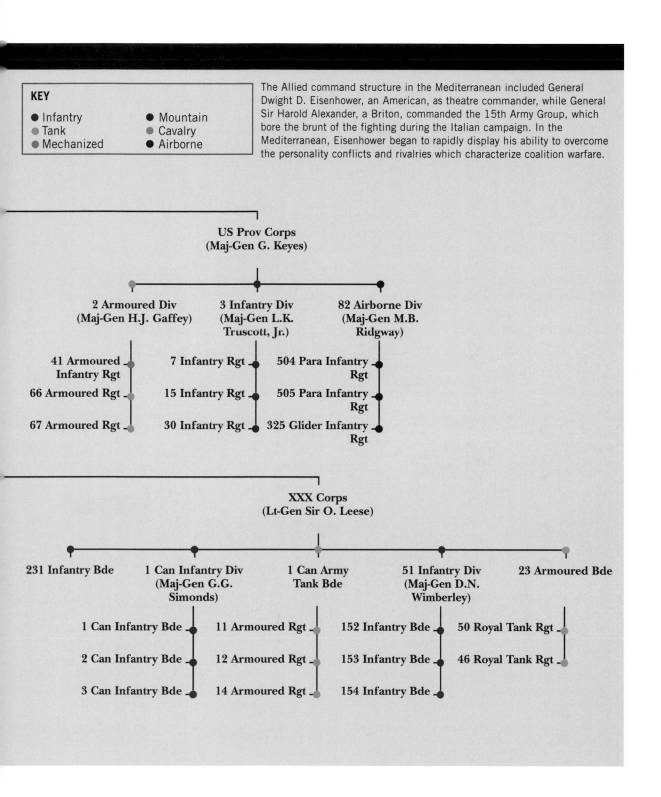

US Prov Corps
(Maj-Gen G. Keyes)

2 Armoured Div
(Maj-Gen H.J. Gaffey)

3 Infantry Div
(Maj-Gen L.K. Truscott, Jr.)

82 Airborne Div
(Maj-Gen M.B. Ridgway)

41 Armoured Infantry Rgt

66 Armoured Rgt

67 Armoured Rgt

7 Infantry Rgt

15 Infantry Rgt

30 Infantry Rgt

504 Para Infantry Rgt

505 Para Infantry Rgt

325 Glider Infantry Rgt

XXX Corps
(Lt-Gen Sir O. Leese)

231 Infantry Bde

1 Can Infantry Div
(Maj-Gen G.G. Simonds)

1 Can Army Tank Bde

51 Infantry Div
(Maj-Gen D.N. Wimberley)

23 Armoured Bde

1 Can Infantry Bde

2 Can Infantry Bde

3 Can Infantry Bde

11 Armoured Rgt

12 Armoured Rgt

14 Armoured Rgt

152 Infantry Bde

153 Infantry Bde

154 Infantry Bde

50 Royal Tank Rgt

46 Royal Tank Rgt

Montgomery eventually succeeded in moving around strong enemy defences near Mount Etna and slugged his way towards Messina. On 17 August, within hours of one another, the Seventh Army and then the Eighth Army entered the city.

Tragic friendly fire

One aspect of Operation Husky which initially went terribly awry was the airborne phase. Rough winds buffeted the 370 transport aircraft carrying the 505th Parachute Infantry Regiment of the US 82nd Airborne Division and the Airlanding Brigade of the British 1st Airborne Division. The Americans were mistakenly fired upon by Allied ships near one of the landing areas, and 33 planes were shot down with 37 damaged and more than 300 casualties. Only a fraction of the airborne troops assigned to the operation reached their assigned drop, or landing, zones.

The development of airborne divisions came during the 1940s for both the British and American armies. Although General Lesley J. McNair, architect of the new US Army during the period, disliked specialized divisions, he authorized the 82nd and 101st Airborne Divisions in 1942 and organized them as small infantry divisions with 8500 troops, organized in one parachute regiment and two glider regiments with light weapons. The British 1st Parachute Brigade had been constituted in 1941 and combined with the 1st Airlanding Brigade to form the 1st Airborne Division. The 6th Airborne Division was formed in 1943. At various times, the divisions numbered from 8500 to 10,000 troops.

10 July–17 August 1943

The attack on Sicily took place on 10 July 1943, on 26 beaches along 240km (150 miles) of Sicily's southeastern coast. In place of the half-hearted resistance expected, the Allied army faced fierce combat from the German divisions on the island. As Montgomery's army advanced north towards Messina, racing Patton's army that had burst through the centre of Sicily and was now driving along the north coast, the Germans decided to evacuate rather than make a last-ditch stand. Vigorous German rearguards gave a foretaste of the bitter fighting that was to come in Italy.

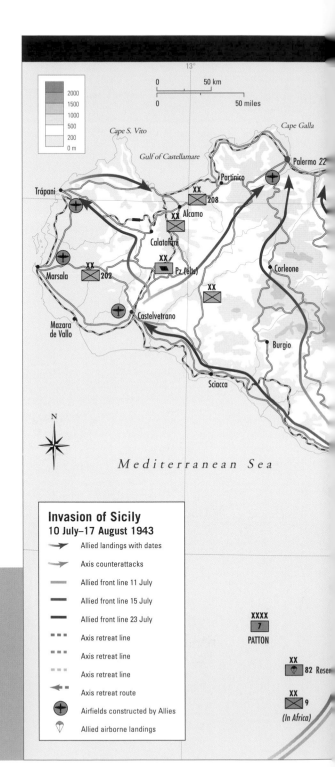

Invasion of Sicily
10 July–17 August 1943

- Allied landings with dates
- Axis counterattacks
- Allied front line 11 July
- Allied front line 15 July
- Allied front line 23 July
- Axis retreat line
- Axis retreat line
- Axis retreat line
- Axis retreat route
- Airfields constructed by Allies
- Allied airborne landings

INVASION OF SICILY

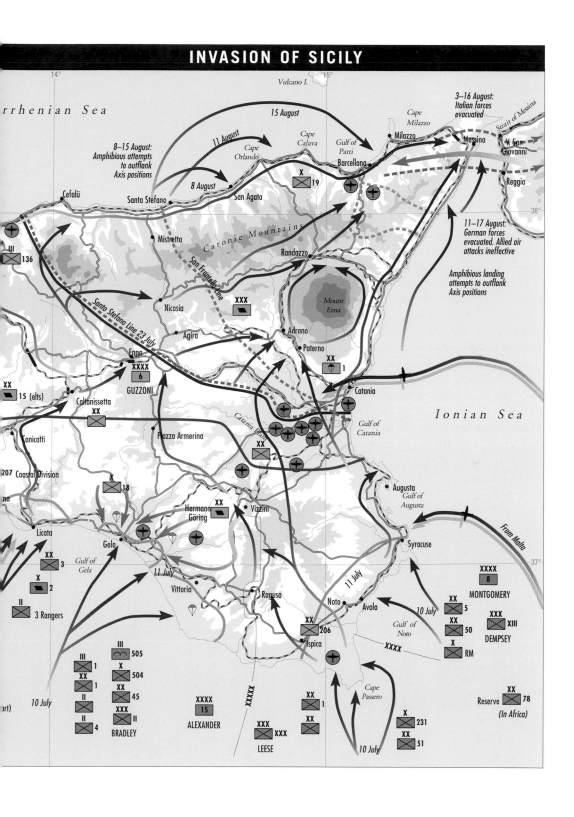

14°

Vulcano I.

15°

Tyrrhenian Sea

15 August

3–16 August:
Italian forces
evacuated

Cape
Milazzo

Strait of Messina

11 August

Cape
Calava

Gulf of
Patti

Milazzo

Messina

V. San
Giovanni

8–15 August:
Amphibious attempts
to outflank
Axis positions

Cape
Orlando

Barcellona

8 August

Reggio

Cefalü

Santa Stefano

San Agata

X
19

38°

11–17 August:
German forces
evacuated. Allied air
attacks ineffective

Mistretta

Caronie Mountains

Randazzo

Amphibious landing
attempts to outflank
Axis positions

III
136

San Frattello Line

Santa Stefano Line 23 July

Nicosia

XXX

Mount
Etna

Agira

Adrano

Paterno

Enna

XX
1

Ionian Sea

XXXX
6
GUZZONI

Catania

XX
15 (elts)

Caltanissetta

XX

Piazza Armerina

Catania Plain

Canicatti

207 Coastal Division

X
18

Hermann
Göring

XX

Vizzini

XX

Augusta
Gulf of
Augusta

Licata

Gela

Syracuse

From Malta

XX
3

Gulf of
Gela

11 July

XXXX
8
MONTGOMERY

37°

X
2

Vittoria

Ragusa

Noto

11 July

10 July

XX
5

II
3 Rangers

Avola

Gulf of
Noto

XX
50

XXX
XIII
DEMPSEY

III
1

III
505

XX
206

Ispica

X
RM

XX
1

XX
1

X
504

Cape
Passero

XX
231

Reserve

XX
78

II
1

XX
45

II
II

XXX

XXXX
15

XXXXX

XX
51

(In Africa)

II
4
BRADLEY

ALEXANDER

10 July

10 July

LEESE

XXX

10 July

(art)

10 July

Invading Italy

British Prime Minister Winston Churchill had long referred to the Mediterranean as the 'soft underbelly' of Axis-controlled Europe. The hard fighting in Sicily proved that, although Benito Mussolini had been deposed on 25 July, the German forces now occupying all of the Italian mainland would continue to stubbornly resist.

With the victory in Sicily, the US Seventh Army was pulled from the front and placed under the command of General Alexander M. Patch within 6th Army Group in order to rest and refit for the invasion of southern France, Operation Dragoon, which was to take place in support of the anticipated landings in northwest Europe in 1944.

By 1943, General McNair had further refined the strength and mobility of the US infantry combat division. While the former divisional organization, referred to as 'square', pre-dated US entry into World War II and included a complement of 22,000 riflemen and support troops, the streamlined 'triangular' division of 1943 numbered slightly more than 14,000. The result was that each fourth regiment taken from an existing square division could be used to constitute a new triangular division, maintaining overall strength but adding to the mobility of the forces in the field.

The triangular divisions were each equipped with enough transport to consider them motorized, with the exception of the infantry components. Their support elements included a headquarters company; a complement of divisional artillery; a battalion of combat engineers; companies of quartermaster, signal, ordnance, and military police; along with a reconnaissance troop. If necessary, the infantry regiments could be motorized with the addition of only six standard trucks.

US ARMORED DIVISIONS (15 SEPTEMBER 1943)		
Division	Tank Battalions	Armoured Infantry Battalions
1 Armored	1, 4, 13	6, 11, 14
4 Armored	8, 35, 37	10, 51, 53
5 Armored	10, 34, 81	15, 46, 47
6 Armored	15, 68, 69	9, 44, 50
7 Armored	17, 31, 40	23, 38, 48
8 Armored	18, 36, 80	7, 49, 50
9 Armored	2, 14, 19	27, 52, 60
10 Armored	3, 11, 21	20, 54, 61
11 Armored	22, 41, 42	21, 55, 63
12 Armored	23, 43, 714	17, 56, 66
13 Armored	24, 45, 46	16, 59, 67
14 Armored	25, 47, 48	19, 62, 68
16 Armored	5, 16, 26	18, 64, 69
20 Armored	9, 20, 27	8, 65, 70

3 September–15 December 1943

Operation Baytown, the step by the British Eighth Army from the eastern tip of Sicily across the Strait of Messina to Calabria on the Italian mainland, began on 3 September 1943. Six days later, Operation Avalanche, the landing of the Allied Fifth Army, under the command of General Mark Clark, took place at Salerno, the furthest point northwards which could be covered by a protective umbrella of Allied fighter aircraft. A small amphibious operation at Taranto and Brindisi, codenamed Operation Slapstick, was carried out by the British 1st Airborne Division as well. The landings at Salerno were hotly contested, as a single German division under General Heinrich von Vietinghoff established strong defensive positions and pounded the landing beaches.

The British and American troops at Salerno clung to their beachhead with grim determination, and naval gunfire beat back repeated German attacks. Meanwhile, the Eighth Army made progress northwards and compelled the German Tenth Army to withdraw towards fortified positions on the Gustav Line, including strong defences anchored at the town of Cassino.

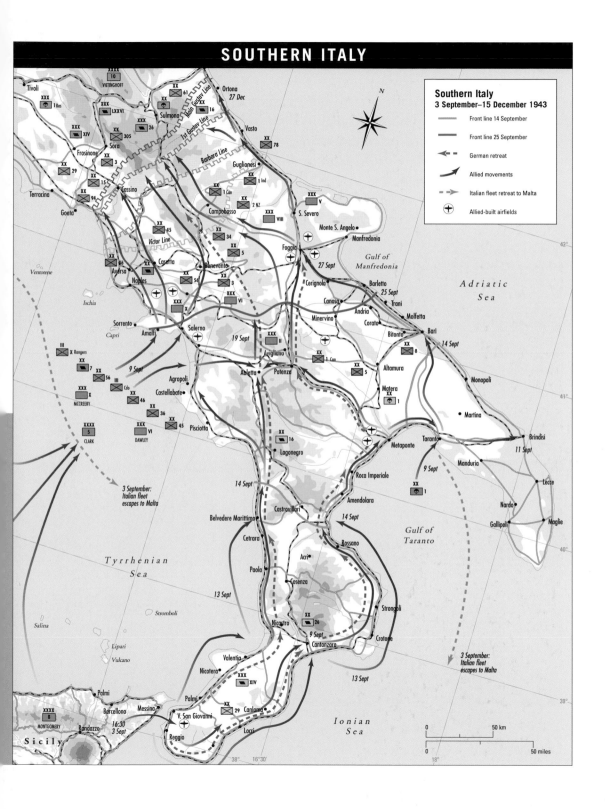

SOUTHERN ITALY

Southern Italy
3 September–15 December 1943

- Front line 14 September
- Front line 25 September
- German retreat
- Allied movements
- Italian fleet retreat to Malta
- Allied-built airfields

N

Tivoli
XXX 1 Res
XXXX 10 VIETINGHOFF
XX 61 Ortona 27 Dec
LXXVI Sulmona
XX 16
XX 26
305 Sora
XIV
Frosinone
Main Gustav Line
1st Gustav Line
XX 3
29 Cassino
XX 15
94 Terracina
Goeta
Barbara Line
Vasto
XX 78
Guglionesi
XX 1 Ind
XX 1 Can
XX 2 NZ
XX 45 Victor Line
XX 34 Campobasso
XX 5
XX VIII
S. Severo
XXX V
Monte S. Angelo
Manfredonia
Foggia 27 Sept
Gulf of Manfredonia
Ventotene
XX 46 Aversa
XX Caserta
Naples
XX 3
XX 56
XXX VI
Benevento
Cerignola
Barletto 25 Sept
Trani
Canosa
Andria
Corato
Molfetta
Bari 14 Sept
Minervino
Bitonto
XX 8
Ischia
Sorrento
Capri
Amalfi
Salerno 19 Sept
9 Sept
XXX II
XXX X
Avigliano
Abletta
Potenza
XX 1 Can
XX 5
Altamura
Matera XX 1
Monopoli
III X Rangers
XX 7
III 56
Cdo
XXX X MCCREERY
XX 46
XX 36
XX 45
Agropoli
Castellabate
Pisciotta
Martina
XXXX 5 CLARK
XXX VI DAWLEY
Lagonegro
XX 16
Metaponte
Taranto
Brindisi 11 Sept
Manduria
Lecce
Nardo
Gallipoli
Maglie
9 Sept
XX 1
14 Sept
Roca Imperiale
Amendolara
Gulf of Taranto
Tyrrhenian Sea
14 Sept
Castrovillari
14 Sept
Belvedere Marittimo
Cetrara
Rossano
Acri
Paola
Cosenza
13 Sept
Strongoli
Stromboli
Salina
Lipari
Vulcano
Nicastro
XX 26
9 Sept
Cantanzaro
Crotone
13 Sept
Valentia
Nicotera
XXX XIV
Ionian Sea
Palmi
Barcellona
Messina
XX 29 Canlama
XXXX 8 MONTGOMERY
Randazzo
16:30 3 Sept
V. San Giovanni
Sicily
Reggio
Locri

3 September: Italian fleet escapes to Malta

3 September: Italian fleet escapes to Malta

Adriatic Sea

42°
41°
40°
39°

16°30'
18°

0   50 km
0   50 miles

Landings at Salerno

The Allied soldiers who landed at Salerno on the mainland of Italy on 9 September 1943 discovered that their German opponents were stubborn and resourceful defenders who gave ground only at a high price.

In the pre-dawn hours of Operation Avalanche, the first Allied troops ashore were three battalions of US Army Rangers, who met little resistance at Maiori. However, the troops of the US VI Corps were under intense and accurate enemy fire from the moment they set foot on the beach. German tanks threatened the thin perimeter. The US 36th Infantry Division, in its first combat operation, was hardest hit. To the south, the British 46th and 56th Divisions of X Corps were at least 8km (5 miles) away.

The heavy resistance that met the British divisions required them to fight directly to their front rather than

9–16 September 1943

During Operation Avalanche at Salerno, troops of the Allied Fifth Army were nearly driven into the sea as the German 29th Panzergrenadier Division fired from the surrounding hills. German reinforcements repeatedly attacked the US 36th and 45th Divisions, which were thinly spread along their perimeter, nearly breaking through to the beach itself. Airborne reinforcements, naval gunfire, artillery and air support eventually stopped the Germans. Further counter-attacks were unsuccessful, and the approach of the Eighth Army from the south contributed to the decision to withdraw German troops to the Gustav Line.

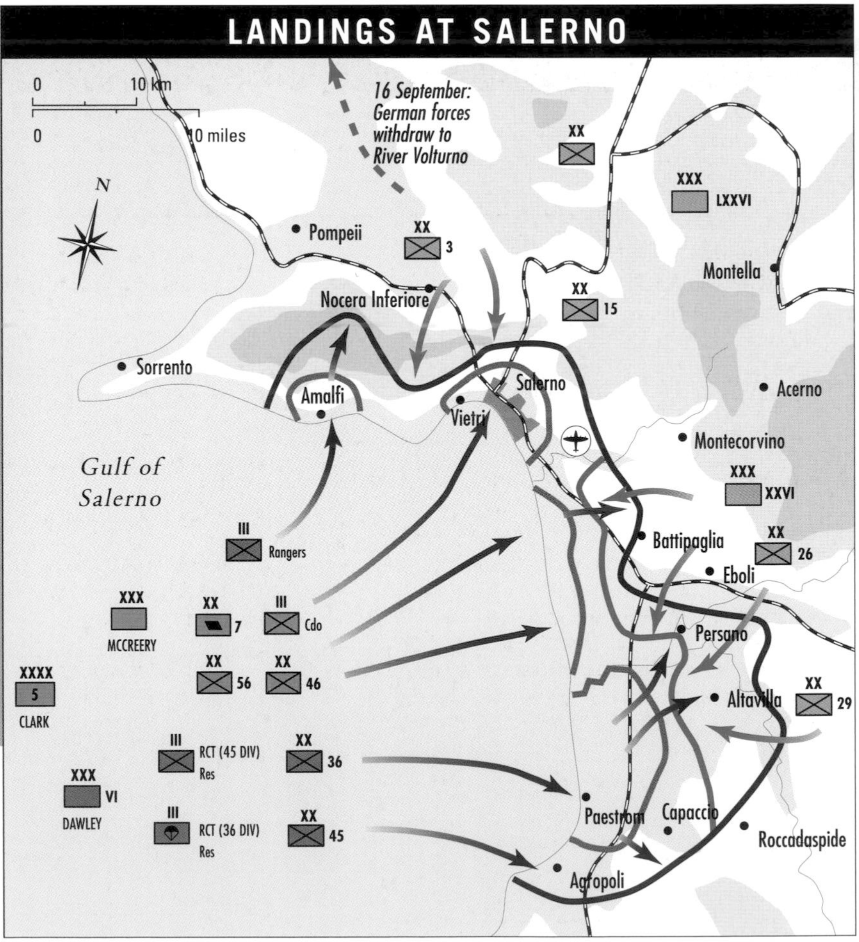
LANDINGS AT SALERNO
0
10 km
0
10 miles
N
16 September: German forces withdraw to River Volturno
Pompeii
Nocera Inferiore
Sorrento
Amalfi
Vietri
Salerno
Gulf of Salerno
Montella
Acerno
Montecorvino
Battipaglia
Eboli
Persano
Altavilla
Paestrom
Capaccio
Roccadaspide
Agropoli
XX 3
XX 15
XX
XXX LXXVI
XXX XXVI
XX 26
XX 29
III Rangers
XXX MCCREERY
XX 7
III Cdo
XX 56
XX 46
XXXX 5 CLARK
III RCT (45 DIV) Res
XX 36
XXX VI DAWLEY
III RCT (36 DIV) Res
XX 45

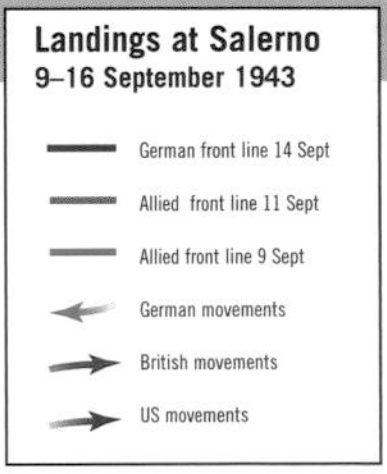
Landings at Salerno
9–16 September 1943
German front line 14 Sept
Allied front line 11 Sept
Allied front line 9 Sept
German movements
British movements
US movements

attempt the planned link-up with the Americans. The junction was not accomplished for two full days, and it was tenuous at best.

Fierce counterattacks, desperate stand

German armour and infantry, including elements of six divisions, counterattacked heavily during the next five days. The 2nd Battalion, 143rd Infantry Regiment, of the 36th Division was cut off by German tanks and virtually annihilated.

In the area of the US 45th Division, the left wing of the VI Corps line collapsed, driving a wedge between the two American divisions. German tanks were then able to drive to within 3.2km (2 miles) of the beach itself on 13 September. To stem the enemy tide, Clark

ordered cooks, musicians, clerks, and staff officers to take up rifles and defend the beachhead. The embattled Allies were reinforced by two battalions of the 82nd Airborne Division, totalling about 1300 troops, on the night of 13 September. This was followed by more than 3000 troops of the 325th Glider and 509th and 504th Parachute Infantry Regiments.

Eighth Army pushes on

Concentrated naval gunfire and efficient Fifth Army artillery combined with the advance of the Eighth Army from the south to force the Germans to withdraw. On 18 September, the VI and X Corps were firmly linked. On the 20th, elements of the Eighth Army made contact with Clark's forces.

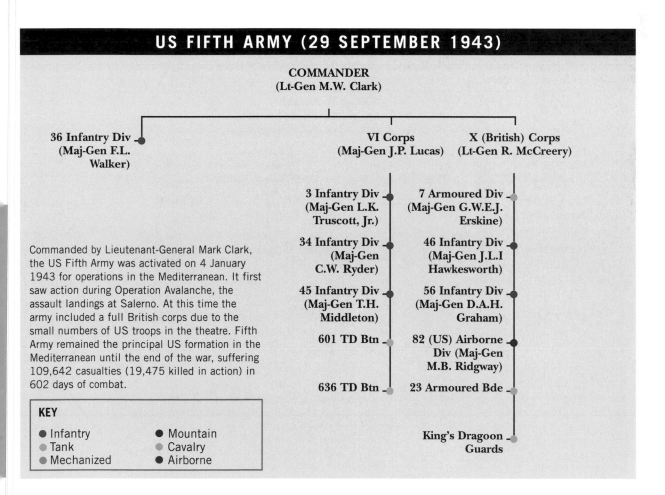

US FIFTH ARMY (29 SEPTEMBER 1943)

COMMANDER
(Lt-Gen M.W. Clark)

36 Infantry Div
(Maj-Gen F.L. Walker)

VI Corps
(Maj-Gen J.P. Lucas)

X (British) Corps
(Lt-Gen R. McCreery)

3 Infantry Div
(Maj-Gen L.K. Truscott, Jr.)

34 Infantry Div
(Maj-Gen C.W. Ryder)

45 Infantry Div
(Maj-Gen T.H. Middleton)

601 TD Btn

636 TD Btn

7 Armoured Div
(Maj-Gen G.W.E.J. Erskine)

46 Infantry Div
(Maj-Gen J.L.I Hawkesworth)

56 Infantry Div
(Maj-Gen D.A.H. Graham)

82 (US) Airborne Div (Maj-Gen M.B. Ridgway)

23 Armoured Bde

King's Dragoon Guards

Commanded by Lieutenant-General Mark Clark, the US Fifth Army was activated on 4 January 1943 for operations in the Mediterranean. It first saw action during Operation Avalanche, the assault landings at Salerno. At this time the army included a full British corps due to the small numbers of US troops in the theatre. Fifth Army remained the principal US formation in the Mediterranean until the end of the war, suffering 109,642 casualties (19,475 killed in action) in 602 days of combat.

KEY

- Infantry
- Tank
- Mechanized
- Mountain
- Cavalry
- Airborne

life. At various times, its strength consisted of a headquarters company, four mountain infantry regiments and three field artillery battalions with pack 75mm (2.95in) howitzers.

Accurate artillery

One aspect of the fighting in Italy that often tipped the balance in favour of the Allies was the presence of superb artillery. Although the guns were difficult to deploy in the mountainous terrain, their concentrated firepower decimated German troop formations and preceded offensive operations, accurately delivering ordnance at unseen enemy positions or engaging simultaneously on target support missions.

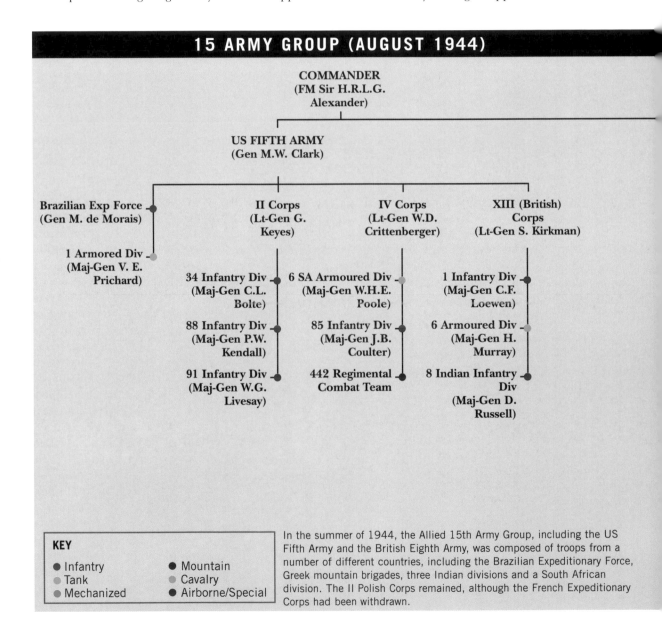

15 ARMY GROUP (AUGUST 1944)

COMMANDER
(FM Sir H.R.L.G. Alexander)

US FIFTH ARMY
(Gen M.W. Clark)

Brazilian Exp Force
(Gen M. de Morais)

II Corps
(Lt-Gen G. Keyes)

IV Corps
(Lt-Gen W.D. Crittenberger)

XIII (British) Corps
(Lt-Gen S. Kirkman)

1 Armored Div
(Maj-Gen V. E. Prichard)

34 Infantry Div
(Maj-Gen C.L. Bolte)

6 SA Armoured Div
(Maj-Gen W.H.E. Poole)

1 Infantry Div
(Maj-Gen C.F. Loewen)

88 Infantry Div
(Maj-Gen P.W. Kendall)

85 Infantry Div
(Maj-Gen J.B. Coulter)

6 Armoured Div
(Maj-Gen H. Murray)

91 Infantry Div
(Maj-Gen W.G. Livesay)

442 Regimental Combat Team

8 Indian Infantry Div
(Maj-Gen D. Russell)

KEY
- Infantry
- Tank
- Mechanized
- Mountain
- Cavalry
- Airborne/Special

In the summer of 1944, the Allied 15th Army Group, including the US Fifth Army and the British Eighth Army, was composed of troops from a number of different countries, including the Brazilian Expeditionary Force, Greek mountain brigades, three Indian divisions and a South African division. The II Polish Corps remained, although the French Expeditionary Corps had been withdrawn.

In the British Army, the greater availability of the 25-pounder gun as the war progressed provided stronger support as the 6-pounder took on the primary anti-tank role. Two officers, Generals Montgomery and Kirkman, were instrumental in recognizing that an increased artillery presence on the battlefield, employing shells in a creeping barrage, would offer tremendous shock value and suppress enemy fire against advancing troops.

The workhorse of the US artillery in Italy and elsewhere was the ubiquitous 105mm (4.1in) howitzer. Pre-war doctrine specified two primary roles for the field artillery: providing depth to the battlefield with counterbattery fire against enemy reserves and support

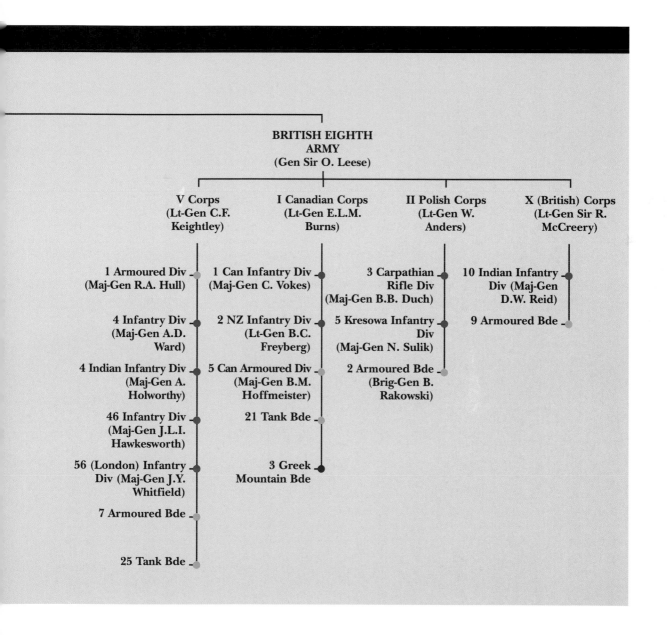

BRITISH EIGHTH ARMY
(Gen Sir O. Leese)

V Corps
(Lt-Gen C.F. Keightley)

I Canadian Corps
(Lt-Gen E.L.M. Burns)

II Polish Corps
(Lt-Gen W. Anders)

X (British) Corps
(Lt-Gen Sir R. McCreery)

1 Armoured Div (Maj-Gen R.A. Hull)

4 Infantry Div (Maj-Gen A.D. Ward)

4 Indian Infantry Div (Maj-Gen A. Holworthy)

46 Infantry Div (Maj-Gen J.L.I. Hawkesworth)

56 (London) Infantry Div (Maj-Gen J.Y. Whitfield)

7 Armoured Bde

25 Tank Bde

1 Can Infantry Div (Maj-Gen C. Vokes)

2 NZ Infantry Div (Lt-Gen B.C. Freyberg)

5 Can Armoured Div (Maj-Gen B.M. Hoffmeister)

21 Tank Bde

3 Greek Mountain Bde

3 Carpathian Rifle Div (Maj-Gen B.B. Duch)

5 Kresowa Infantry Div (Maj-Gen N. Sulik)

2 Armoured Bde (Brig-Gen B. Rakowski)

10 Indian Infantry Div (Maj-Gen D.W. Reid)

9 Armoured Bde

formations, and supporting those units assigned the tasks of taking and holding ground by firing on targets which impeded progress. The towed 105mm (4.1in) howitzer was accurate, capable of withstanding a great deal of battlefield wear, and produced in great

numbers after 1940. A total of 8536 of the 105s were built from 1941 to 1945.

Victory in northern Italy

In December 1944, General Clark assumed command

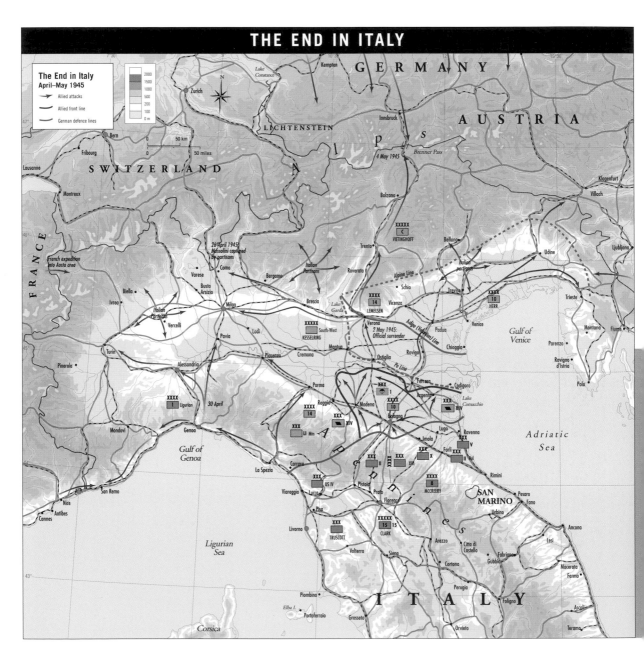

of the 15th Army Group following Field Marshal Alexander's promotion to command of the Allied forces in the Mediterranean theatre. Subsequently, General Truscott took command of the Fifth Army while Leese was succeeded by General Sir Richard McCreery in command of the Eighth Army.

Six months of near stalemate were broken with Allied attacks in April 1945. Within three weeks, German forces were retreating towards the Alps despite orders from Hitler that they fight along the lines of the Po and Adige rivers. On 21 April, Polish troops entered Bologna. Three days later, the German commander, General Heinrich von Vietinghoff, ignored Hitler's order and authorized a general withdrawal.

Surrender

On 29 April 1945, the surrender of all Axis forces in Italy was signed at Alexander's headquarters near Naples, and on 6 May, Allied troops transited the Brenner Pass into Austria. For the Allies, the Italian campaign had succeeded in keeping large numbers of German and Italian forces occupied so that they could not oppose the primary offensive in Northwest Europe or the relentless advance of the Soviet Red Army from the east.

April–May 1945

Following the breach of the Gothic Line by the Eighth Army in September 1944, German forces withdrew to positions south of the city of Bologna, and the Allies were unable to achieve further appreciable gains before the onset of harsh winter weather.

With the renewal of Allied offensive operations in April 1945, German troops were subjected to continual harassment from the air, while the Eighth Army advanced eastwards of Bologna and captured the city. Fifth Army advances in the west compelled the Germans to abandon defensive positions in the Po River Valley. As the Germans retreated, Allied troops cut them off before they could fully cross the Po.

On 2 May, German forces in Italy surrendered, and four days later the Allies were through the Brenner Pass and into Austria.

MARK W. CLARK (1896–1984)

The primary American command figure in Italy, Clark led the US Fifth Army during most of the two-year campaign. His controversial decisions ordering the 36th Infantry Division to cross the Rapido River and to divert forces from pursuit of the German Tenth Army to capture Rome are debated today.

• Prior to Operation Torch, Clark was appointed deputy commander of US Army forces in the Mediterranean.

• At Salerno, Clark's Fifth Army landings were seriously challenged by strong German resistance.

• In December 1944, Clark succeeded Field Marshal Sir Harold Alexander as commander of the Allied 15th Army Group.

• At the end of World War II, Clark was commander of all Allied troops in Italy.

After the war, Clark was appointed High Commissioner to Austria and served as Deputy to the US Secretary of State. He also served as commander of United Nations forces during the Korean War.

Northwest Europe: 1942–44

The Allies learned lessons from the disastrous raid on Dieppe in 1942, which were to bear fruit with the successful landings in Normandy on 6 June 1944. From there, it would be another 11 months before Nazi Germany was finally defeated.

British Churchill and Sherman tanks pass each other on a country road in Normandy following the invasion. Although no match for the German Tigers and Panthers, Allied tanks could normally assume a local superiority of at least four to one.

Since the evacuation of the British Expeditionary Force (BEF) from the European continent in 1940, Allied military planners had determined that the return of their forces to France and the defeat of the Germans on land would be a primary objective of the future prosecution of World War II. In December 1943, General Dwight D. Eisenhower had been named supreme commander of Allied forces in Europe. Eisenhower was charged with maintaining relations between the British and American commanders, which were sometimes strained, and with forging the coalition armies into a fighting force capable of defeating the Nazis in Western Europe.

Second front

Even while Allied forces were fighting the Axis in the deserts of North Africa, across Sicily, and up the torturous boot of Italy, the Soviets clamoured for the opening of a second front in Western Europe. The Nazis had taken a heavy toll in Soviet lives and treasure, and the efforts of the Western Allies to relieve the heavy pressure on the Red Army were deemed inadequate by Soviet Premier Josef Stalin.

Among the senior British and American commanders, the timing of an invasion across the English Channel and the strength required for its success were hotly debated. Many of the Americans argued for an attack in 1943; however, the British countered that available troops and supplies were inadequate. Eventually, the operation was planned for 1944.

Still, numerous raids by British commandos and other Allied forces – most notably the costly effort at Dieppe in August 1942 – obliged the Germans to guard thousands of kilometres of coastline and to fortify a large portion of it, which Hitler referred to as the Atlantic Wall. By the spring of 1944, the build-up of troops, tanks, artillery, aircraft and supplies in England had been deemed sufficient to launch Operation Overlord, the invasion of Nazi-occupied France. Within 10 months of landing on the beaches of Normandy, the Allied Expeditionary Force entered Germany, and World War II in Europe had come to an end.

Dieppe Raid: 1942

A dress rehearsal for the invasion of Nazi-occupied Europe, the Dieppe raid revealed numerous flaws in Allied planning.

British Combined Operations, led by Lord Louis Mountbatten, conceived the raid on Dieppe as an opportunity to validate tactics and test equipment for the future large-scale invasion of the European continent. Operation Jubilee was undertaken by Canadian and British forces numbering just over 6000 troops. The objective of the raid, scheduled for 19 August 1942, was to seize the port of Dieppe, opposite the southern coast of England, destroy gun emplacements and installations, and return safely.

Canadians to the fore

The Canadian 2nd Division, commanded by General J.H. 'Ham' Roberts, was selected for Operation Jubilee. The entire Allied force consisted of the Canadian 4th and 6th Infantry Brigades, the Canadian 14th Tank Battalion (Calgary Regiment), British No. 3 and No. 4 Commandos, Royal Marine A Commando and a contingent of 50 US Army Rangers. Additionally, 70 squadrons of Royal Air Force (RAF) fighters and fighter-bombers were employed to provide protection and a ground-attack capability.

Commando raiders

The original commando units had been formed in the British Army in 1940 in response to a call to arms by Prime Minister Winston Churchill. Each commando unit was initially composed of three officers and six troops of 65 soldiers, which included a heavy weapons troop. During the course of World War II, some

OMAHA BEACH	
Unit	**Commander**
1ST INFANTRY DIVISION	Maj-Gen C.R. Huebner
16th Infantry Rgt	Col G.A. Taylor
18th Infantry Rgt	Col G. Smith, Jr.
26th Infantry Rgt	Col J.F.R. Seitz
ATTACHMENTS	
741st Tank Battalion	Lt-Col R.N. Skaggs
745th Tank Battalion	Lt-Col W. Nichols
635th Tank Destroyer Btn	Lt-Col W. Smith
16th Rgtl Combat Team	Col C.D.W. Canham
115th Rgtl Combat Team	Col E.N. Slappey
29TH INFANTRY DIVISION	Maj-Gen C. H. Gerhardt
115th Infantry Rgt	Col E.N. Slappey
116th Infantry Rgt	Col C.D.W. Canham
175th Infantry Rgt	Col P.R. Goode
ATTACHMENTS	
743rd Tank Battalion	Lt-Col J.S. Upham, Jr
747th Tank Battalion	Lt-Col S.G. Fries
26th Rgtl Combat Team	Col J.F.R. Seitz

UTAH BEACH	
Unit	**Commander**
4TH INFANTRY DIVISION	Maj-Gen R.O. Barton
8th Infantry Rgt	Col J.A. Van Fleet
12th Infantry Rgt	Col R.P. Reeder, Jr
22nd Infantry Rgt	Col H.A. Tribolet
1st Engineer Special Bde	Brig-Gen J.W. Wharton
531st Engineer Shore Rgt	–
6TH ARMORED GROUP	Col F.F. Fainter
70th Tank Btn	Lt-Col J.C. Welborn
746th Tank Btn	Lt-Col C.G. Hupfer
ATTACHMENTS	
359th Infantry Rgt	Col C.K. Fales

armed and generally without armour, the airborne divisions were meant to act as shock troops, seizing objectives and holding them for limited periods until relieved by advancing infantry formations.

On the beaches

The Overlord amphibious operations began at about 6.30 a.m., an hour after the naval bombardment had begun and while up to 9000 aircraft bombed and strafed German positions in 14,000 sorties. More than 50,000 vehicles and 1000 tanks were scheduled to land in support of the ground effort, which was undertaken by 53,800 British, 21,400 Canadian and 57,500 American troops along with a contingent of French commandos.

Although the Atlantic Wall defences were incomplete in some areas, the Germans had sown thousands of mines and erected beach obstacles, some of them topped with mines and capable of tearing the bottoms out of landing craft. Specially trained Allied demolition teams had done what they could to eliminate some of these obstacles.

Good fortune at Utah

The first Allied soldiers to hit the beach in large numbers were men of the 4th Infantry Division's 8th Regiment, carried to the shore in 20 landing craft called Higgins boats, named after their designer, and grouped into 30-man assault teams. These were to be followed by a second wave with additional troops, combat engineers and naval demolition units.

When the navy patrol craft that was to guide them to the beach struck a mine and sank rapidly, the Utah invasion force drifted more than 1.6km (1 mile) to the south and actually came ashore in the wrong area. However, the misdirected assault proved a stroke of luck, and Brigadier-General Theodore Roosevelt, Jr. ordered his troops to 'start the war from here!'

Against light resistance, the 4th Division moved inland and captured several of the vital causeways by 8 a.m., linking up with airborne troops. By the end of the day, 23,000 American soldiers and 1700 vehicles had come ashore at Utah Beach.

Ordeal at Omaha

The situation at Omaha Beach was in stark contrast to Utah. The veterans of the German 352nd Infantry Division manned strong defences along high cliffs that dominated the beach and covered its exits.

On the western side of Omaha, two battalions of the US 29th Infantry Division's 116th Regimental Combat Team (RCT) were to land, followed half an hour later by a third battalion. To the east, the 16th RCT of the 1st Infantry Division was to follow the same pattern. About 220 members of the US 2nd Ranger Battalion were to

SWORD BEACH	
Unit	**Commander**
3RD INFANTRY DIVISION	Maj-Gen T.G. Rennie
8th Infantry Brigade	Brigadier E.E.E. Cass
9th Infantry Brigade	Brigadier J.G. Cunningham
185th Infantry Brigade	Brigadier K.P. Smith
27TH ARMOURED BRIGADE	Brigadier G.E. Prior-Palmer
13th/18th Royal Hussars	Lt-Col Harrap
The Staffordshire Ymn	Lt-Col J.A. Eadie
22nd Dragoons	Lt-Col A.D.B. Cocks
1ST SPECIAL SERVICE BDE	Brig Lord Lovat
3 Commando	Lt-Col P. Young
4 Commando	Lt-Col R.W.P. Dawson
6 Commando	Lt-Col D. Mills-Roberts
45 RM Commando	Cpt R.M.N.C. Ries
4TH SPECIAL SERVICE BDE	Brigadier B.W. Leicester
41 RM Commando	Lt-Col T.M. Gray
46 RM Commando	Lt-Col C.R. Hardy

JUNO BEACH	
Unit	**Commander**
3RD CANADIAN INFANTRY DIV	General R.F.L. Keller
7th Canadian Infantry Bde	Brigadier H.W. Foster
Royal Winnipeg Rifles	Lt-Col J.M. Meldram
Regina Rifle Regiment	Lt-Col F.M. Matheson
Canadian Scottish Rgt	Lt-Col F.N. Cabeldu
8th Canadian Infantry Bde	Brigadier K.G. Blackadder
Queen's Rifles of Canada	Lt-Col J.G. Spragge
New Shore Regiment	Lt-Col D.B. Buell
Régiment de la Chaudière	Lt-Col J.E.G.P. Mathieu
9th Canadian Infantry Bde	Brigadier D.G. Cunningham
Highland Light Inf of Can	Lt-Col F.M. Griffiths
Dundas, Stormont and	
Glengarry Highlanders	Lt-Col G.H. Christiansen
North Novia Scotia	
Highlanders	Lt-Col C. Petch
Cameron Highlanders	
of Ottawa	Lt-Col P.C. Klaehn
2ND CANADIAN ARMOURED BDE	Brigadier R.A. Wyman
6th Can Arm Rgt (1st Hsrs)	Lt-Col R.J. Colwell
10th Canadian Arm Rgt	Lt-Col R.E.A. Morton
27th Canadian Arm Rgt	Lt-Col M.B.K. Gordon
48 RM Commando	Lt-Col J.L. Moulton

GOLD BEACH	
Unit	**Commander**
50TH INFANTRY DIVISION	Maj-Gen D.A.H. Graham
231st Infantry Brigade	Brigadier A.G.B. Stanier
56th Infantry Brigade	Brigadier E.C. Pepper
69th Infantry Brigade	Brigadier F.Y.C. Knox
151st Infantry Brigade	Brigadier R.H. Senior
8TH ARMOURED BRIGADE	Brigadier B. Cracroft
4th/7th Dragoon Guards	Lt-Col R. Byron
Notts Yeomanry	Lt-Col J. Anderson
24th Lancers	Lt-Col W.A.C. Anderson
47 RM Commando	Lt-Col C.F. Phillips

scale the sheer cliffs of Pointe du Hoc to the west and silence heavy German guns that could threaten both Omaha and Utah beaches.

The Americans at Omaha were under constant fire as accurate artillery hit some landing craft well off the beach. Those who made it ashore unscathed were often pinned down and had lost much of their equipment. For several hours, the situation appeared grim on Omaha Beach; however, the command initiative exhibited by several officers spurred soldiers into action. By 9 a.m., exits had been secured. At the end of the day, the Omaha beachhead reached just 3.2km (2 miles) inland, and nearly 3000 casualties had been suffered.

DD tank disaster

One contributing factor to the difficulties on Omaha Beach was the inability of specially modified amphibious tanks to reach the shore in numbers. Each of the RCTs at Omaha was to have been supported by two tank battalions, consisting of three companies of 16 tanks and two battalions of attached Rangers. The DD (Duplex Drive) tanks were M4 Shermans mounting 75mm (2.95in) cannon and fitted with propeller systems and canvas shields that could be raised and lowered to manoeuvre briefly in water. Designed to reach the beach and provide heavy fire support, many of the DD tanks

drifted and foundered in the choppy English Channel, while others were hit before they came out of the water.

US combat organization

Below the division level, the US Army of 1944 was organized into regiments, battalions, companies platoons and squads. Within the standard regiment, at

D-DAY LANDINGS: PLANS AND OBJECTIVES

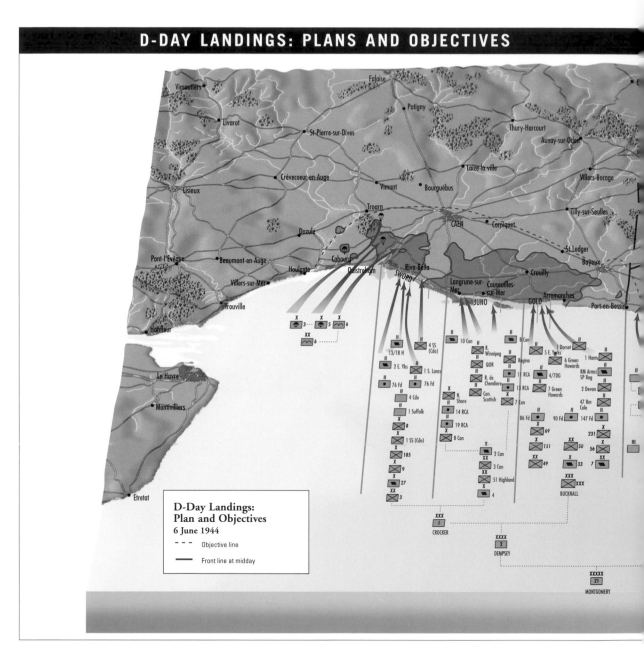

**D-Day Landings:
Plan and Objectives**
6 June 1944

- - - Objective line

Front line at midday

least three battalions of infantry totalling 600–900 men were equipped with six 105mm (4.1in) howitzers, nine 57mm (2.2in) anti-tank guns, 55 heavy .50-calibre machine guns and a number of light .30-calibre machine guns. The standard company included about 200 soldiers with 15 Browning automatic rifles (BARs),

two .30-calibre machine guns plus one .50-calibre, and six additional automatic weapons. An infantry platoon contained 41 soldiers with three BARs, and the standard rifle squad usually included 12 soldiers.

At 7.25 a.m., the 231st and 69th Infantry Brigades of the British 50th (Northumbrian) Infantry Division

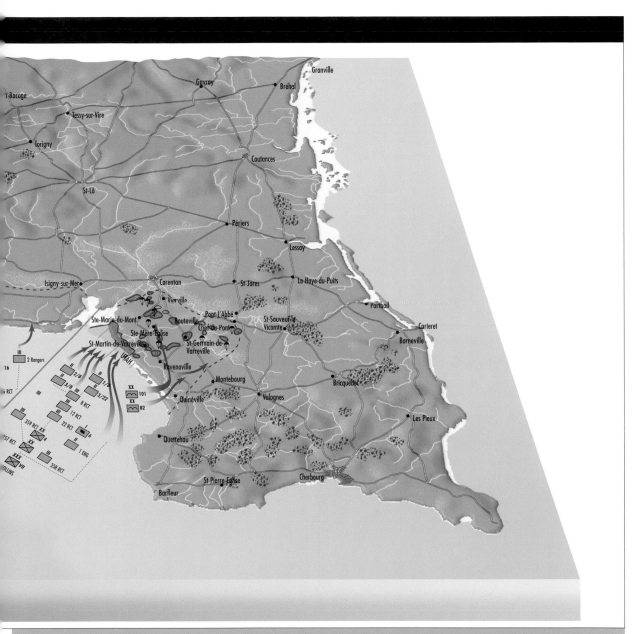

6 June 1944

The Allied D-Day landings took place across a 96.5km (60-mile) front. In the west, the US 4th Infantry Division assaulted Utah Beach and encountered light resistance, while further east elements of the 1st and 29th Infantry Divisions met the tough German 352nd Division at Omaha Beach. The British 50th Infantry Division at Gold Beach sustained only 400 casualties and put 25,000 soldiers ashore. The 3rd Canadian Infantry Division at Juno Beach overcame fierce defence from the German 716th Division and advanced further than any other Allied force on D-Day, approximately 15km (9.3 miles). At Sword Beach, the British 3rd Infantry Division was advancing beyond the shore within 45 minutes.

assaulted Gold Beach, near the centre of the Allied operations area. These were supported by the 8th Armoured Brigade of the 79th Armoured Division and No. 47 Royal Marine Commando. The 56th and 151st Infantry Brigades were to follow closely.

Although fierce German resistance was encountered at Le Hamel, the decision was made to land the DD tanks of units such as the 7th Dragoons and the Westminster Dragoons directly on the beach to provide fire support. Steady progress was made along the beach, and with 25,000 troops ashore by midnight the British had taken Arromanches and pushed towards Bayeux with only 400 casualties.

British armoured organization

The employment of British armour played a decisive role in the success achieved at Gold Beach on D-Day. The standard British armoured division of 1944

included 14,695 troops equipped with 1398 automatic weapons, 48 heavy artillery pieces, 380 anti-tank weapons, 2500 vehicles for the transport of soldiers and supplies, and 336 tanks. Often, large British tank formations were referred to as 'armoured brigades' and fielded tank strength equivalent to that of a division.

Jump-off at Juno

The primary Allied force at Juno Beach, east of the main road linking the coast to the strategically important town of Caen, was the 3rd Canadian Infantry Division supported by the 2nd Canadian Armoured Brigade. The 7th Canadian Infantry Brigade and 6th Canadian Armoured Regiment landed in the west and the 8th Canadian Infantry Brigade with the 10th Canadian Armoured Regiment landed to the east at 7.35 a.m.

Resistance on Juno Beach, which was heavily defended by the German 716th Division, inflicted casualty rates as

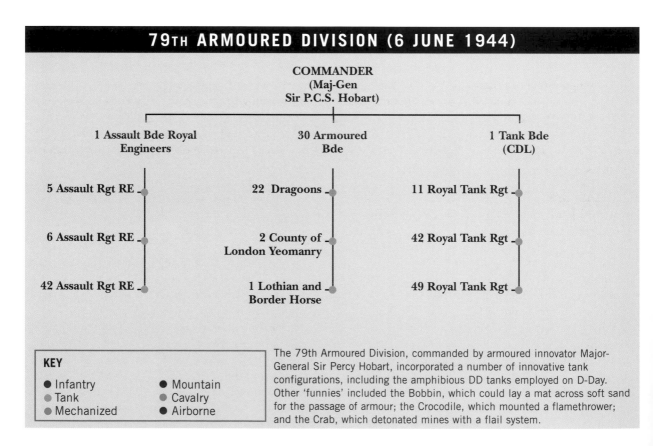

79TH ARMOURED DIVISION (6 JUNE 1944)

COMMANDER
(Maj-Gen Sir P.C.S. Hobart)

1 Assault Bde Royal Engineers	30 Armoured Bde	1 Tank Bde (CDL)
5 Assault Rgt RE	22 Dragoons	11 Royal Tank Rgt
6 Assault Rgt RE	2 County of London Yeomanry	42 Royal Tank Rgt
42 Assault Rgt RE	1 Lothian and Border Horse	49 Royal Tank Rgt

KEY
- Infantry
- Tank
- Mechanized
- Mountain
- Cavalry
- Airborne

The 79th Armoured Division, commanded by armoured innovator Major-General Sir Percy Hobart, incorporated a number of innovative tank configurations, including the amphibious DD tanks employed on D-Day. Other 'funnies' included the Bobbin, which could lay a mat across soft sand for the passage of armour; the Crocodile, which mounted a flamethrower; and the Crab, which detonated mines with a flail system.

2ND CANADIAN ARMOURED BDE, 1ST HUSSARS, 'B' SQN

The 19 DD Tanks of B Squadron, 1st Hussars, were assigned to support the Regina Rifles on the western side of Juno Beach on D-Day. Launched 4000m (4400 yards) from the beach, 15 of the tanks reached the shore, a number of them remaining hull-down with low silhouettes and engaging German gun emplacements ringing the beach. Clearing the area of Courseulles-sur-Mer, B Squadron then reached open country and engaged German 88mm (3.46in) guns, which knocked out six tanks and killed seven crewmen within minutes. Following this encounter, B Squadron retired. At the end of the day, just four of its tanks remained operational.

Sherman DD tanks x 19

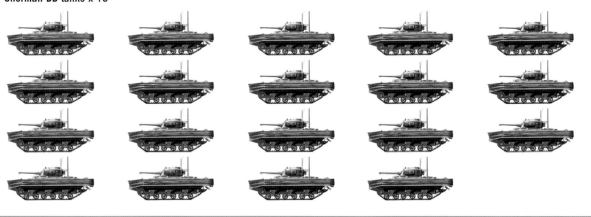

high as 50 per cent on the attackers. Nevertheless, by the end of the day the Canadians had broken through the German defences and battled to the edge of Caen. By the end of 6 June, the 3rd Canadian Division had completed the deepest Allied penetration of D-Day, advancing 15km (9.3 miles).

Swift seizure of Sword

Resistance on Sword Beach was comparatively light, with troops of the British 3rd Infantry Division and the 27th Armoured Brigade landing at 7.25 a.m. while commandos landed on the extreme left flank of the invasion beaches. Within 45 minutes, the British were advancing inland. By 1.30 p.m., they had linked up with the paras of the 6th Airborne Division, who had held the bridges over the Caen Canal and the Orne River since before daylight.

In the afternoon, two infantry regiments, the King's Shropshire Light Infantry and the Staffordshire Yeomanry, had set off in the direction of Caen and were attempting to join with the Canadians fighting their way off Juno Beach. By 4 p.m., the British met the only

determined counterattack by German armoured forces on D-Day as tanks of the 21st Panzer Division rolled forward from the vicinity of Caen all the way to the beach, dangerously driving a wedge between Juno and Sword. However, reinforcements did not materialize and the Germans lost 54 tanks in the process, eventually forcing them to withdraw. As D-Day ended, the British had put 29,000 soldiers ashore at Sword Beach, at a cost of only 630 dead and wounded.

D-Day assessment

The bloody contests on Omaha and Juno aside, Allied casualties on D-Day were comparatively light. Allied troops were firmly ashore on all five beaches by the end of 6 June; however, gaps still existed in several areas. The Germans had been taken by surprise, although the prospect of counterattack, particularly at Omaha, remained very real. Caen, a primary objective of D-Day, had not been captured, and it would remain in German hands for another month. But an important objective had been achieved: the Allies had returned to Northwest Europe in force.

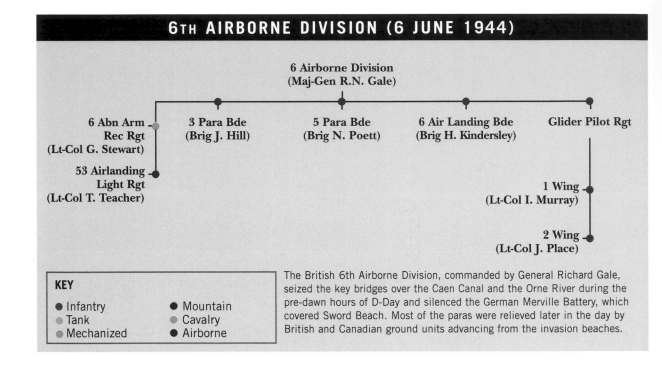

6TH AIRBORNE DIVISION (6 JUNE 1944)

6 Airborne Division
(Maj-Gen R.N. Gale)

6 Abn Arm
Rec Rgt
(Lt-Col G. Stewart)

3 Para Bde
(Brig J. Hill)

5 Para Bde
(Brig N. Poett)

6 Air Landing Bde
(Brig H. Kindersley)

Glider Pilot Rgt

53 Airlanding
Light Rgt
(Lt-Col T. Teacher)

1 Wing
(Lt-Col I. Murray)

2 Wing
(Lt-Col J. Place)

KEY

● Infantry   ● Mountain
● Tank   ● Cavalry
● Mechanized ● Airborne

The British 6th Airborne Division, commanded by General Richard Gale, seized the key bridges over the Caen Canal and the Orne River during the pre-dawn hours of D-Day and silenced the German Merville Battery, which covered Sword Beach. Most of the paras were relieved later in the day by British and Canadian ground units advancing from the invasion beaches.

Operation Dragoon

Originally conceived in the summer of 1943 as Operation Anvil, the invasion of southern France was intended to support Operation Overlord in Normandy and was scheduled to take place concurrently.

The Americans were strongly in favour. However, the British were bitterly opposed, particularly Prime Minister Winston Churchill who advocated a thrust into the Balkans or a reinvigorated push through Italy.

Eventually, the American view prevailed. Churchill is said to have insisted that the effort be renamed Operation Dragoon, reflecting his original reluctance – but this is questionable. A shortage of landing craft and other materiel resulted in the postponement of Operation Dragoon until 15 August 1944, a full nine weeks after the D-Day landings in Normandy.

Despite the delay, General Eisenhower remained convinced that Operation Dragoon was essential to the

prospects for the success of Operation Overlord. Fighting on two fronts in France would require the Germans to keep large numbers of troops in the south, which might otherwise be transferred to Normandy.

The demands of Dragoon

As they girded for the invasion of Southern France, the American and British planners drew upon three battle-hardened infantry divisions from Italy and North Africa in June 1944. These were the 3rd, 36th and 45th, which formed the nucleus of the Seventh Army under General Alexander M. Patch and included VI Corps, commanded by General Lucian Truscott, who had

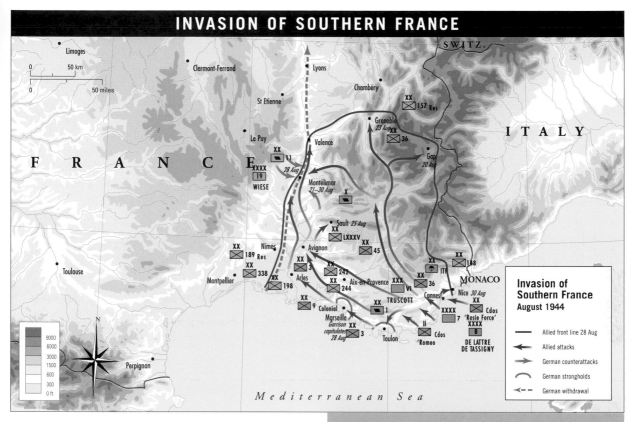

INVASION OF SOUTHERN FRANCE

Invasion of Southern France
August 1944

— Allied front line 28 Aug
← Allied attacks
→ German counterattacks
⌒ German strongholds
◄-- German withdrawal

Mediterranean Sea

August 1944

Originally intended as a support effort for Operation Overlord in Normandy, the invasion of southern France, codenamed Operation Dragoon, did not get underway until 15 August 1944. German resistance to the landings of three American infantry divisions between Cannes and St Tropez was surprisingly light, and French infantry and armour advanced rapidly towards the cities of Toulon and Marseille as the Germans retreated northwards. Airborne forces advanced eastwards from their landing zones near Le Muy and captured Nice. Within four weeks, the French had linked up with the US Third Army advancing eastwards, and the Sixth Army Group had assumed the southern flank of the Allied armies in the West.

transferred from Italy. Six days before they hit the French beaches, the infantry divisions boarded transport craft at ports in Italy and North Africa. Their trek first took them in the direction of Genoa before turning westwards towards the invasion area.

In addition to the three infantry divisions, the 1st Airborne Task Force was created under the command of General Robert T. Frederick. It included his former command, the Canadian-American 1st Special Service Force, the British 2nd Independent Parachute Brigade, the 551st Parachute Infantry Regiment and the 517th Parachute Regimental Combat Team. French Army B, later to be designated the French First Army, was also formed under General Jean de Lattre de Tassigny, and consisted of six divisions of Free French infantry grouped into two corps along with the attached French 1st Armoured Division.

Seventh Army and French Army B were gathered under the auspices of the US 6th Army Group,

commanded by General Jacob L. Devers. At peak strength, the Allied forces engaged in Operation Dragoon numbered nearly 200,000. The overall plan included 4000 aircraft and an armada of nearly 900 ships, 47 of them warships that would fire

15,900 shells at targets near the landing beaches. Along a 72.5km (45-mile) front in the region of Provence, the three US infantry divisions landed between St Tropez and Cannes, beginning at 8 a.m. on 15 August. The airborne phase of Dragoon, initiated just after 4 a.m., included parachute and glider landings primarily near the town of Le Muy.

By the end of the first day, more than 60,000 Allied soldiers and 6700 vehicles had come ashore in southern France. Within two days, orders for a general withdrawal were issued to the bulk of the German troops in the invasion area.

1st Special Service Force

A somewhat unique formation that was employed in the Aleutians, during the Italian campaign, and in southern France was the 1st Special Service Force. Formed in 1942 from both American and Canadian soldiers, the unit was composed of 1800 highly trained soldiers who excelled in stealth and hand-to-hand combat. Organized into three regiments and a service battalion, the force earned the nickname of the Devil's Brigade. Their leader, then-Colonel Robert T. Frederick, helped to design the V-42 fighting knife, which was made originally for the men of the 1st Special Service Force.

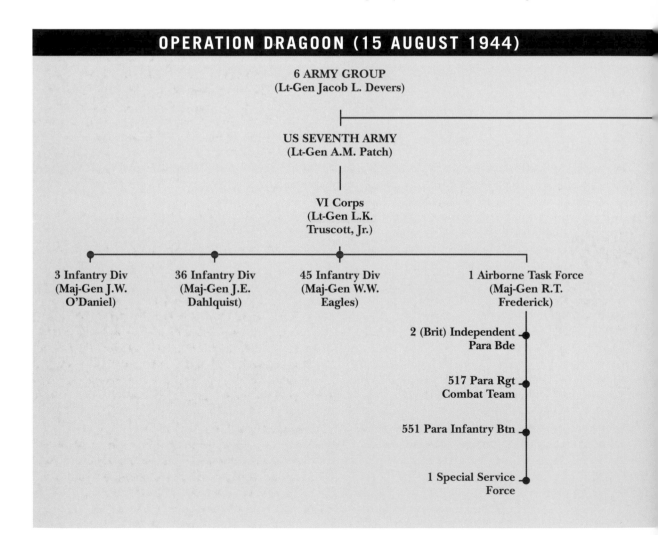

OPERATION DRAGOON (15 AUGUST 1944)

6 ARMY GROUP
(Lt-Gen Jacob L. Devers)

US SEVENTH ARMY
(Lt-Gen A.M. Patch)

VI Corps
(Lt-Gen L.K. Truscott, Jr.)

3 Infantry Div
(Maj-Gen J.W. O'Daniel)

36 Infantry Div
(Maj-Gen J.E. Dahlquist)

45 Infantry Div
(Maj-Gen W.W. Eagles)

1 Airborne Task Force
(Maj-Gen R.T. Frederick)

2 (Brit) Independent Para Bde

517 Para Rgt Combat Team

551 Para Infantry Btn

1 Special Service Force

During Operation Dragoon, the Devil's Brigade was assigned to the 1st Airborne Task Force, capturing the islands of Port Cros and Levant, south of the landing beaches, and disabling the coastal artillery batteries. As the campaign progressed, the unit accounted for 12,000 enemy casualties, including 7000 prisoners.

The 1st Special Service Force was disbanded on 5 December 1944. Its Canadian veterans were assigned to the 1st Canadian Parachute Battalion and other units, while the Americans were dispersed to airborne regiments or were assigned to the 474th Infantry Regiment, attached to General Patton's Third Army.

The Maquis

Throughout Operation Dragoon and beyond, the French Resistance harassed the Germans at every opportunity. Along with the Free French Forces of the Interior (FFI), thousands of French men and women formed bands of Maquis, irregular fighters who had often chosen to flee into the mountains of southern France rather than be conscripted into the Vichy government's forced labour programme. The Maquis also came to the aid of downed Allied airmen, and during Operation Dragoon they engaged in pitched battles with retreating German columns.

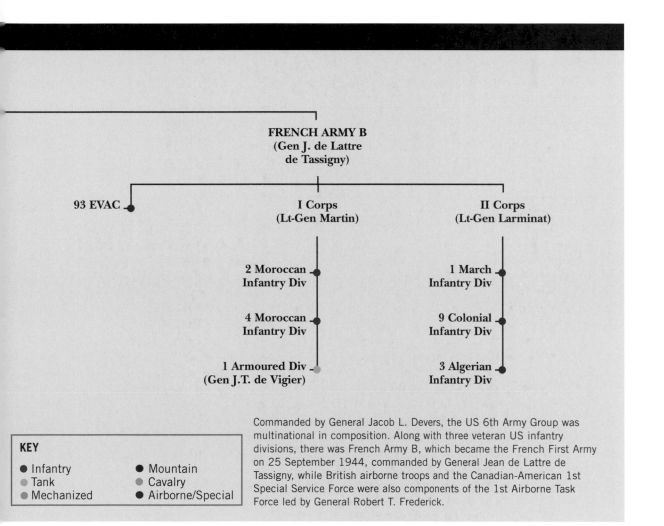

FRENCH ARMY B
(Gen J. de Lattre de Tassigny)

93 EVAC

I Corps
(Lt-Gen Martin)

II Corps
(Lt-Gen Larminat)

2 Moroccan Infantry Div

4 Moroccan Infantry Div

1 Armoured Div
(Gen J.T. de Vigier)

1 March Infantry Div

9 Colonial Infantry Div

3 Algerian Infantry Div

KEY
- Infantry
- Tank
- Mechanized
- Mountain
- Cavalry
- Airborne/Special

Commanded by General Jacob L. Devers, the US 6th Army Group was multinational in composition. Along with three veteran US infantry divisions, there was French Army B, which became the French First Army on 25 September 1944, commanded by General Jean de Lattre de Tassigny, while British airborne troops and the Canadian-American 1st Special Service Force were also components of the 1st Airborne Task Force led by General Robert T. Frederick.

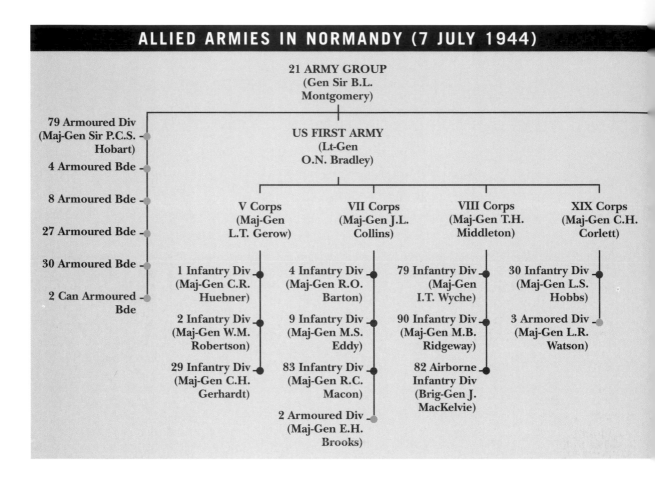

ALLIED ARMIES IN NORMANDY (7 JULY 1944)

21 ARMY GROUP
(Gen Sir B.L. Montgomery)

79 Armoured Div (Maj-Gen Sir P.C.S. Hobart)

4 Armoured Bde

8 Armoured Bde

27 Armoured Bde

30 Armoured Bde

2 Can Armoured Bde

US FIRST ARMY
(Lt-Gen O.N. Bradley)

V Corps (Maj-Gen L.T. Gerow)

VII Corps (Maj-Gen J.L. Collins)

VIII Corps (Maj-Gen T.H. Middleton)

XIX Corps (Maj-Gen C.H. Corlett)

1 Infantry Div (Maj-Gen C.R. Huebner)

2 Infantry Div (Maj-Gen W.M. Robertson)

29 Infantry Div (Maj-Gen C.H. Gerhardt)

4 Infantry Div (Maj-Gen R.O. Barton)

9 Infantry Div (Maj-Gen M.S. Eddy)

83 Infantry Div (Maj-Gen R.C. Macon)

2 Armoured Div (Maj-Gen E.H. Brooks)

79 Infantry Div (Maj-Gen I.T. Wyche)

90 Infantry Div (Maj-Gen M.B. Ridgeway)

82 Airborne Infantry Div (Brig-Gen J. MacKelvie)

30 Infantry Div (Maj-Gen L.S. Hobbs)

3 Armored Div (Maj-Gen L.R. Watson)

Rapid Allied advance

Little German resistance was encountered during the opening hours of Operation Dragoon, enabling the French divisions to rapidly exploit the beachhead behind the Americans. Fanning out towards the naval facilities at Toulon and the great Mediterranean port of Marseille, the French had taken both cities by the end of the month. As the Germans retreated northwards through the valley of the Rhone River, attempts by the 36th Division to cut them off failed, due to difficult terrain and a lack of manpower. Meanwhile, Allied airborne forces advanced eastwards from Le Muy and captured Nice on 30 August. By mid-September, the French I Corps had made a junction with Patton's US Third Army, completely cutting off the remaining German forces in southwest France. The German soldiers who had been left behind in the south and west were primarily garrison troops defending the French port cities and numbered more than 85,000. Only those at St Nazaire and Lorient held out beyond September, and these cities would remain in German hands until the end of the war.

An overwhelming success, Operation Dragoon came to an official end on 15 September. The 6th Army Group effectively became the extreme right flank of the Allied line on the Western Front and was tasked with operating from the Mediterranean through the rugged Vosges Mountains, along the Swiss border and to the right of Third Army.

Only one month in duration, Dragoon had netted 79,000 German prisoners at a cost of 14,000 Allied casualties. As a result, the 6th Army Group strengthened the Allied push to the frontier of the Third *Reich*.

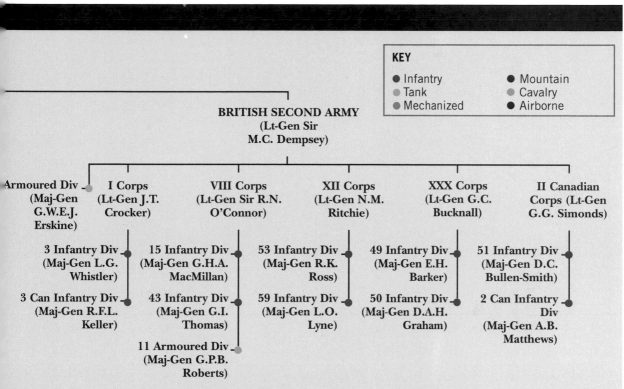

BRITISH SECOND ARMY
(Lt-Gen Sir
M.C. Dempsey)

Armoured Div (Maj-Gen G.W.E.J. Erskine)

I Corps (Lt-Gen J.T. Crocker)

VIII Corps (Lt-Gen Sir R.N. O'Connor)

XII Corps (Lt-Gen N.M. Ritchie)

XXX Corps (Lt-Gen G.C. Bucknall)

II Canadian Corps (Lt-Gen G.G. Simonds)

3 Infantry Div (Maj-Gen L.G. Whistler)

3 Can Infantry Div (Maj-Gen R.F.L. Keller)

15 Infantry Div (Maj-Gen G.H.A. MacMillan)

43 Infantry Div (Maj-Gen G.I. Thomas)

11 Armoured Div (Maj-Gen G.P.B. Roberts)

53 Infantry Div (Maj-Gen R.K. Ross)

59 Infantry Div (Maj-Gen L.O. Lyne)

49 Infantry Div (Maj-Gen E.H. Barker)

50 Infantry Div (Maj-Gen D.A.H. Graham)

51 Infantry Div (Maj-Gen D.C. Bullen-Smith)

2 Can Infantry Div (Maj-Gen A.B. Matthews)

The strength of Allied forces in Normandy grew steadily during the weeks following D-Day. By the first week of July, the 21st Army Group, led by Allied ground forces commander General Sir Bernard L. Montgomery, was composed of nine army corps in the US First Army, under General Omar Bradley, and the British Second Army under General Sir Miles Dempsey.

Falaise Pocket

When Allied forces achieved the breakout from the French hedgerow country, thousands of German troops were trapped in a killing zone.

While the D-Day landings had been successful, Allied plans to expand and ultimately break out of the confines of the French bocage, or hedgerow country, were frustrated for days. The road and communications centre of Caen, which Overlord planners had expected to capture on the day of the invasion, held out for weeks before falling to British and Canadian forces.

Bloody actions such as Operation Epsom and Operation Charnwood had cost General Sir Richard O'Connor's VIII Corps hundreds of tanks, to no avail.

Finally, Operation Goodwood commenced on 17 July. Caen was secured three days later, but not before VIII Corps had lost another 200 tanks.

The Sherman saga
The horrendous losses that the Allies experienced in armour throughout the fighting in Western Europe may be attributed to several factors. While German factories produced heavily armoured tanks such as the medium Mark V Panther with its high velocity 75mm (2.95in)

BREAKOUT PLAN

Breakout Plan
22 July–6 August 1944

Front line 18 July 1944
Front line 24 July 1944
Front line 6 August 1944

gun and the massive Mark VI Tiger with its 88mm (3.46in) cannon, the most prevalent Allied tank was the M4 Sherman.

Compared with the Panther and Tiger, the Sherman was lightly armoured and its 75mm (2.95in) gun did not pack the penetrating punch of the German weapons.

Although many Shermans were upgunned by the British with the 17-pounder anti-tank cannon as main armament, these tanks, nicknamed the Firefly, remained susceptible to the long range of the German weapons.

The development of the Sherman tank lay in the pre-war US doctrine relating to the employment of armour

22 July–6 August 1944

Although the continuous battering by the British and Canadian forces around Caen had degraded the German forces combat strength, the Germans were also troubled by American forces on their left flank. The Germans maintained only 11 understrength divisions in front of the US First Army, with the majority of their armour concentrated on their right, facing British and Canadian units. British General Sir Bernard L. Montgomery, commander of the Allied 21st Army Group, launched Operation Goodwood against Caen on 17 July. The city fell on the 20th, while plans for the American breakout effort, Operation Cobra, were being finalized. On 25 July, following saturation bombing along a narrow front, American units poured through the gap in the German defences near St Lô. In less than three weeks, Allied pincers had encircled 60,000 German troops at Falaise.

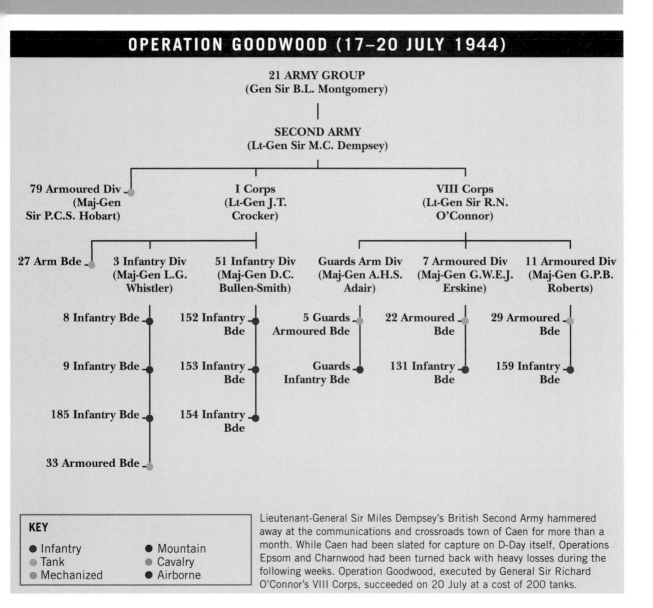

OPERATION GOODWOOD (17–20 JULY 1944)

21 ARMY GROUP
(Gen Sir B.L. Montgomery)

SECOND ARMY
(Lt-Gen Sir M.C. Dempsey)

79 Armoured Div (Maj-Gen Sir P.C.S. Hobart)

I Corps (Lt-Gen J.T. Crocker)

VIII Corps (Lt-Gen Sir R.N. O'Connor)

27 Arm Bde

3 Infantry Div (Maj-Gen L.G. Whistler)

51 Infantry Div (Maj-Gen D.C. Bullen-Smith)

Guards Arm Div (Maj-Gen A.H.S. Adair)

7 Armoured Div (Maj-Gen G.W.E.J. Erskine)

11 Armoured Div (Maj-Gen G.P.B. Roberts)

8 Infantry Bde — 152 Infantry Bde — 5 Guards Armoured Bde — 22 Armoured Bde — 29 Armoured Bde

9 Infantry Bde — 153 Infantry Bde — Guards Infantry Bde — 131 Infantry Bde — 159 Infantry Bde

185 Infantry Bde — 154 Infantry Bde

33 Armoured Bde

KEY
- ● Infantry
- ● Tank
- ● Mechanized
- ● Mountain
- ● Cavalry
- ● Airborne

Lieutenant-General Sir Miles Dempsey's British Second Army hammered away at the communications and crossroads town of Caen for more than a month. While Caen had been slated for capture on D-Day itself, Operations Epsom and Charnwood had been turned back with heavy losses during the following weeks. Operation Goodwood, executed by General Sir Richard O'Connor's VIII Corps, succeeded on 20 July at a cost of 200 tanks.

on the battlefield. General Lesley J. McNair, who exerted great influence on the development of the US Army in World War II and served as commander of Army Ground Forces, had concluded that tanks should be used in support of infantry formations, rather than to engage enemy armour in open combat. Therefore, the first American tanks were built for mobility and armed with only machine guns. Later, light tanks were armed with 37mm (1.45in) cannon. One other dismaying drawback was that the Sherman was powered by a gasoline engine and tended to erupt in flames when hit by enemy fire.

What the Sherman lacked in firepower, it made up for in speed and sheer weight of numbers. During World War II, up to 48,000 Shermans were built. Their performance on the battlefield was mixed, and often a platoon of four Shermans engaging a single Tiger or Panther would sacrifice at least two of their number to direct enemy fire while a third Sherman worked around to the German rear, where its armour was thinnest, to fire a single shot.

The experience of the US 3rd Armored Division is indicative of the disparity between the Sherman tank and German designs. According to its organizational strength table, the 3rd Armored was assigned a complement of 232 Shermans. During 10 months of fighting, a total of 648 were lost in combat while 1100 needed repair – 700 of these due to battle damage. In total, the 3rd Armored Division alone lost nearly 1350 tanks. In the end, a war of attrition, which included dominant Allied air power, overwhelmed the German armour. Quantity, some said, had triumphed over quality. The debate continues.

Operation Cobra

While the German defenders in Normandy

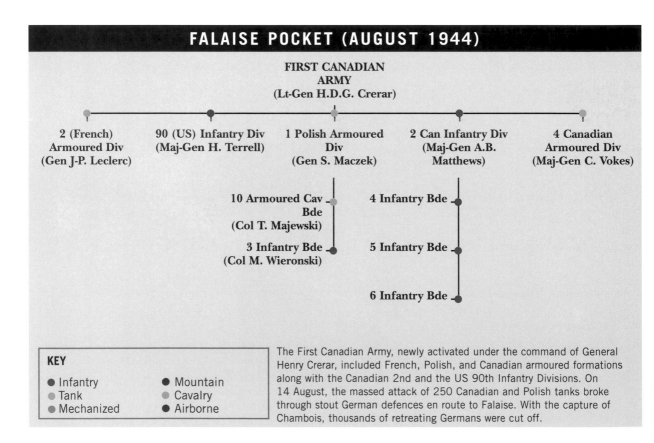

FALAISE POCKET (AUGUST 1944)

FIRST CANADIAN ARMY
(Lt-Gen H.D.G. Crerar)

| 2 (French) Armoured Div (Gen J-P. Leclerc) | 90 (US) Infantry Div (Maj-Gen H. Terrell) | 1 Polish Armoured Div (Gen S. Maczek) | 2 Can Infantry Div (Maj-Gen A.B. Matthews) | 4 Canadian Armoured Div (Maj-Gen C. Vokes) |

10 Armoured Cav Bde (Col T. Majewski)

4 Infantry Bde

3 Infantry Bde (Col M. Wieronski)

5 Infantry Bde

6 Infantry Bde

KEY
- Infantry
- Tank
- Mechanized
- Mountain
- Cavalry
- Airborne

The First Canadian Army, newly activated under the command of General Henry Crerar, included French, Polish, and Canadian armoured formations along with the Canadian 2nd and the US 90th Infantry Divisions. On 14 August, the massed attack of 250 Canadian and Polish tanks broke through stout German defences en route to Falaise. With the capture of Chambois, thousands of retreating Germans were cut off.

US LIGHT TANK COMPANY

The standard US light tank company in 1944 included headquarters and maintenance troops with two jeeps, a single truck, and an M3 halftrack for the movement of personnel and supplies along with a pair of M5 Stuart light tanks and a recovery tank constructed on the chassis of an M4 Sherman. Fifteen M3A3s were arranged in three platoons of five tanks. Mounting 37mm (1.45in) main armament and three .30-calibre Browning machine guns, the light tanks were often employed in a reconnaissance role.

HQ (1 Jeep, 1 x truck, 2 x M5A3 light tanks)

Maintenance (1 x Jeep, 1 x M3 halftrack, 1 x recovery tank)

1 Platoon (5 x M5A3 light tanks)

2 Platoon (5 x M5A3 light tanks)

3 Platoon (5 x M5A3 light tanks)

concentrated much of their infantry and armoured strength against the British Second Army in the north and stymied attempts to take Caen, the Germans opposed the Americans to the south with only 11 understrength divisions. Therefore, Allied planners decided to change their primary focus for breakout to the US sector.

South of the town of St Lô, on a 6400m (7000-yard) front, hundreds of Allied bombers would saturate the area while artillery joined in. Following the heavy bombardment, troops and tanks of the US VII and XIX Corps would charge through the breach in the German line and at long last break into open country. An unfortunate short bombing resulted in friendly fire casualties, among them General McNair. However, Operation Cobra succeeded and the race was on to encircle retreating German troops.

Destruction at Falaise

Although their momentum at times was agonizingly slow, the overall pace of the Allied advance was impressive. By mid-August, Patton's Third Army had reached Argentan, and Canadian and Polish troops slammed the door shut at Falaise, trapping at least

FALAISE POCKET

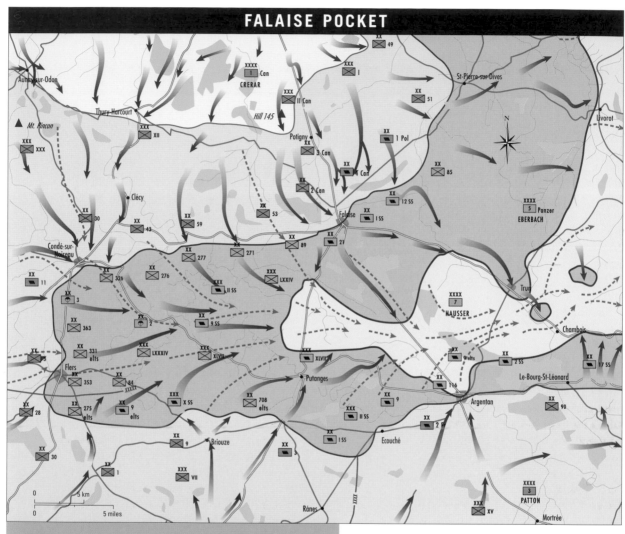

6–19 August 1944

While American spearheads halted at Argentan, the progress of General Henry Crerar's First Canadian Army towards Falaise, in order to close the northern hinge of a giant pincer movement, was slowed by stubborn German resistance. On 16 August, elements of the 4th Canadian and 1st Polish Armoured Divisions reached Falaise, and four days later they occupied the village of Chambois to complete the encirclement of 60,000 German troops, trapping them in a killing zone just 65km (40 miles) long and 20km (12 miles) wide. Allied air and ground attacks slaughtered 10,000 enemy soldiers in the Falaise Pocket; however, the victory was not complete as 40,000 enemy soldiers escaped the closing ring of death.

Falaise Pocket
6–19 August 1944

—— Front line 6 August

—— Front line 16 August

—— Front line 19 August

60,000 Germans in what came to be known as the Falaise Pocket. About 40,000 German soldiers had slipped through the gap between the Allied forces, but those who were caught suffered mightily from repeated air and ground attack. More than 10,000 Germans were killed and 50,000 taken prisoner. With the Allied triumph at Falaise, the campaign in Normandy had come to an end.

Paris liberated

After four years of bitter occupation, Paris, the City of Light, was freed from Nazi occupation on 25 August after almost a week of fighting.

On 14 July 1944, the headquarters of the US 12th Army Group was established in London under the command of General Omar N. Bradley. Composed of the First, Third and later the Ninth and Fifteenth Armies, this was the largest organization of American troops ever to take to the battlefield. Up to that time, the American forces had been under the command of British General Sir Bernard Montgomery's 21st Army Group. By the end of the war, the strength of the US 12th Army Group had reached 1.3 million combat and support troops.

Among the units under American control was the French 2nd Armoured Division, commanded by General Jacques-Philippe Leclerc. As news of the approaching Allied armies filtered into Paris during the summer, irregular fighters, many of them under communist-controlled members of the Free French Forces of the Interior (FFI), fomented unrest in the French capital. More than 400 barricades were erected in the streets, and open rebellion against the German occupiers ensued.

Race to the capital

After the gruelling battle in Normandy and the rapid exploitation of the breakthrough at St Lô, Allied forces advanced steadily across France. By 20 August, elements of General Patton's Third Army were only 50km (30 miles) from Paris, the City of Light. As chaos gripped the city, the Germans initially refused to evacuate, and Hitler's order to destroy its historically significant buildings had not been carried out.

Alarmed by the civil uprising and a possible communist seizure of power, General Charles de Gaulle, the de facto head of the Free French Forces, appealed to General Eisenhower, the Supreme Allied Commander, for an all-out effort to take Paris. Eisenhower was wary of de Gaulle and his political aspirations, however, and further recognized that a

major battle in Paris might destroy the city in order to liberate it.

In response, de Gaulle instructed Leclerc and the French 2nd Armoured Division to make an independent advance on Paris, without authorization from Bradley. Leclerc quickly put 17 tanks and 10 armoured cars, under the command of Captain Raymond Dronne, on the road towards the capital. When Bradley realized what was happening, he informed Eisenhower, who reluctantly authorized the release of the remainder of the 2nd Armored Division and the US 4th Infantry Division to support the drive.

US armoured divisions

The original configuration of the US armoured divisions during World War II consisted of two armoured regiments grouped into four medium tank battalions and two battalions of light tanks accompanied by an armoured infantry regiment of three battalions. Later designated as 'heavy' divisions, two of these, the 2nd and 3rd Armored, remained with the heavy configuration throughout the war. Fourteen other US armoured divisions were reorganized with a 'light' order of battle, which included three tank battalions with three medium tank companies each, along with one light tank company and three battalions of motorized infantry.

The French 2nd Armoured Division

Organized along a structure similar to that of a US light armoured division, the French 2nd Armoured was officially formed in August 1943, many of its personnel having seen combat in North Africa under the leadership of Leclerc in 1941. With a total strength of 14,454 men, its ranks included Moroccans and Algerians, as well as a contingent of Spaniards.

On 1 August 1944, the 2nd Armoured came ashore at Utah Beach in Normandy. Within weeks, the French

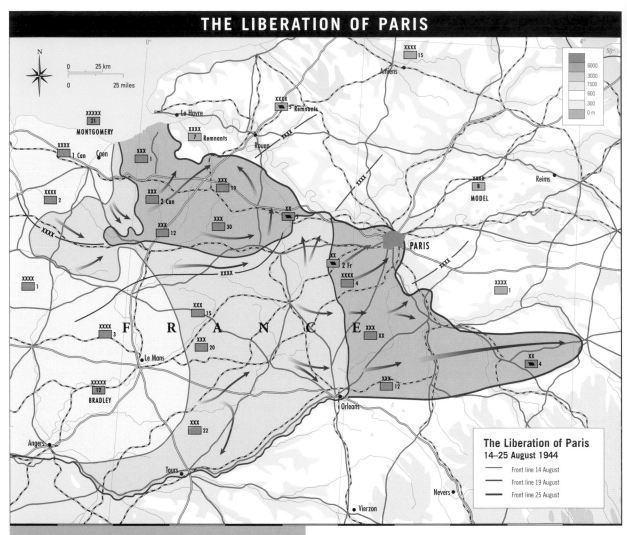

THE LIBERATION OF PARIS

The Liberation of Paris
14–25 August 1944

Front line 14 August
Front line 19 August
Front line 25 August

14–25 August 1944

The swift advance of Allied forces which followed the breakout from Normandy led to the encirclement of 60,000 German soldiers in the Falaise Pocket in mid-August, and the news that liberation might well be at hand electrified the citizens of Paris. Hundreds of them, including members of the Free French Forces of the Interior (FFI), rose against the Germans, who had occupied the city during four long years. Detaching from the US 12th Army Group, the French 2nd Armoured Division, commanded by General Jacques-Philippe Leclerc and supported by the US 4th Infantry Division, liberated the City of Light on 25 August.

unit had experienced heavy combat, participating in Operation Cobra and the subsequent breakout from the hedgerow country, during which it inflicted more than 13,000 German casualties, including 4500 dead. Less than a week after receiving de Gaulle's order, the 2nd Armoured had fought its way into Paris at a cost of 35 tanks, six assault guns and 750 other vehicles of various types. The German garrison surrendered on 25 August, and 20,000 were taken prisoner.

A day later, de Gaulle led a victory parade along the Champs Elysées and ignored fire from German snipers as he entered the cathedral of Notre Dame. Although

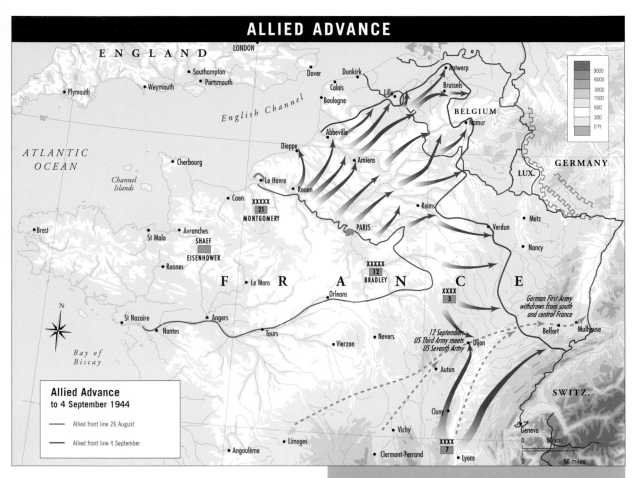

ALLIED ADVANCE

Allied Advance
to 4 September 1944

—— Allied front line 26 August

—— Allied front line 4 September

he had been a thorn in the side of the British and American military establishments, de Gaulle had become the living symbol of French defiance and nationalism. His personal intervention in the liberation of Paris may well have prevented the accession of a communist government.

Crossing the Seine
By the autumn of 1944, Allied troops were across the Seine River in force, and there was growing optimism among both the military and civilian leadership that the war might be won by the end of the year. However, lengthening supply lines and the strained capacity of port facilities along the Channel coast were beginning to present problems as the Allied spearheads strained eastwards.

4 September 1944
By the first week of September 1944, the US First Army was across the Seine River and approaching the German border near the Ardennes Forest, while the US Third Army, further south, was preparing to assault the fortress city of Metz and enter the French province of Lorraine.

On 4 September, British troops of Montgomery's 21st Army Group liberated Brussels, the Belgian capital. The following day, the Germans were driven from the Scheldt Estuary, opening the great seaport of Antwerp.

Some Allied leaders believed the Germans were beaten and that the war might be won by Christmas. Although recent events were cause for optimism, the onset of winter and supply difficulties contributed to an appreciable slowdown of offensive momentum.

Operation Market Garden

The largest airborne operation in the history of warfare, Market Garden, the offensive into Holland to seize numerous important bridges in mid-September 1944, ended in disaster for the Allies.

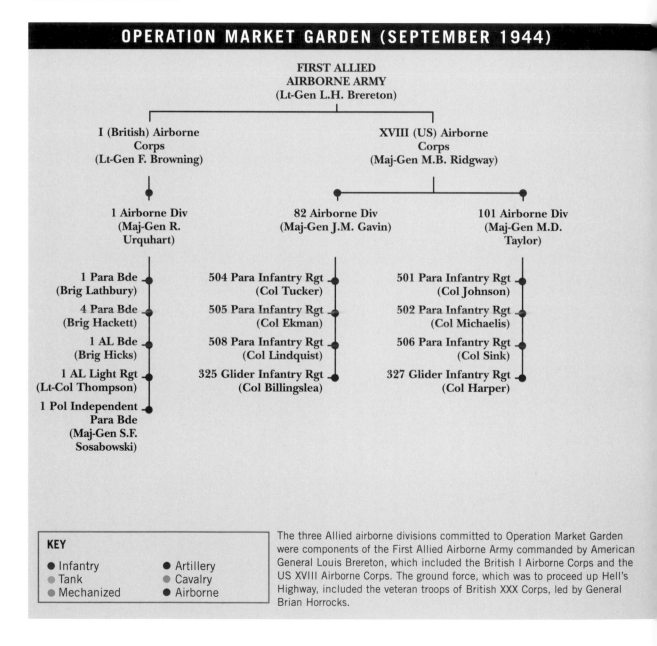

OPERATION MARKET GARDEN (SEPTEMBER 1944)

FIRST ALLIED AIRBORNE ARMY
(Lt-Gen L.H. Brereton)

I (British) Airborne Corps
(Lt-Gen F. Browning)

XVIII (US) Airborne Corps
(Maj-Gen M.B. Ridgway)

1 Airborne Div
(Maj-Gen R. Urquhart)

82 Airborne Div
(Maj-Gen J.M. Gavin)

101 Airborne Div
(Maj-Gen M.D. Taylor)

1 Para Bde (Brig Lathbury)
4 Para Bde (Brig Hackett)
1 AL Bde (Brig Hicks)
1 AL Light Rgt (Lt-Col Thompson)
1 Pol Independent Para Bde (Maj-Gen S.F. Sosabowski)

504 Para Infantry Rgt (Col Tucker)
505 Para Infantry Rgt (Col Ekman)
508 Para Infantry Rgt (Col Lindquist)
325 Glider Infantry Rgt (Col Billingslea)

501 Para Infantry Rgt (Col Johnson)
502 Para Infantry Rgt (Col Michaelis)
506 Para Infantry Rgt (Col Sink)
327 Glider Infantry Rgt (Col Harper)

KEY
- Infantry
- Tank
- Mechanized
- Artillery
- Cavalry
- Airborne

The three Allied airborne divisions committed to Operation Market Garden were components of the First Allied Airborne Army commanded by American General Louis Brereton, which included the British I Airborne Corps and the US XVIII Airborne Corps. The ground force, which was to proceed up Hell's Highway, included the veteran troops of British XXX Corps, led by General Brian Horrocks.

Field Marshal Sir Bernard L. Montgomery was known for exercising caution during his long military career, but in September 1944 he believed that the time was right for bold action. The Allied drive towards Germany and the Rhine River, the last great natural barrier to the east, had been halted by shortages of fuel and other supplies.

Montgomery believed that his 21st Army Group could, if given strategic priority over the American armies to the south, strike deep into Germany and occupy the Ruhr, the industrial heart of the Third *Reich*. The first blow would be a coordinated offensive by airborne troops landing in Holland via parachute and glider and seizing

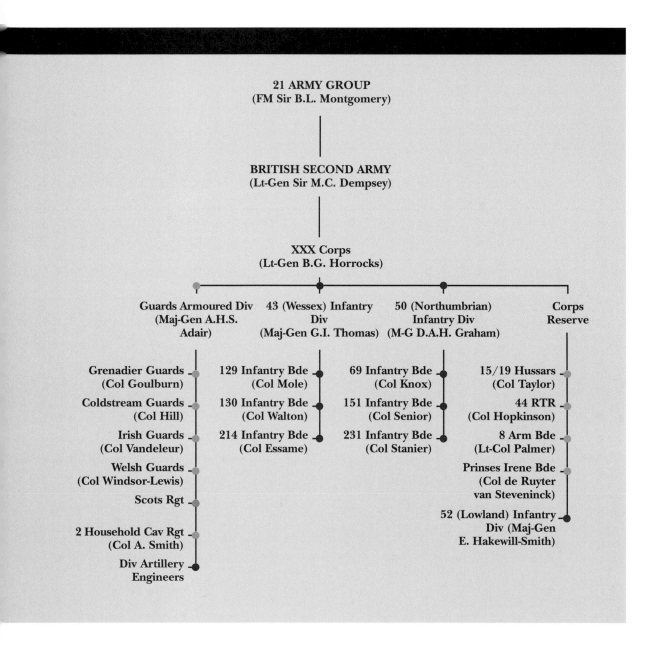

21 ARMY GROUP
(FM Sir B.L. Montgomery)

BRITISH SECOND ARMY
(Lt-Gen Sir M.C. Dempsey)

XXX Corps
(Lt-Gen B.G. Horrocks)

| Guards Armoured Div (Maj-Gen A.H.S. Adair) | 43 (Wessex) Infantry Div (Maj-Gen G.I. Thomas) | 50 (Northumbrian) Infantry Div (M-G D.A.H. Graham) | Corps Reserve |

Grenadier Guards
(Col Goulburn)

Coldstream Guards
(Col Hill)

Irish Guards
(Col Vandeleur)

Welsh Guards
(Col Windsor-Lewis)

Scots Rgt

2 Household Cav Rgt
(Col A. Smith)

Div Artillery
Engineers

129 Infantry Bde
(Col Mole)

130 Infantry Bde
(Col Walton)

214 Infantry Bde
(Col Essame)

69 Infantry Bde
(Col Knox)

151 Infantry Bde
(Col Senior)

231 Infantry Bde
(Col Stanier)

15/19 Hussars
(Col Taylor)

44 RTR
(Col Hopkinson)

8 Arm Bde
(Lt-Col Palmer)

Prinses Irene Bde
(Col de Ruyter
van Steveninck)

52 (Lowland) Infantry
Div (Maj-Gen
E. Hakewill-Smith)

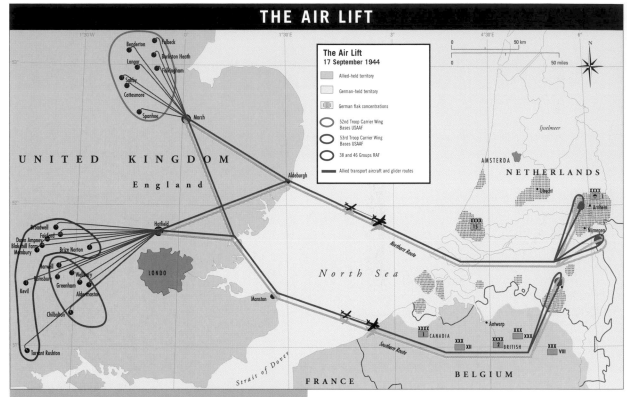

THE AIR LIFT

The Air Lift
17 September 1944

- Allied-held territory
- German-held territory
- German flak concentrations
- 52nd Troop Carrier Wing Bases USAAF
- 53rd Troop Carrier Wing Bases USAAF
- 38 and 46 Groups RAF
- Allied transport aircraft and glider routes

17 September 1944

The vast air armada that delivered three Allied airborne divisions into Holland during Operation Market Garden consisted of more than 2000 aircraft. Transports of the IX Troop Carrier Command USAAF were required both to carry paratroops and to tow gliders, but these functions could not be carried out at the same time, so the initial elements of the Market phase were completed over three days.

The early air landings took place during daylight hours and encountered relatively light German resistance, but the British 1st Airborne near Arnhem experienced immediate difficulties when many of its vehicles failed to arrive and radios proved inoperable. Delayed by two days of bad weather, the Polish 1st Independent Parachute Brigade did not enter the fighting until 21 September.

key bridges across several waterways, including the Waal, Maas and Neder (Lower) Rhine rivers.

Montgomery's plan called for three airborne divisions – the US 82nd and 101st and the British 1st – to take the bridges and hold them until relieved by infantry and armoured units of British XXX Corps, commanded by General Sir Brian Horrocks. The Americans would take the spans over the Wilhelmina Canal near Eindhoven, the Maas-Waal Canal, and the Maas and Waal rivers in the vicinity of Grave and Nijmegen. Three bridges across the Neder Rhine at Arnhem, the furthest north, would be taken by the British paras.

Meanwhile, the three divisions and 50,000 troops of XXX Corps would be in a race against time, driving in column up the narrow Highway 69 to relieve the lightly armed airborne troops at each bridge along the way. Should Market Garden succeed as planned, the path into Germany lay open. Allied forces would not be required to assault the fixed fortifications of the Siegfried Line, and the war might well be brought to a speedy close. Operation Market Garden began auspiciously enough, with hundreds of transport and glider aircraft delivering their human cargoes against relatively light resistance. Most of the landings, although they were divided into

AIRBORNE DROP ZONES

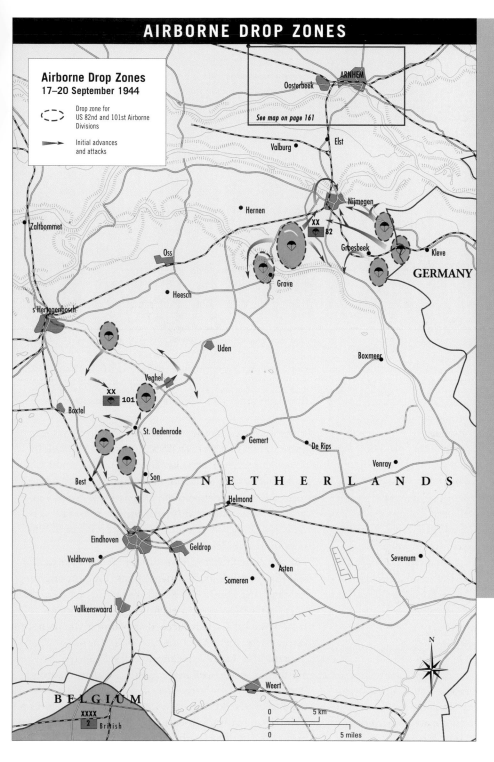

Airborne Drop Zones
17–20 September 1944

- - - Drop zone for
US 82nd and 101st Airborne
Divisions

→ Initial advances
and attacks

ARNHEM

Oosterbeek

See map on page 161

Valburg

Elst

Hernen

Nijmegen

XX 82

Zaltbommel

Oss

Groesbeek

Kleve

Grave

GERMANY

Heesch

s'Hertogenbosch

Uden

Boxmeer

Veghel

XX 101

Boxtel

St. Oedenrode

Gemert

De Rips

Venray

Best

Son

N E T H E R L A N D S

Helmond

Eindhoven

Geldrop

Veldhoven

Sevenum

Someren

Asten

Vallkenswaard

N

BELGIUM

Weert

0   5 km

XXXX
2   British

0   5 miles

17–20 September 1944

By 2 p.m. on
17 September, more
than 20,000 Allied
airborne troops were on
the ground in Holland.
US paratroopers of the
101st Division dropped
with near perfection
into zones north of
Eindhoven and
liberated the town. The
Germans, however,
denied them the Son
bridge, blowing the
span sky high moments
before the paratroopers
arrived. The following
evening, Canadian
engineers erected a
temporary span,
allowing XXX Corps to
pass to the north. The
82nd Airborne
captured three bridges
rather quickly, over the
Maas River at Grave,
the Maas-Waal Canal
bridge at Heumen, and
the bridge on the road
between Nijmegen and
Groesbeek. The
Nijmegen Highway
bridge was not in
American hands until
the evening of
20 September.

US AIRBORNE INFANTRY PLATOON

US airborne and infantry organization changed periodically throughout World War II. Originally two squads of airborne infantrymen, the US airborne infantry platoon was later augmented with a third squad, to total 36 paratroopers. Specialized platoons included those which deployed 81mm (3.18in) mortars, gathered intelligence or performed reconnaissance duties. Some glider troops served in anti-tank platoons, using such weapons as the 37mm (1.45in) and 57mm (2.24in) guns. Three rifle platoons and a weapons platoon constituted an airborne company, while three rifle companies and a service company were included in a battalion. Three battalions made up a parachute infantry regiment.

Platoon (36 men)

multiple airlift efforts covering consecutive days, were on target. Several of the bridges were seized intact. However, due to a combination of difficulties at Arnhem, including delays caused by German defenders, breakdowns in communication and the sheer distance from the drop zones to the town, only the 2nd Parachute Battalion of the 1st Airborne Division, under Lieutenant-Colonel John Frost, reached the main bridge.

Aside from the difficulties encountered by the 1st Airborne Division at Arnhem, the ground phase of Operation Market Garden was in trouble from the start. Highway 69, or Hell's Highway as it came to be known, was a two-lane road raised above the surrounding polder country. The high silhouettes of Sherman tanks made excellent targets for German gunners, and the leading 2nd Battalion, Irish Guards, was obliged to halt and deploy infantry and tanks into combat formations to dislodge the stubborn Germans.

British Army organization
In 1944, the standard British Army division numbered more than 18,000 troops in three infantry brigades with three battalions each. A total of 54 heavy 25-pounder guns and 48 anti-tank weapons, either 6-pounder or

17-pounder, were grouped into three artillery regiments. The infantry battalion consisted of 821 soldiers in four rifle companies and a headquarters company of several specialized units, including engineers and those in signal and mortar platoons. The concurrent British armoured division included an armoured brigade of 336 tanks grouped into three armoured regiments of 112 tanks each. Two field artillery regiments and an anti-tank regiment were assigned along with a mechanized infantry brigade of three battalions.

Days of disappointment
The American 101st Airborne, commanded by General Maxwell Taylor, took the Wilhelmina Canal bridge. Although the Son bridge was destroyed by the Germans, XXX Corps was rolling forwards on the night of 18 September. To the north, the 82nd, led by General James Gavin, captured the Grave bridge and another over the Maas-Waal Canal. The advance to Nijmegen was slowed due to German resistance, and by the time the 82nd had taken the bridge there on 20 September, XXX Corps had already come up. The Germans were then astride the highway in force and nearly 48 hours elapsed before XXX Corps could advance further.

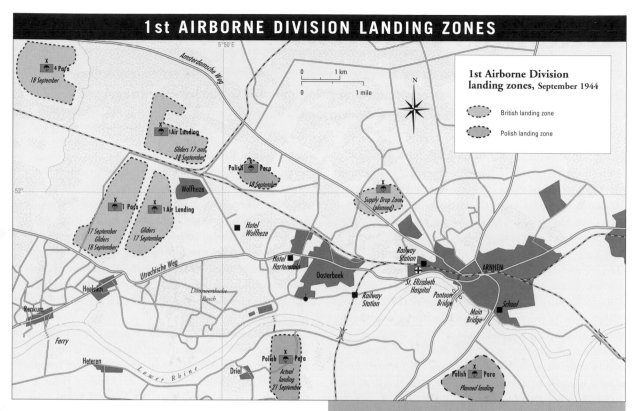

1st AIRBORNE DIVISION LANDING ZONES

1st Airborne Division landing zones, September 1944

British landing zone

Polish landing zone

4 Para
18 September

1 Air Landing
Gliders 17 and 18 September

Polish Para
18 September

Wolfheze

Supply Drop Zone (planned)

1 Para
17 September Gliders 18 September

1 Air Landing
Gliders 17 September

Hotel Wolfheze

Hotel Hartenstein

Oosterbeek

Railway Station

St. Elizabeth Hospital

Pontoon Bridge

ARNHEM

School

Main Bridge

Railway Station

Heelsum

Renkum

Doorwerthsche Bosch

Utrechische Weg

Ferry

Heteren

Driel

Polish Para
Actual landing 21 September

Lower Rhine

Polish Para
Planned landing

Amsterdamsche Weg

September 1944

Due to mistaken intelligence which indicated that the Arnhem area was heavily defended by German anti-aircraft guns, drop zones at least 13km (8 miles) west of the town were chosen for the British 1st Airborne Division. Available transport aircraft were insufficient in number; therefore, the complicated plan involved delivery of troops and supplies over a period as long as three days. Glider and parachute formations were to land near Heelsum on the afternoon of 17 September, while an additional brigade was scheduled to follow the next day. By 20 September, the Polish 1st Independent Parachute Brigade would drop south of the Lower Rhine and eventually link up with the infantry and armour of XXX Corps advancing along the narrow corridor of Highway 69.

At Arnhem bridge, Frost's 745 men had no weapon heavier than the anti-tank PIAT and their organic machine guns. Isolated and without reinforcement, they were cut off and surrounded by elements of the German II SS Panzer Corps, which included the 9th and 10th SS Panzer Divisions. Casualties mounted, and the remnants of the 2nd Battalion finally surrendered to the Germans on 21 September. The bulk of General Roy Urquhart's 1st Airborne Division held an ever-shrinking perimeter around the Hartenstein Hotel, 5km (3 miles) from the embattled Arnhem bridge.

By 25 September, Montgomery conceded that Operation Market Garden had failed and authorized Urquhart to withdraw as best he could. He had gone into the Arnhem area with nearly 10,000 men. Slightly more than 2000 made good their escape through German lines. More than 6600 were wounded or captured, and 1200 were dead. Further, the American airborne divisions had lost a quarter of their number – killed, wounded, or captured.

The failure of Operation Market Garden was a serious blow to Allied confidence, shattering the possibility of an end to the war in 1944 and confirming the original broad front strategy advocated by the supreme commander, General Eisenhower.

heavy forest and limited reconnaissance efforts in a sector thought to be relatively safe from attack. On the morning of 16 December, German artillery

erupted and was followed by probing actions to identify areas of lightest resistance. The Germans were stalled by the 99th Division but managed to outflank the

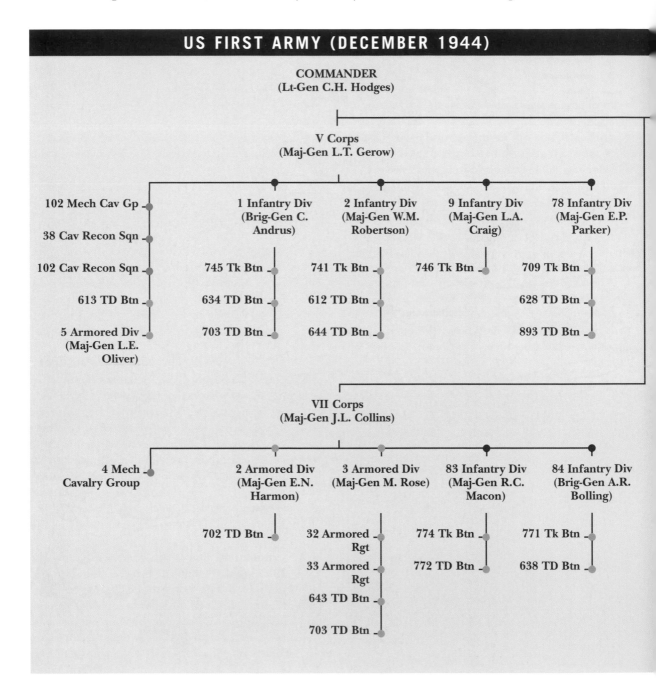

US FIRST ARMY (DECEMBER 1944)

COMMANDER
(Lt-Gen C.H. Hodges)

V Corps
(Maj-Gen L.T. Gerow)

102 Mech Cav Gp	1 Infantry Div (Brig-Gen C. Andrus)	2 Infantry Div (Maj-Gen W.M. Robertson)	9 Infantry Div (Maj-Gen L.A. Craig)	78 Infantry Div (Maj-Gen E.P. Parker)
38 Cav Recon Sqn				
102 Cav Recon Sqn	745 Tk Btn	741 Tk Btn	746 Tk Btn	709 Tk Btn
613 TD Btn	634 TD Btn	612 TD Btn		628 TD Btn
5 Armored Div (Maj-Gen L.E. Oliver)	703 TD Btn	644 TD Btn		893 TD Btn

VII Corps
(Maj-Gen J.L. Collins)

4 Mech Cavalry Group	2 Armored Div (Maj-Gen E.N. Harmon)	3 Armored Div (Maj-Gen M. Rose)	83 Infantry Div (Maj-Gen R.C. Macon)	84 Infantry Div (Brig-Gen A.R. Bolling)
	702 TD Btn	32 Armored Rgt	774 Tk Btn	771 Tk Btn
		33 Armored Rgt	772 TD Btn	638 TD Btn
		643 TD Btn		
		703 TD Btn		

106th through the Losheim Gap, while tanks in the centre of the offensive crossed the Our River and forced open a direct route to the vital Belgian crossroads town of Bastogne. On the southern shoulder of a rapidly expanding German salient, the 4th Infantry and 9th Armored Divisions stood firm.

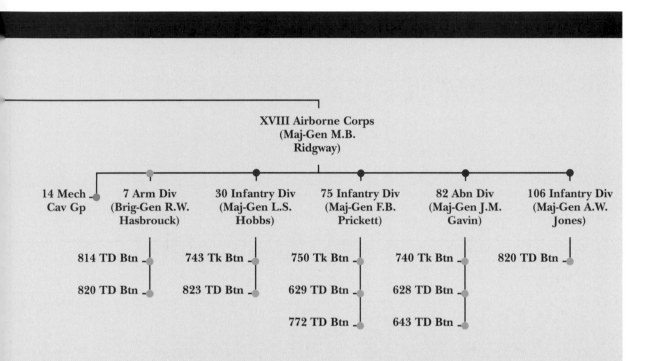

XVIII Airborne Corps
(Maj-Gen M.B.
Ridgway)

14 Mech Cav Gp	7 Arm Div (Brig-Gen R.W. Hasbrouck)	30 Infantry Div (Maj-Gen L.S. Hobbs)	75 Infantry Div (Maj-Gen F.B. Prickett)	82 Abn Div (Maj-Gen J.M. Gavin)	106 Infantry Div (Maj-Gen A.W. Jones)
	814 TD Btn	743 Tk Btn	750 Tk Btn	740 Tk Btn	820 TD Btn
	820 TD Btn	823 TD Btn	629 TD Btn	628 TD Btn	
			772 TD Btn	643 TD Btn	

KEY

- Infantry
- Tank
- Mechanized
- Mountain
- Cavalry
- Airborne

On the eve of the Battle of the Bulge, the US First Army, commanded by General Courtney Hodges, included the V, VII and XVIII Airborne Corps. The need for continuing armoured support to counter heavy German tanks had necessitated the attachment of numerous tank and tank destroyer battalions to each of the First Army's infantry divisions. Separate tank battalions allowed the US Army ultimate flexibility in the employment of its armoured forces.

Meanwhile, more than 100 tanks and 4000 SS troops led by Lieutenant-Colonel Joachim Peiper, rolled through the Losheim Gap, towards Stavelot. Fuel shortages plagued Peiper's advance, while small groups of American soldiers fought desperate delaying actions. The efforts of combat engineers were particularly effective, demolishing bridges and blocking roads.

Peiper was finally stopped near La Gleize, short of the Meuse. During their advance, the SS troops committed numerous atrocities. The most publicized of these was the execution by machine-gun fire of about 100 American prisoners in a field near the Belgian town of Malmedy. Most of the casualties belonged to the 285th Field Artillery Observation Battalion.

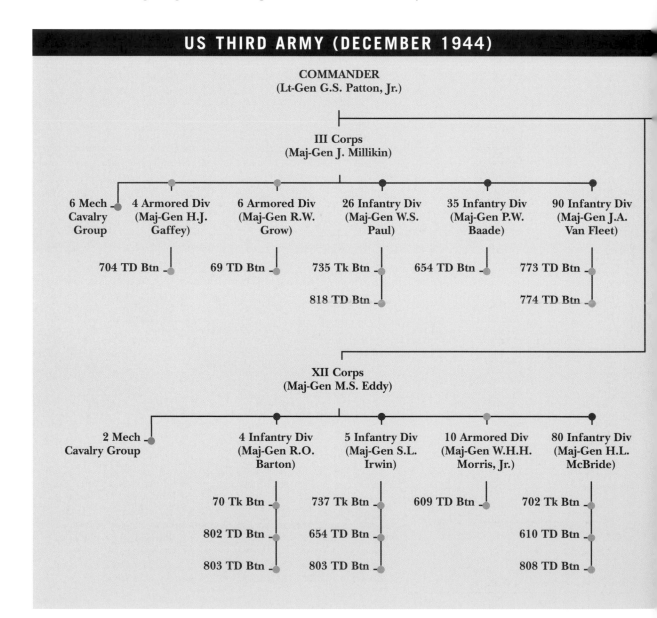

US THIRD ARMY (DECEMBER 1944)

COMMANDER
(Lt-Gen G.S. Patton, Jr.)

III Corps
(Maj-Gen J. Millikin)

| 6 Mech Cavalry Group | 4 Armored Div (Maj-Gen H.J. Gaffey) | 6 Armored Div (Maj-Gen R.W. Grow) | 26 Infantry Div (Maj-Gen W.S. Paul) | 35 Infantry Div (Maj-Gen P.W. Baade) | 90 Infantry Div (Maj-Gen J.A. Van Fleet) |

704 TD Btn   69 TD Btn   735 Tk Btn   654 TD Btn   773 TD Btn

818 TD Btn   774 TD Btn

XII Corps
(Maj-Gen M.S. Eddy)

| 2 Mech Cavalry Group | 4 Infantry Div (Maj-Gen R.O. Barton) | 5 Infantry Div (Maj-Gen S.L. Irwin) | 10 Armored Div (Maj-Gen W.H.H. Morris, Jr.) | 80 Infantry Div (Maj-Gen H.L. McBride) |

70 Tk Btn   737 Tk Btn   609 TD Btn   702 Tk Btn

802 TD Btn   654 TD Btn   610 TD Btn

803 TD Btn   803 TD Btn   808 TD Btn

US cavalry squadron

Outgunned by superior German forces, elements of the US 14th Cavalry Group had been unable to hold the 8km (5-mile) wide Losheim Gap during the opening hours of the Battle of the Bulge.

The traditional horse cavalry had disappeared by World War II, and the US Army was arguably the most highly mechanized fighting force in the world. The need for mobile reconnaissance remained, however, and in heavy armoured divisions this duty was fulfilled by armoured reconnaissance battalions. In the light armoured divisions, the responsibility for such activities fell to the modern mechanized cavalry squadron. This meant that cavalry squadrons were lightly armoured

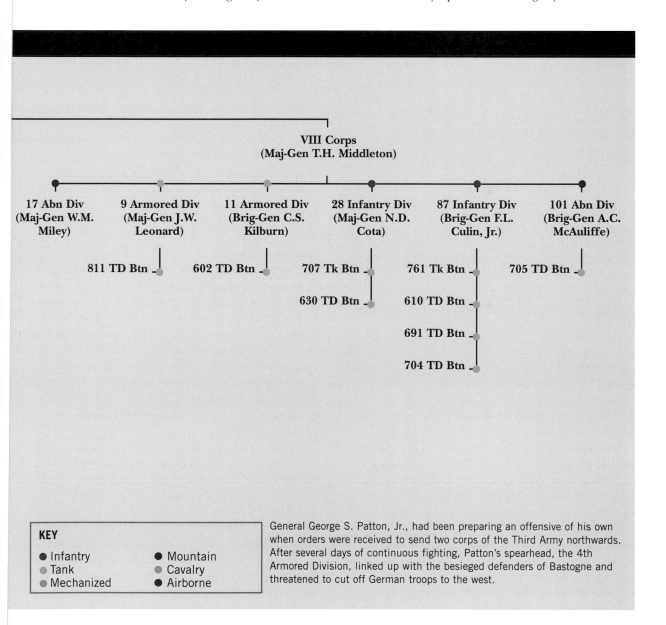

VIII Corps
(Maj-Gen T.H. Middleton)

17 Abn Div
(Maj-Gen W.M. Miley)

9 Armored Div
(Maj-Gen J.W. Leonard)

811 TD Btn

11 Armored Div
(Brig-Gen C.S. Kilburn)

602 TD Btn

28 Infantry Div
(Maj-Gen N.D. Cota)

707 Tk Btn

630 TD Btn

87 Infantry Div
(Brig-Gen F.L. Culin, Jr.)

761 Tk Btn

610 TD Btn

691 TD Btn

704 TD Btn

101 Abn Div
(Brig-Gen A.C. McAuliffe)

705 TD Btn

KEY

● Infantry
● Tank
● Mechanized
● Mountain
● Cavalry
● Airborne

General George S. Patton, Jr., had been preparing an offensive of his own when orders were received to send two corps of the Third Army northwards. After several days of continuous fighting, Patton's spearhead, the 4th Armored Division, linked up with the besieged defenders of Bastogne and threatened to cut off German troops to the west.

Invading the Reich: 1945

The final spring offensive in March–April 1945 carried the armies of the Western Allies to the heart of Nazi Germany, eventually linking up with the Soviet Red Army.

US infantry move past barriers and obstacles designed to hinder armour as they enter Germany, March 1945.

The unexpected German offensive in the Ardennes upset the Allied timetable for the resumption of the drive for the great natural barrier of the Rhine River and deep into the Third *Reich* towards Berlin. Postponed by at least four weeks, the offensive General Eisenhower envisioned embraced the broad front strategy once again, employing his three army groups in cooperative efforts to bring the war to a conclusion.

Despite the fact that Operation Market Garden, his plan for a concentrated strike into Germany, had ended in failure the previous autumn, Field Marshal Montgomery once again raised the notion of a single thrust into the Ruhr.

This time, the high-level disagreement threatened to fracture the Anglo-American coalition even while the Germans were still inside what remained of the Ardennes salient. Tension between the commanders was elevated to the point that it appeared Montgomery might be forced to resign before a semblance of cooperation returned.

Eisenhower prevails

The renewal of the Allied broad front offensive took shape in January 1945, the primary responsibility for success resting with Montgomery in the north. Troops of the 21st Army Group were closest to the Rhine and would open the offensive with Operation Veritable, a thrust by General Henry Crerar's First Canadian Army from Nijmegen through the dense forest of the Reichswald and to the Rhine at Emmerich. Operation Grenade was to be launched concurrently, with the US Ninth Army, under the command of General Simpson, driving northeast to meet the Canadians at Wesel, where it was expected Montgomery would lead the first Allied troops across the Rhine.

South of the 21st Army Group, General Bradley's 12th Army Group was to proceed through the heavily wooded Eifel to the Rhine between Koblenz and Cologne, effecting a second crossing. The 6th Army Group, commanded by General Jacob L. Devers, was to advance towards the Rhine near Mainz and Mannheim, clearing the Saar of Germans in the process.

The beginning of the end

With the opening of the offensive, Allied commanders no longer harboured any illusions that the German Army was finished as a formidable military force, even with the added pressure of the Soviet juggernaut that was rolling relentlessly from the east. In fact, it was clear that the Germans were likely to fight with even greater resolve on their own soil. Operation Veritable commenced on 8 February 1945, with a 1000-gun artillery barrage.

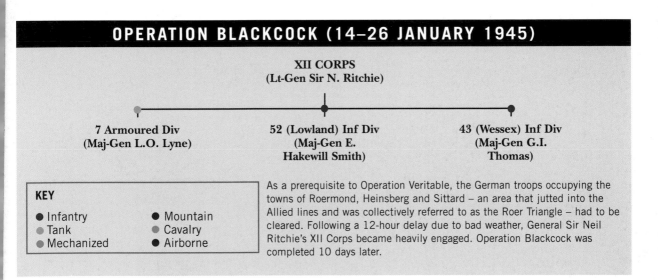

OPERATION BLACKCOCK (14–26 JANUARY 1945)

XII CORPS
(Lt-Gen Sir N. Ritchie)

7 Armoured Div	52 (Lowland) Inf Div	43 (Wessex) Inf Div
(Maj-Gen L.O. Lyne)	(Maj-Gen E. Hakewill Smith)	(Maj-Gen G.I. Thomas)

KEY
- Infantry
- Tank
- Mechanized
- Mountain
- Cavalry
- Airborne

As a prerequisite to Operation Veritable, the German troops occupying the towns of Roermond, Heinsberg and Sittard – an area that jutted into the Allied lines and was collectively referred to as the Roer Triangle – had to be cleared. Following a 12-hour delay due to bad weather, General Sir Neil Ritchie's XII Corps became heavily engaged. Operation Blackcock was completed 10 days later.

8 February – 21 March 1945

In February 1945, the task for the Allied armies was to cross the Rivers Roer, Our and Saar and to reach the Rhine. By 21 February, Goch, Cleve and Calcar were in British and Canadian hands, and the Americans took Moenchengladbach on 1 March, and Cologne five days later. On 7 March, the US First Army took the Ludendorff bridge at Remagen. On 23 March, Montgomery's 21st Army Group stormed the Rhine at Wesel, preceded by two divisions of paratroopers. By nightfall, the ground troops had joined up with the paratroopers, and the Rhine bridgeheads were secure. Further south, the Americans launched their own crossings, mostly mounted by fewer men with limited resources. Patton, eager to beat Montgomery across the river, had sent an assault regiment of the US 5th Division, part of his Third Army, to cross the Rhine, in rubber boats, between Nierstein and Oppenheim. Securing the far bank, they were joined by the rest of the division. By the end of March, Darmstadt and Wiesbaden were in American hands, and US armoured columns were driving for Frankfurt-am-Main. Further south, the French had put an Algerian division across the river at Gemersheim. Most German troops knew that the war was lost and were ready to surrender, though a few young volunteers along with diehard SS men continued to fight.

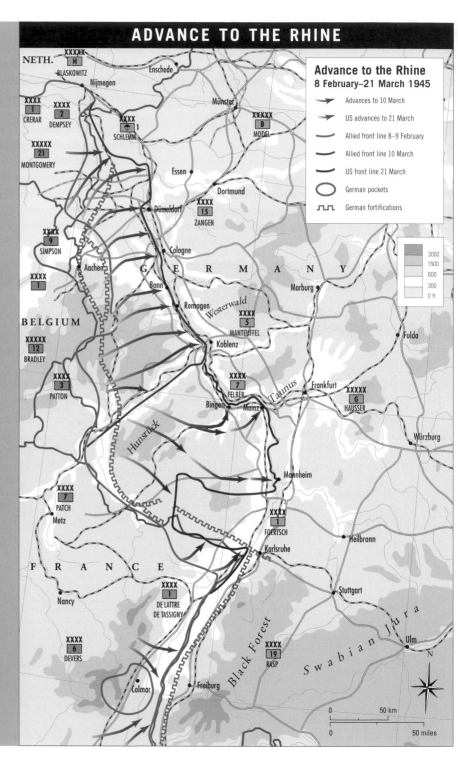

ADVANCE TO THE RHINE

Advance to the Rhine
8 February–21 March 1945

- Advances to 10 March
- US advances to 21 March
- Allied front line 8–9 February
- Allied front line 10 March
- US front line 21 March
- German pockets
- German fortifications

3000
1500
600
300
0 ft

NETH.

XXXXX H BLASKOWITZ
XXXX 1 CRERAR
XXXX 2 DEMPSEY
XXXX 1 SCHLEMM
XXXXX B MODEL
XXXXX 21 MONTGOMERY
XXXX 15 ZANGEN
XXXX 9 SIMPSON
XXXX 1
XXXXX 12 BRADLEY
XXXX 3 PATTON
XXXX 5 MANTEUFFEL
XXXX 7 FELBER
XXXXX 6 HAUSSER
XXXX 7 PATCH
XXXX 1 FOERTSCH
XXXX 1 DE LATTRE DE TASSIGNY
XXXX 6 DEVERS
XXXX 19 RASP

Enschede
Nijmegen
Münster
Essen
Dortmund
Düsseldorf
Cologne
Aachen
Bonn
Remagen
Koblenz
Marburg
Fulda
Westerwald
Bingen
Mainz
Frankfurt
Würzburg
Taunus
Hunsrück
Mannheim
Metz
Karlsruhe
Heilbronn
Nancy
Stuttgart
Black Forest
Freiburg
Ulm
Swabian Jura
Colmar

GERMANY
BELGIUM
FRANCE

0   50 km
0   50 miles

led by the armoured infantry of the Royal Tank Regiment, the 15th and 51st Scottish Divisions, and a Second Army commando brigade in conjunction with Operation Varsity, an airborne drop by the British 6th and the US 17th Airborne Divisions. Within 72 hours, the Wesel bridgehead had been expanded 45km (28 miles) beyond the east bank of the Rhine and encompassed a front of 40km (25 miles).

The US Third Army, meanwhile, unleashed against the Siegfried Line during the first week of March, drove hell for leather towards the Rhine after clearing the Eifel and taking 5000 prisoners during the opening hours of the advance. On 10 March, General Patton reached the Rhine at Koblenz; however, the advance was stymied when the bridges were blown up by the retreating Germans.

Undeterred, Patton changed direction and struck south, crossing the Moselle River and trapping a large number of enemy troops in their Siegfried Line defences. On the night of 22 March, Third Army troops crossed the Rhine at Oppenheim. In five days, 18–22 March, Patton's troops captured 68,000 Germans and eliminated the last enemy positions west of the Rhine. In the 6th Army Group operations area, the XV Corps of General Alexander M. Patch's Seventh Army crossed the Rhine at Worms on 26 March and formed a continuous line with the right flank of Third Army the following day.

The superb combat engineers

Numerous crossings of the Rhine were accomplished by combat engineers who, often under fire, completed

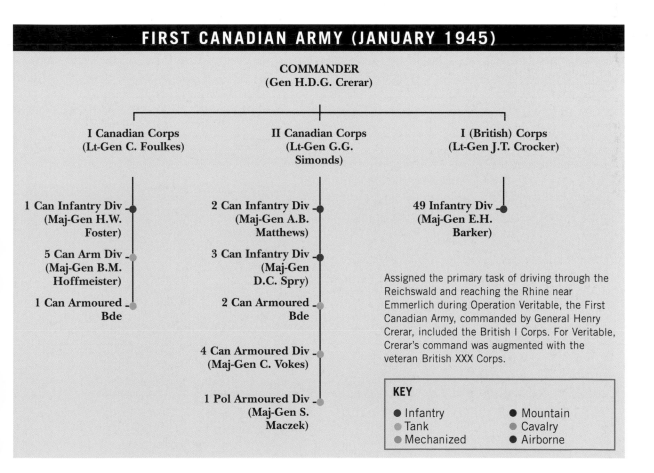

FIRST CANADIAN ARMY (JANUARY 1945)

COMMANDER
(Gen H.D.G. Crerar)

I Canadian Corps
(Lt-Gen C. Foulkes)

II Canadian Corps
(Lt-Gen G.G. Simonds)

I (British) Corps
(Lt-Gen J.T. Crocker)

1 Can Infantry Div
(Maj-Gen H.W. Foster)

5 Can Arm Div
(Maj-Gen B.M. Hoffmeister)

1 Can Armoured Bde

2 Can Infantry Div
(Maj-Gen A.B. Matthews)

3 Can Infantry Div
(Maj-Gen D.C. Spry)

2 Can Armoured Bde

4 Can Armoured Div
(Maj-Gen C. Vokes)

1 Pol Armoured Div
(Maj-Gen S. Maczek)

49 Infantry Div
(Maj-Gen E.H. Barker)

Assigned the primary task of driving through the Reichswald and reaching the Rhine near Emmerlich during Operation Veritable, the First Canadian Army, commanded by General Henry Crerar, included the British I Corps. For Veritable, Crerar's command was augmented with the veteran British XXX Corps.

KEY
- Infantry
- Tank
- Mechanized
- Mountain
- Cavalry
- Airborne

temporary spans of numerous types. The typical US combat engineer battalion was permanently assigned to an infantry division, and included 623 officers and men grouped into three companies as well as headquarters and service units. A number of larger engineer regiments were included at the corps and field army levels.

Aside from building bridges, the engineers also performed demolition, fortification construction and road-building assignments. If necessary, combat engineers could also serve as infantry.

Reaching the Ruhr

On 25 March, General Hodges' US First Army struck beyond the Remagen bridgehead in force. As VII Corps penetrated 19km (12 miles), both III Corps and V Corps also made substantial gains. Within days, the breakthrough was complete and the First Army had managed a junction with General Simpson's US Ninth Army to the north. All that remained of German Army Group B was encircled in the heavily industrialized Ruhr. The surrender of such a large number of German troops would be catastrophic.

Push into Bavaria and Austria

Within three weeks of the closure of the ring around the Ruhr, German Army Group B ceased to exist as 325,000 soldiers surrendered to the Americans. Meanwhile, Montgomery, expecting 21st Army Group to continue its leading role in the campaign, began planning for a major offensive across the plain of northern Germany to Berlin.

General Eisenhower, however, revised Allied strategy and shifted the major focus of the offensive into Germany southwards to the operational area of General Bradley's 12th Army Group. The primary objective of the offensive was dramatically altered. No longer would the Anglo-American coalition drive for Berlin.

Pragmatic progress

The objective for General Simpson's Ninth Army was the Elbe River near Magdeburg, while General Hodges' First Army drove for the city of Leipzig, 210km (130 miles) to the east. General Patton's Third Army was to continue eastwards, through southern Germany and into Czechoslovakia and Austria.

In the south, General Devers' 6th Army Group was to transit the Black Forest and reach the Alps, thwarting any German attempt to organize a guerrilla resistance. Montgomery's 21st Army Group was to consolidate the Allied hold on the plain in northern Germany, invest or capture major German ports, and prevent the transfer of enemy troops from Norway or Denmark.

Eisenhower's rationale, which was at first vehemently opposed by the British, was understandable. Political factors were already influencing the conduct of the

March–April 1945

Launching out of the huge bridgehead stretching up the east bank of the Rhine from Bonn, Allied troops drove deep into Germany. Elements of the US Ninth Army crossed the Weser on 4 April. By 10 April, they were approaching the Elbe. On 24 April, the US First Army reached its stop line on the Mulde, and the next day sought to link up with Soviet forces at Torgau. Germany had been divided in two. Soon afterwards, on 3 May, troops from the Second British Army of Montgomery's 21st Army Group met the spearheads of Rokossovsky's 2nd Belorussian Front at Wismar on the Baltic. The third act in the dismemberment of the Third *Reich* came with the Vienna Offensive, which ended on 13 April 1945 with the Soviet capture of the city. The US Seventh Army occupied the Tyrol early in May, linking up with the US Fifth Army, which had advanced from northern Italy.

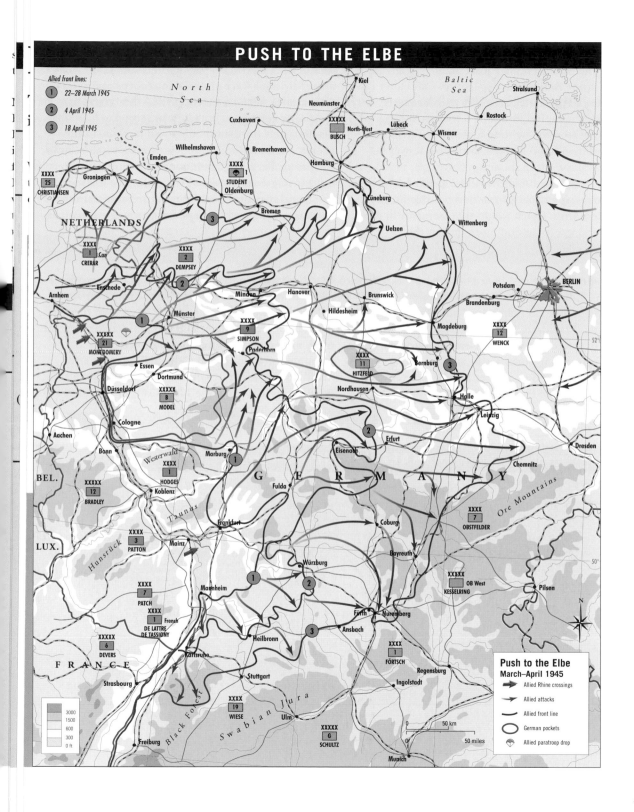

PUSH TO THE ELBE

Allied front lines:
1. 22–28 March 1945
2. 4 April 1945
3. 18 April 1945

North Sea

Baltic Sea

Kiel

Neumünster

Stralsund

Cuxhaven

North-West

Lübeck

Rostock

XXXX
BUSCH

Wismar

Wilhelmshaven

Bremerhaven

Hamburg

Emden

XXXX 1
STUDENT
Oldenburg

XXXX
25
CHRISTIANSEN

Groningen

Bremen

Lüneburg

Wittenberg

NETHERLANDS

Uelzen

XXXX 1
Can
CRERAR

XXXX
2
DEMPSEY

Minden

Hanover

Brunswick

Potsdam

BERLIN

Enschede

Münster

Hildesheim

Brandenburg

Arnhem

XXXX
SIMPSON

Magdeburg

XXXX
12
WENCK

XXXXX
21
MONTGOMERY

Paderborn

Essen

Dortmund

XXXX
11
HITZFELD

Bernburg

Düsseldorf

XXXXX
B
MODEL

Nordhausen

Halle

Cologne

Leipzig

Aachen

Bonn

Westerwald

Marburg

Eisenach

Erfurt

Dresden

BEL.

XXXXX
12
BRADLEY

XXXX
1
HODGES

Koblenz

Fulda

GERMANY

Chemnitz

Ore Mountains

Taunus

Coburg

XXXX
7
OBSTFELDER

LUX.

XXXX
3
PATTON

Mainz

Frankfurt

Bayreuth

Pilsen

Hunsrück

XXXX
7
PATCH

Mannheim

Würzburg

XXXXX
OB West
KESSELRING

XXXX
1
French
DE LATTRE
DE TASSIGNY

Fürth

Nuremberg

XXXXX
6
DEVERS

Heilbronn

Ansbach

FRANCE

Karlsruhe

XXXX
1
FÖRTSCH

Regensburg

Strasbourg

Stuttgart

Ingolstadt

XXXX
19
WIESE

Swabian Jura

Ulm

Freiburg

Black Forest

XXXXX
G
SCHULTZ

Munich

Push to the Elbe
March–April 1945

➤ Allied Rhine crossings
→ Allied attacks
— Allied front line
⬭ German pockets
☂ Allied paratroop drop

3000
1500
600
300
0 ft

0   50 km
0   50 miles

Brigades de Cavalerie, 1re *43*
Brigades de Spahis
  1er *51*
  2e *55*
  3e *43*
Commands
  Middle East Mobile Forces
    41
  Tunisia *41*
Corps d'Armée
  Ire *40, 42*, 145, 146, *183*
  IIe *40, 43*, 145, *183*
  IIIe *40, 42*
  IVe *40, 42*
  Ve *40, 42*
  VIe *41, 51*
  VIIe *41, 55*
  VIIIe *41, 50*
  IXe *41, 50*
  Xe *40, 43*
  XIe *40, 43*
  XIIe *41, 50*
  XIIIe *41, 55*
  XIVe *41, 57*
  XVe *41, 57*
  XVIe *40, 42*, 54
  XVIIe *41, 50*
  XVIIIe *40, 43*
  XIXe *86, 88*
  XXe *41, 50*
  XXIe *40*
  XXIIIe *40*
  XXIVe *41, 51*
  XLIe *40, 43*
  XLIIe *41, 51*
  XLIIIe *41, 50*
  XLIV de Forteresse *55*
  XLIVe *41*
  XLV de Forteresse *55*
  XLVe *41*
Cavalerie *42*
Colonial *41, 51*
Franc d'Afrique *88*
Corps Expeditionnaire Francais
  en Scandinavie *29, 41*
Divisions Cuirassée de Réserve
  1re *42*
  4e *49*
Divisions d'Infanterie
  1re Coloniale *43*
  1re Légère *29, 41*
  1re March *145*
  1re Motorisée *42, 44*
  1re Polonaise *50*
  2e *51, 57*
  2e Marocaine *58, 145, 183*
  3e Algérienne *145, 183*
  3e Coloniale *43*
  3e Marocaine *58*
  3e Motorisée *44*
  4e *42*
  4e Coloniale *50*
  4e Marocaine *145, 183*
  4e Nord-Africaine *43*
  5e Motorisée *43, 44, 47*
  6e *51*
  6e Coloniale *51*
  6e Nord-Africaine *51*
  7e *51*
  8e *51*
  9e Coloniale *145, 183*
  9e Motorisée *42, 44*
  10e *183*
  11e *50*
  12e Motorisée *44*
  13e *55*
  14e 56, *183*
  15e Motorisée *42, 44*
  16e *50*
  18e *43*, 47
  19e *55*
  20e *51*
  21e *42*
  22e *43*
  24e *50*
  25e Motorisée *42, 44*
  26e *51*
  27e 55, *183*
  30e *50*
  31e *50*
  35e *50*

41e *43*
42e *51*
47e *50*
51e *51*
52e *50*
53e *43*
54e *55*
55e *47*
56e *51*
57e *55*
58e *51*
60e *42*
61e *43*
62e *50*
63e *55*
64e *57*
65e *57*
66e *57*
67e *55*
70e *50*
81e d'Afrique *56*
82e *50*
83e d'Afrique *56*
84e d'Afrique *56*
85e d'Afrique *56*
87e d'Afrique *50*
88e d'Afrique *56*
103e de Forteresse *50*
104e de Forteresse *55*
105e de Forteresse *55*
180e d'Afrique *56*
181e d'Afrique *56*
182e d'Afrique *56*
183e d'Afrique *56*
Alger d' *88*
du Maroc *88*
Oran d' *88*
organization 38
Divisions Légère de Chasseurs
  1re *29, 38, 41, 43*
  2e *29, 38, 41, 43*
  3e *38, 51*
  4e *38, 43*
  5e *38, 43*
  6e *56*
Divisions Légère Mécanique
  1re *39, 42, 44, 52*
  2e *42, 44, 52*
  3e *42, 44, 52*, 53
  4e *44, 52*
  7e *52*
  organization *39, 52*
Free French Brigade, 1st
  72, *73, 77, 78*
Free French Division, 1st 116
French Army B 143, *145*
French Expeditionary Corps
  116
Fronts
  Est Saharien *56*
  Sud Tunisien *56*
Groupes de Bataillons
  de Chars de Combat
  501 *50*
  502 *50*
  503 *43*
  504 *50*
  506 *55*
  508 *50*
  510 *42*
  511 *51*
  513 *51*
  514 *57*
  515 *42*
  517 *50*
  518 *43*
  519 *42*
  520 *51*
  522 *58*
  532 *51*
Légion Etrangère 64
  13e Demi Brigade *29, 72*
Motorized Division, 1st *183*
Region Militaire, XIX *56*
Secteurs Défensif Nice *57*
Secteurs Fortifiée
  Alpes-Maritime *57*
  Altkirch *55*
  Boulay *51*
  Dauphinée *57*
  Jura Central *55*

Montbéliard *55*
Savoie *57*
Theatres of Operations
  Eastern Mediterranean *41*
  North African *41*
  Northeastern 40
  Southeastern *41*
Troupes de Maroc *58*

Greece
First Army 96, 98
Cavalry Division *94*
Evzones Royal Guard 98
Infantry Brigades
  2nd *74*
  3rd Mountain *127*
  5th *94*
Infantry Corps
  I *95*
  II *94*
  III *94*
Infantry Divisions
  1st *94*
  2nd *95*
  3rd *95*
  4th *94*
  5th *94*
  6th *94*
  7th *95*
  8th *95*
  9th *94*
  10th *94*
  11th *94*
  12th *95*
  13th *94*
  14th *95*
  15th *94*
  16th *94*
  17th *94*
  18th *95*
  19th Motorised *95*
  20th *95*
National Popular Liberation
  Army (ELAS) 104, 105
National Republican Greek
  League (EDES) 104
Royal Hellenic Army *94–5*

Holland
Commando Luchtverdediging
  32
Infantry Divisions
  1re *32, 33*
  2e *32, 33*
  3e *32, 33*
  4e *32, 33*
  5e *32, 33*
  6e *32, 33*
  7e *32, 33*
  8e *32, 33*
  Lichte *32*
  Peel *32*
Legerkorps
  I *32*
  II *32*
  III *32*
  IV *32*
Prinses Irene Brigade *157*
Royal Dutch Army *32*, 33
Vesting Holland (Fortress
  Holland) 30, *32*

India
Infantry Brigades
  5th 62, *66, 69, 77*
  7th 62, *69, 77*
  9th 62, 75
  10th 62, 72
  11th 62, *65, 66, 69*
  18th 75
  26th *74*
  29th 62
  123rd 62
  161st 62, *77*
Infantry Divisions
  4th 62, *65, 66, 69, 77*, 87,
    88, *104, 123, 127*
  5th 62
  8th *122, 126*
  10th 65, *123, 127*
  organization 62

Italy
28th Garibaldi Brigade *127*
Combat Groups
  Cremona *127*
  Folgore *126*
  Friuli *127*
  Legnano *126*

New Zealand
4th Armoured Brigade *74*
Infantry Brigades
  2nd *96*
  4th *69*, 100
  5th *69, 77, 96*, 100
  6th *69, 75, 77, 96*
  9th *77*
  10th 100
Infantry Division, 2nd *69*, 76,
  77, 78, 87, *96*, 98, *100*,
  123, 127

Norway
Infantry Divisions
  1st *28*, 30
  2nd *28*, 30
  3rd *28*, 30
  4th *28*, 30
  5th *28*, 30
  6th *28*
Royal Norwegian Army 27, *28*,
  30

Poland
Armies
  Karpaty 16, *18*
  Kraków 16, *19*, 21, 23
  Lódz 16, *19*, 21
  Modlin 16, *19*
  Narew *18*
  Pomorze 16, *18*, 21–2
  Poznan 16, *18*, 21–2, 23
  Prusy 16, *19*, 21
  Warszawa 21, *22*
  Wyszków *19*
Armoured Brigade, 2nd
  117, 123, 127
Armoured Division, 1st
  150, 152, *175, 184*
Army Corps
  II 116, *117*, 120, *122, 123,
    127*
  Bielsko *19*
  Czersk *18*
  Kruszewo *19*
  Piotrków *19*
  Skwarczynski *19*
  Slask *19*
  Slowacja *18*
  Wegry *19*
  Wschod *18*
Artillery Group *117*
Cavalry Brigades 14
  10th Armoured *150*
  10th Motorized *19*
  Combined *22*
  Krakowska *19, 22, 23*
  Kresowa *19, 22*
  Mazowiecka *19, 22*
  Nowogrodzka *19, 22*
  organization 23
  Podlaska *18, 22*
  Podolska *18, 22*
  Pomorska *18, 22*
  Suwalska *18, 22*
  Wielkopolska *18, 22*
  Wilenska *19, 22*
  Wolynska *19, 22*
Grodno Fortified Zone *19*
Independent Parachute
  Brigade, 1st *156*, 158, 161
Infantry Brigades
  1st Carpathian Rifle *117*
  1st Mountain *117*
  2nd Carpathian Rifle *117*
  2nd Mountain *117*
  3rd *150*
  3rd Carpathian Rifle *117*
  3rd Mountain *18*
  5th Wolno *117*
  6th Lvov *117*
  Independent Carpathian
    Rifle Brigade 69

Karpacka *18*
Infantry Divisions
  1st *17, 19*
  2nd *17, 19, 22*
  3rd *17, 19*
  3rd Carpathian *117, 123, 127*
  4th *17, 18*
  5th *17, 22*
  5th Kresowa *117, 123, 127*
  6th *17, 19*
  7th *17, 19*
  8th *17, 19*, 21, *22*
  9th *17, 18*
  10th *17, 19*
  11th Karpaty *17, 18*
  12th *17, 19*
  13th *17, 19, 22*
  14th *17, 18*
  15th *17, 18, 22*
  16th *17, 18*
  17th *17, 18*
  18th *17, 18*
  19th *17, 19*
  20th *17, 19, 22*
  21st Mountain *17, 19*
  22nd Mountain *17, 19*
  23rd *17, 19*
  24th *17, 18*
  25th *17, 18, 22*
  26th *17, 18*
  27th *17, 18*
  28th *17, 19, 22*
  28th Reserve *18*
  29th *17, 19*
  30th *17, 19, 22*
  33rd Reserve *18*
  35th Reserve *19*
  36th Reserve *19*
  39th Reserve *19*
  41st Reserve *19*
  44th *22*
  44th Reserve *19*
  45th Reserve *19*
  55th Reserve *19*
Modlin Fortress *19*, 21, *22*
Pultusk Bridgehead *19*
Rózan Bridgehead *19*

South Africa
6th Armoured Division *122, 126*
Infantry Brigades
  1st *69, 77*
  2nd *77*
  3rd *69, 72, 75, 77*
  4th *69*
  5th *69*
  6th *69, 72*
Infantry Divisions
  1st *69, 72*, 76, *77*
  2nd *69, 72*

United Kingdom *see* Britain
United States
93rd Evacuation Hospital *145*
Airborne Divisions
  17th *167, 175, 181*
  82nd *109*, 110, *115, 134–5*,
    146, 156, 158, 159, 160,
    165, 185
  101st 110, *134–5, 156*,
    158, 159, 160, 162, *167*,
    168–9
  organization 110, *160*
Anti-Aircraft Brigade, 49th *134*
Armies
  First
    Germany, assault on
      162, *164–5*, 174, 176,
      178, *180, 182*
    Normandy landings
      131, 134, *146*, 149,
      153, 155
  Third 146, 151, 153, 155,
    162, *166–7*, *168–9*, 174,
    175, 178, *181, 182*
  Fifth *106*, 112, 115, 116,
    118, 120, *122, 125, 126*,
    176, 178
  Seventh 107, *108–9*, 110,
    142, *144*, 175, 176, 178,
    182

Ninth 153, 162, 171, 176,
  178, *180*, 183
Fifteenth 153, 178, *181*
Armored Divisions
  1st *80*, 86, *88, 112, 118*,
    122, 126
  2nd *80*, 109, *146*, 153, *164*,
    180
  3rd *80*, *146*, 150, 153, *164*,
    180
  4th *80*, 112, *166, 167, 181*
  5th *80*, 112, *164, 185*
  6th *80*, 112, *166, 180*
  7th *80*, 112, *165, 185*
  8th *80*, 112, *180*
  9th *80*, 112, 162, 165, *167*,
    173, *181*
  10th *80*, 112, *166, 182*
  11th *80*, 112, *167, 181*
  12th *80*, 112, *182*
  13th *80*, 112, *181*
  14th *80*, 112, *181*
  16th *80*, 112, *181*
  20th *80*, 112, *182*
  organization *80*, 153
Army Corps
  II 86, 87, 88, *88*, 107, *108*,
    118, 120, *122, 126*
  III *166*, 176, *181*
  IV 120, *122, 126*
  V *134, 146, 164*, 176, *181*
  VI 114, 115, *118*, 119, 120,
    142, *144, 182*
  VII *134, 146*, 151, *164*, 176,
    180
  VIII *146, 167, 180*
  XII *166, 181*
  XIII *180*
  XV 175, *182*
  XVI *180*
  XVIII Airborne *156, 165, 185*
  XIX *146*, 151, *180*
  XX *181*
  XXI *182*
  XXII *181*
  XXIII *181*
  organization 178
  Provisional 107, *109*
Army Groups
  1st 134
  6th 112, 143, *144–5*, 146,
    171, 172–3, 176, *178*,
    182–3
  12th 153, 154, 168, *169*,
    171, 172, 176, *178*,
    180–1, 183
Cavalry Divisions
  1st *80*
  organization 167–8
Combat Commands 85
Command, Middle East *83*
Engineer Special Brigades
  1st *134, 136*
  Provisional *134*
  Forces X, Y and Z *85*
Infantry Divisions
  1st *81, 88, 108, 134, 135*,
    136, 139, *146, 164, 181*
  2nd *80, 81, 134, 146, 162*,
    164, 181
  3rd *81, 109, 115, 116, 118*,
    119, 142, *144, 182*
  4th *81, 134*, 136, 139, *146*,
    153, 154, 162, 165, *166*,
    180
  5th *81, 166, 174, 181*
  6th *81*
  7th *81*
  8th *81, 185*
  9th *81*, 84, *88, 108, 134*,
    146, 164, 180
  10th Mountain 120, 122,
    126, 182
  23rd Americal *81*
  24th *81*
  25th *81*
  26th *81, 166, 181*
  27th *81*
  28th *81*, 162, *167, 181*
  29th *81, 134*, 136, 139,
    146, 180

30th *81, 146, 165, 180*
31st *81*
32nd *81*
33rd *81*
34th *81, 88, 115, 118, 122, 126*
35th *81, 166, 180*
36th *81, 114, 115, 116, 118,* 125, 142, *144, 182*
37th *81*
38th *81*
40th *81*
41st *81*
42nd *182*
43rd *81*
44th *81, 182*
45th *81, 108,* 114, 115, *118,* 142, *144, 182*
63rd *81, 182*
65th *181*
66th *81, 181*
69th *81, 180,* 183
70th *81, 180*
71st *181*
75th *81, 165, 180*
76th *81, 180*
77th *81*
78th *81, 164, 180*
79th *81, 146, 180*
80th *81, 166, 181*
81st *81*
82nd *81*
83rd *81, 146, 164, 180*
84th *81, 164, 180*

85th *81, 118, 122, 126*
86th *81, 182*
87th *81, 167, 180*
88th *81, 118, 122, 126*
89th *180*
90th *81, 134, 146, 150, 166, 181*
91st *81, 122, 126*
92nd *81, 126*
93rd *81*
94th *81, 181*
95th *81, 180*
96th *81*
97th *81, 181*
98th *81*
99th *81, 162, 181*
100th *81, 182*
101st *81*
102nd *81, 180*
103rd *81, 182*
104th *81, 180*
106th *81, 162, 165, 168, 181*
organization 80, *81,* 112
Mechanized Cavalry Groups
2nd *166*
4th *164*
6th *166*
14th *165,* 167
102nd *164*
Regimental Combat Teams
16th *136*
26th *85,* 136
39th *85*
66th *85*

115th *136*
116th *136*
168th *85*
442nd *122*
517th Parachute *143*
Tank Battalions
70th *166*
702nd *166*
707th *167*
709th *164*
735th *166*
737th *166*
740th *165*
741st *164*
743rd *165*
745th *164*
746th *164*
750th *165*
761st *167*
771st *164*
774th *164*
Tank Destroyer Battalions
69th *166*
601st *115, 117*
602nd *167*
609th *166*
610th *166, 167*
612th *164*
613th *164*
628th *164, 165*
629th *165*
630th *167*
634th *164*
635th *136*

636th *115*
638th *164*
643rd *164, 165*
644th *164*
654th *166*
691st *167*
702nd *164*
703rd *164*
704th *166, 167*
705th *167*
772nd *164, 165*
773rd *166*
774th *166*
802nd *166*
803rd *166*
808th *166*
811th *167*
814th *165*
818th *166*
820th *165*
823rd *165*
893rd *164*
Task Forces
Central *82, 85*
Eastern *82, 85*
Green *85*
Sub Task Force Goalpost
84–5
Western *82, 84, 85*

Yugoslavia
Armies
First *92*
Second *92*

Third *93*
Third Territorial *93*
Fourth *92*
Fifth Independent *93*
Sixth Independent *93*
Seventh *92*
Coastal *92*
1st Armoured Battalion *93*
Army Groups
1 *92*
2 *92*
3 *93*
Banatiski Brigade *93*
Cavalry Divisions
1st *92*
2nd *93*
3rd *92*
Infantry Brigades
Ormozki *92*
Pozaveracki *93*
Risnajaski Mountain *92*
Sencan *92*
Smederevski *93*
Strumiki *93*
Subotica *92*
Sumbor *92*
Infantry Divisions
1st Cerska *93*
3rd Dunavska *93*
5th Sumadijska *93*
7th Potiska *92*
8th Krajinska *93*
9th Timocka *93*
10th Basanka *92*

12th Jadranska *92*
13th Hercegovacka *93*
15th Zetska *93*
17th Vrbaska *92*
20th Bregalnicka *93*
22nd Ibarska *93*
25th Vardarska *93*
27th Savska *92*
30th Osjecka *92*
31st Kosovska *93*
32nd Triglavski *92*
33rd Licka *92*
34th Toplicka *93*
40th Slavonska *92*
42nd Murska *92*
44th Unska *93*
46th Moravska *93*
47th Dinarska *93*
49th Sremska *93*
50th Drinska *93*
Komski Cavalry Brigade *93*
National Liberation Army
101, 102
Partisan Detachments *102*
Partisan Divisions *103*
Royal Yugoslav Army 91, *92–3,* 94
Savski Brigade *93*
Supreme Command Reserve *93*

Index of Commanders

Page numbers in *italics* refer to tables and illustrations.

Abraham, General R. *18, 22*
Adair, Major-General A.H.S. *149, 157, 169, 172, 185*
Adam, Lieutenant-General Sir A. *46*
Adamovic, Lieutenant-General K. *93*
Alexander, Field Marshal Sir Harold R.L.G.
  Italy 107, *108, 109,* 120, *122,* 125, *126,* 182
  North Africa *74,* 75
  pre-war *7, 8*
Alimpic, Lieutenant-General M. *92*
Allen, Brigadier A.S. 66, *96*
Allen, Major-General R.R. *182*
Allen, Major-General T. de la M. *85, 88, 108, 180*
Allfrey, Lieutenant-General C. *88*
Almond, Major-General E.M. *126*
Alter, Major-General F. *17, 18, 22*
Anders, General W. *19, 117, 123, 127*
Anderson, Lieutenant-Colonel J. *137*
Anderson, Major-General J.B. *180*
Anderson, Major-General J.W. *85*
Anderson, Lieutenant-General Kenneth A.N. *85,* 86
Anderson, Lieutenant-Colonel W.A.C. *137*
Andrews, Lieutenant-Colonel *130*
Andrus, Brigadier-General C. *164, 181*
Antic, Lieutenant-General J. *93*
Arbuthnott, Major-General K. *126*
Arnold, General Henry 'Hap' *81*
Arras, Major-General d' *43*
Aubry, Lieutenant-Colonel *42*
Auchinleck, General Sir Claude 71, *74–5,* 76
Audet, Lieutenant-General S.G. *29, 41*

Baade, Major-General P.W. *166, 180*
Bakopoulos, Lieutenant-General K. *95*
Bakos, Major-General G. *95*
Balmer, Brigadier-General J.D. *181*
Barbe, Major-General *43*
Barber, Major-General C.M. *172, 185*
Barker, Major-General E.H. *147, 173, 175, 185*
Barnett, Major-General A.J. *180*
Barrowclough, Brigadier *96*
Bartholomew, General W.H. *8*
Barton, Major-General R.O. *134, 136, 146, 166*
Beauchesne, Colonel de *42*
Beauman, General Archibald P. *46, 57*
Bent, Major-General *32*
Beresford-Peirse, Major-General P. *65, 66*

Berney-Ficklin, Major-General H.P.M. *108*
Berniquet, Major-General *43*
Besson, General A.M.B. *43*
Béthouart, General M.A. *29, 41, 183*
Beynet, General *41*
Billingslea, Colonel *156*
Billotte, General G.H.G. *40, 42*
Billotte, General P. *183*
Birk, Lieutenant-Colonel H. *68*
Bischoff von Heemskerk, Colonel W.F.K. *33*
Blackadder, Brigadier K.G. *137*
Blakeley, Major-General H.W. *180*
Blanc, Lieutenant-General A.F.A. *56*
Blanchard, General Georges *40, 42, 43*
Bloch, Lieutenant-General *40, 42*
Boissau, General R. *88*
Boissieres, Lieutenant-Colonel *42*
Bolling, Major-General A.R. *164, 180*
Bols, Lieutenant-General B.G. *169*
Bols, Major-General E.L. *185*
Bolte, Major-General C.L. *122, 126*
Boltuc, Major-General M. *18*
Boncza-Uzdowski, Major-General W. *17, 18, 19*
Bonham-Carter, General Sir C. *10*
Boris, Lieutenant-General *40, 42*
Bortnowski, Lieutenant-General Wladyslaw 16, *18*
Boruta-Spiechowicz, Major-General M. *19*
Bosville, Brigadier T.J.B. *77*
Bouffet, Major-General *40, 43*
Bougrain, Brigadier-General *42*
Boulakas, Colonel K. *94*
Bourret, General V. *41, 50*
Bozic, Lieutenant-General Z. *92*
Bradley, Lieutenant-General Omar N.
  Germany, assault on 171, *178, 180, 181,* 183
  Italy 107, *108*
  Normandy landings *131, 134, 146, 147,* 153
Brahnos, Major-General B. *94*
Brasic, General I. *93*
Brereton, Lieutenant-General L.H. *83, 156, 178*
Briggs, Major-General R. *77, 88*
Brink, Major-General G. *69*
Brojat, Lieutenant-Colonel *50*
Broniewski, General *22*
Brooke, Lieutenant-General Sir Alan *46,* 57
Brooks, Major-General E.H. *146, 182*
Brooks, Brigadier W.T. *10*
Brown, Major-General A.E. *181*
Browning, Lieutenant-General F. *156*

Bruneau, Brigadier-General *42*
Brzechwa-Ajdukiewicz, Major-General A. *17, 18*
Bucknall, Lieutenant-General G.C. *133, 147*
Buell, Lieutenant-Colonel D.B. *137*
Bullen-Smith, Major-General D.C. *133, 147, 149*
Burczak, Colonel K. *19*
Burns, Lieutenant-General E.L.M. *123*
Burress, Major-General W.A. *137*
Burrough, Vice-Admiral Sir H. *84*
Byron, Lieutenant-Colonel R. *137*

Cabeldu, Lieutenant-Colonel F.N. *137*
Caffey, Colonel F. *85*
Camas, Major-General de *42*
Campbell, Lieutenant-Colonel John *65,* 67
Canham, Colonel D.D.W. *136*
Carpentier, General M.M. *183*
Carstens, Major-General *32*
Cass, Brigadier E.E.E. *85, 137*
Cato, Lieutenant-Colonel *130*
Caunter, Brigadier J.L.A. *8, 11, 66*
Cehak, Major-General L. *17, 19, 22*
Champion, Major-General *41, 55*
Chanoine, Major-General *43*
Chapman, Major-General E. *178*
Chappel, Brigadier *100*
Charrington, Brigadier *96*
Christiansen, Lieutenant-Colonel G.H. *137*
Clark, General Mark W. 112, *115,* 116, *118,* 119, 120, *122,* 124–5, *126,* 182
Clarke, Brigadier W.S. *169*
Clutterbuck, Major-General W.E. *88*
Cocks, Lieutenant-Colonel A.D.B. *137*
Collins, Major-General J.L. *134, 146, 164, 180, 182*
Collins, Major-General R.J. *7, 9*
Colwell, Lieutenant-Colonel R.J. *137*
Combe, Lieutenant-Colonel John *68*
Conde, General *41, 51*
Connolly, Major-General D.H. *83*
Corap, General A.G. *40, 43*
Corlett, Major-General C.H. *146, 180*
Cota, Major-General N.D. *167, 181*
Couchet, Lieutenant-Colonel de *50*
Coulter, Major-General J.B. *118, 122, 126*
Cracroft, Brigadier B. *133, 137*
Craig, Major-General L.A. *164, 180*
Creagh, Major-General M. O'M. *65, 66*
Crerar, Lieutenant-General H.D.G. *150,* 152, 171, *175,* 184

Crittenberger, Lieutenant-General W.D. *122, 126*
Crocker, Lieutenant-General J.T. *88, 133, 147, 149, 175*
Cukavac, General V. *93*
Culin, Major-General F.L. Jr. *167, 180*
Cunningham, General Alan 62, 68, *69,* 70, 71
Cunningham, Admiral Sir Andrew
Cunningham, Brigadier J.G. *137*
Currie, Brigadier *77*
Curtis, Major-General H.O. *46*
Custance, Brigadier E.C.N. *77*
Czuma, General W. 21, *22,* 23

Dab-Biernacki, Lieutenant-General Stefan 16, *19*
Dager, Major-General H.E. *181*
Dahlquist, Major-General J.E. *144, 182*
Daille, Lieutenant-General M. *41, 55*
Dalby, Major-General T.G. *7, 9*
Dalton, Admiral Jean Francois 83, 84
Dawson, Lieutenant-Colonel R.W.P. *137*
de Gaulle, Colonel Charles 49, *56,* 58, 153, 154–5
Dean, Major-General W.F. *182*
Demaratos, Colonel S. *94*
Demestihas, Lieutenant-General P. *95*
Dempsey, Lieutenant-General Miles
  Germany, assault on *157, 172, 173, 185*
  Italy 107, *108*
  Normandy landings *131, 133, 147, 149*
Dentz, General *41, 50*
Desclaurens, Brigadier-General *42*
Devers, General Jacob L. 143, *144, 145,* 171, 176, *178, 182*
Devine, Major-General J. *180*
Dickinson, Major-General D.P. *10*
Didelet, Major-General *42*
Dimitrijevic, Lieutenant-General A. *93*
Dindorf-Ankowicz, Major-General F. *17, 19*
Djordevic, Lieutenant-General K. *93*
Dojan-Surówka, Colonel E. *17, 19*
Doolittle, Brigadier-General J.H. *84*
Drake-Brockman, Brigadier G.P.L. *9, 11*
Drapella, Major-General J. *17, 18*
Drew, Major-General W.F. *182*
Dronne, Captain Raymond 153
Drucki-Lubecki, Colonel K. *19*
Duch, General B.B. *50, 117, 123, 127*
Duchemin, Major-General F.G.A. *29, 41*
Durand, Colonel *29, 41*
Durnford-Slater, Lieutenant-Colonel J. *130*

Index of Commanders

Eadie, Lieutenant-Colonel J.A. *137*
Eagles, Major-General W.W. *118, 144*
Earnest, Major-General H.L. *181*
Eddy, Major-General M.S. *88, 108, 134, 146, 166, 181*
Eisenhower, General Dwight D.
  Germany, assault on 161, 168, 171, 176, 178, 179, 182, 184
  Italy 107, *109*, 116, 129
  Normandy landings *131*, 134, 153
  North Africa *84*
  Operation Dragoon 142
Ekman, Colonel *156*
Endel-Ragis, Major-General L. *17, 19*
Erichsen, Brigadier-General C. *28*
Erskine, Major-General G.W.E.J. *115, 147, 149*
Erskine, Brigadier I. *65*
Essame, Colonel *157*
Evans, Major-General R. *9*
Evelegh, Major-General V. *88, 108*

Fabrycy, Lieutenant-General K. *18*
Fagalde, Major-General *40, 42*
Fainter, Colonel F.F. *136*
Fales, Colonel C.K. *136*
Filipowicz, Colonel J. *19*
Finley, Major-General T.D. *180*
Fisher, Brigadier A.F. *77*
Fisher, Lieutenant-General B.D. *9*
Flavigny, Lieutenant-General *40*
Fleischer, Brigadier-General C.G. *28*
Fleury, Lieutenant-Colonel *43*
Floyer-Acland, Major-General A.N. *7, 9*
Foer, Major-General H.W. *127*
Fonblanque, Major-General P. de *46*
Fornel de la Laurencie, General de *40, 42*
Fortune, Major-General V.M. *7, 8, 51*
Foster, Major-General H.W. *137, 175, 184*
Foulkes, Lieutenant-General C. *127, 175, 184*
Francois, Lieutenant-General M.J.V.L. *58*
Franklyn, Major-General Harold E. *7, 8, 46*, 52
Fraser, Brigadier W. *29*
Fredenhall, Major-General Lloyd R. 82, *85*
Frederick, General Robert T. 143, 144, 145, *182*
Freeman-Attwood, Major-General H.A. *88*
Frere, General *41, 50*
Freyberg, Lieutenant-General Bernard Cyril *69, 77*, 87, *91, 96*, 98–9, *100, 123, 127*
Freydenberg, Major-General *41, 51*
Fries, Lieutenant-Colonel S.G. *136*
Frost, Lieutenant-Colonel John 160, 161
Fuller, Colonel J.F.C. 7
Furgalski, General T. *17, 19, 22*

Gaffey, Major-General H.J. *109, 166, 181*
Gailliard, General *43*
Gairdner, Major-General C.H. *77*
Galadyk, Colonel J. *19*
Gale, Major-General R.N. *133, 142*
Gamelin, General Maurice 47, 52
Garbay, General P. *183*
Garchery, General J.J.M. *41, 55*
Gasiorowski, Major-General J.T. *17, 19*
Gatehouse, Major-General A.H. *65, 77*
Gavin, Major-General J.M. *156*, 160, *165, 185*
Gazes, Major-General I. *94*
Gentry, Brigadier *77*
Gerhardt, Major-General C.H. *134, 136, 146, 180*
Germain, Major-General *40*
Gerow, Major-General Leonard T. *134, 146, 164, 178, 181*
Gill, Lieutenant General J.G. *8*
Gillem, Major-General A.C. Jr. *180*
Girard, Lieutenant-Colonel *51*
Giraud, General H.H. *40, 42*
Godfrey, Brigadier *77*
Godwin-Austen, Lieutenant-General A.R. *7, 10*
Goode, Colonel P.R. *136*
Gordon, Lieutenant-Colonel M.B.K. *137*
Gort, General John Vereker, Viscount *40*, 45, *46*, 52
Gostling, Lieutenant-Colonel *130*
Gott, Major-General W.H.E. *66, 69*
Goudot, Lieutenant-General V.N. *56*
Goulburn, Colonel *157*
Graham, Major-General D.A.H. *115, 133, 137, 147, 157, 169, 173*
Gransard, Lieutenant-General *40*
Grant, General C. *8*
Gray, Lieutenant-Colonel T.M. *137*
Gregson-Ellis, Major-General P.G.S. *118*
Griffiths, Lieutenant-Colonel F.M. *137*
Grow, Major-General R.W. *166, 180*
Grzmot-Skotnicki, Major-General S. *18*
Guillaume, General A. *183*

Hackett, Brigadier *156*
Haig, General Sir Douglas 7
Haining, Lieutenant-General R.H. *8*
Haislip, Major-General W. *182*
Hakewill-Smith, Major-General E. *157, 171, 185*
Halsey, Brigadier-General M.B. *181*
Hanka-Kulesza, Colonel S. *19*
Harberts, Major-General *32*
Harding, Major-General Sir J. *77*
Hardy, Lieutenant-Colonel C.R. *137*
Hargest, Brigadier *96, 100*
Harmon, Major-General E.N. *85, 118, 164, 181*
Harper, Colonel *156*
Harrap, Lieutenant-Colonel *137*
Harvey, Brigadier C.B.C. *169*
Hasbrouck, Brigadier-General R.W. *165, 185*
Hawkesworth, Lieutenant-General J.L.I. *46, 88, 115, 123, 127*
Hays, Major-General G.P. *126, 182*
Herbert, Major-General W.N. *8, 46*
Hesdin, General R. de *183*
Hewitt, Rear-Admiral H.K. *84*
Hibbs, Major-General L.E. *182*
Hickey, Brigadier-General D.O. *180*
Hicks, Brigadier *156*
Hill, Brigadier J. *142*
Hill, Colonel *157*
Hobart, Major-General Percy C.S. 7, *10, 133, 140, 146, 149*
Hobbs, Major-General L.S. *146, 165, 180*
Hodges, General Courtney 162, *164, 165*, 172, 176, 178, *180*, 182
Hoffmeister, Major-General B.M. *123, 127, 175, 184*
Hoge, Brigadier-General W.M. *134*
Holmes, Major-General W.G. *7, 8, 46*
Holworthy, Major-General A. *104, 123, 127*
Hopkinson, Colonel *157*
Hopkinson, Major-General G.F. *108*
Horrocks, Lieutenant-General Sir Brian G. *77, 156, 157*, 158, *169, 185*
Houston, Major-General T. *108*
Hubert, Lieutenant-General *41, 50*
Hudry, Lieutenant-Colonel *55*
Huebner, Major-General C.R. *134, 135, 136, 146, 181*
Hughes, Major-General J.T.P. *77*
Hull, Major-General R.A. *123, 185*
Huntziger, General C.L.C. *40, 43*
Hupfer, Lieutenant-Colonel C.G. *136*
Hvinden-Haug, Brigadier-General J. *28*

Inglis, Colonel *100*
Irwin, Major-General S.L. *166*

Jagmin-Sadowski, Major-General J. *19*
Jakovic, General M. *92*
Jansen, Colonel F.B.A.J. *33*
Jasperson, Lieutenant-Colonel *130*
Johnson, Colonel *156*
Johnson, Major-General D.G. *7, 9, 46*
Jones, Major-General A.W. *165*
Jouferault, Colonel *51*
Jovanovic, Lieutenant-General B. *92*
Juin, Major-General Alfonse *42*, 116

Kalabinski, Colonel S. *19*
Kales, Colonel A. *94*
Kalina-Zieleniewski, Colonel T. *18*
Karabatos, Colonel G. *95*
Karassos, Major-General K. *95*
Karcz, Colonel J. *19*
Katsemetros, Major-General K. *95*
Keall, Major-General P.W. *126*
Keating, Major-General F.A. *180*
Keefler, Major-General R.H. *184*
Keightley, Major-General C.F. *88, 123, 127*
Keller, Major-General R.F.L. *133, 137, 147*
Kenchington, Brigadier A.G. *77*
Kendall, Major-General P.W. *122*
Keyes, Major-General Geoffrey 107, *109, 118, 122, 126*
Kilburn, Brigadier-General C.S. *167*
Kindersley, Brigadier H. *142*
Kippenberger, Brigadier *77, 100*
Kirkman, General Sir S. *108*, 116, *122, 126*
Klaehn, Lieutenant-Colonel P.C. *137*
Klopper, Major-General H.B. *72*
Kmicica-Skrzynski, Brigadier-General L. *18*
Knox, Brigadier F.Y.C. *137*
Knox, Colonel *157*
Koeltz, Lieutenant-General M.L. *88*
Koenig, Major-General Pierre 72, 73
Kopanski, General S. *69*
Kossecki, Colonel S. *17, 18*
Kostic, Lieutenant-General V. *93*
Kotoulas, Lieutenant-General I. *95*
Kotowicz, Colonel J.S. *18*
Kotzebue, Lieutenant Albert 183
Kowalski, Major-General W. *17, 19*
Kraak, Colonel L.H. *33*
Kramer, Major-General H.F. *181*
Krok-Paszkowski, Colonel H. *19*
Krstic, Lieutenant-General D. *93*
Krukowicz-Przedrzymirski, Major-General Emil 16, *19*
Kruszewski, Major-General S. *19*
Krzyzanowski, Major-General B. *17, 18*
Kukavicic, Lieutenant-General J. *92*
Kustron, Major-General J. *17, 19*
Kutrzeba, General Tadeusz 16, *18*, 23
Kwaciszewski, Major-General J. *17, 19*

Laake, General Kristian 25, 29
Labatt, Lieutenant-Colonel *130*
Langlois, Major-General *42*
Langner, Brigadier-General W. *18*
Lanquetot, Brigadier-General *42*
Larminat, Lieutenant-General *145*
Lathbury, Brigadier *156*
Lattre de Tassigny, General Jean de 56, 143, *145, 183*
Lauer, Major-General W.E. *181*
Laurantzon, Brigadier-General J. *28*
Laure, General *41, 50*
Lavdas, Major-General G. *95*
Leclerc, General J-P. *150*, 153, *154, 183*
Leese, General Sir O. *77*, 107, *109*, 116, 120, *123*, 125
Le Fanu, Major-General R. *7, 8*
Leicester, Brigadier B.W. *133, 137*
Leigh-Mallory, Air Chief Marshal Sir Trafford L. *131*
Leonard, Major-General J.W. *167, 181*
Lescanne, General *41, 50*
Lett, Brigadier S. *130*
L'Huillier, Lieutenant-Colonel *50*
Liardet, Major-General C.F. *9*
Libaud, Major-General *40, 43*
Liddell, Governor *10*
Liddell Hart, Colonel Basil 7
Liljedahl, Brigadier-General E. *28*
Lindquist, Colonel *156*
Lindsay, Major-General G.M. *7, 8*
Lioumpas, Major-General *95*
Liszka-Lawicz, General W. *17, 19, 22*
Livesay, Major-General W.G. *122, 126*
Ljubicic, Lieutenant-General P. *93*
Lloyd, Brigadier W.L. *66*
Loewen, Major-General C.F. *122, 126*
Loiseau, General *51*
Loizeau, General *41, 51*
Lomax, Brigadier C.E.N. *66*
Loon, Colonel A.M.M. van *33*
Lovat, Lieutenant-Colonel Lord *130, 133, 137*
Loyd, Major-General H.C. *7, 8*
Lucas, Major-General L.K. *115, 118*, 119, 120
Lukoski, Major-General K. *18*
Lumsden, Lieutenant-General H. *77*
Lyne, Major-General L.O. *147, 171, 172, 185*

McAuliffe, Major-General A.C. *167*, 168, *182*
McBride, Major-General H.L. *166, 181*
McCreery, Lieutenant-General R. *115, 123*, 125, *127*
Mackay, Major-General I.G. *66, 96*
MacKelvie, Brigadier-General J. *134, 146*
Mackesey, Major-General P.J. *7, 8*
MacMichael, Sir H.A. *10*
MacMillan, Major-General G.H.A. *147, 185*
McNair, General Lesley J. 80, 110, 112, 150, 151
MacNarney, Lieutenant-General J.T. *126*
Macon, Major-General R.C. *146, 164, 180*
Maczek, General S. *19, 150, 175, 184*
Magnan, General P.J. *88, 183*
Magrin-Verneret, Colonel *29*
Majendie, Major-General V.H.B. *8*
Majewski, Colonel T. *150*
Majstorovic, Lieutenant-General M. *93*
Majstorovic, Lieutenant-General Z. *92*
Malony, Major-General H.J. *181*
Marc, Colonel *43*
Maric, Lieutenant-General A. *92*
Marinkovic, Lieutenant-General G. *93*
Markou, Major-General P. *94*
Marriott, Brigadier J.C.O. *69*
Marshall, General George C. 80, 81, 131
Martel, Major-General G. Le Q. *8, 46*
Martin, Lieutenant-General *40, 43, 145*
Mason-MacFarlane, Lieutenant-General F.N. *85*
Massy, Lieutenant-General H.R.S. *29*
Mast, Major-General C.E. *88*
Mathenet, Lieutenant-General M. *88*
Matheson, Lieutenant-Colonel F.M. *137*
Mathieu, Lieutenant-Colonel J.E.P.G. *137*
Matthews, Major-General A.B. *147, 150, 175, 184*
Maxwell, Major-General R.L. *83*
Melasky, Major-General H.M. *182*
Meldram, Lieutenant-Colonel J.M. *137*
Menard, Lieutenant-Colonel *130*
Merritt, Lieutenant-Colonel *130*
Messervy, Major-General F. *69*
Metaxas, Major-General A. *94*
Michaelis, Colonel *156*
Middleton, Major-General T.H. *115, 146, 167, 180*
Mihajlovic, Lieutenant-General M. *93*
Milburn, Major-General F.W. *182*
Milenkovic, Lieutenant-General M. *93*
Milenkvoic, Colonel S. *92*
Miley, Major-General W.M. *167, 181*
Miljkovic, General D. *92*
Millikin, Major-General J. *166*
Mills-Roberts, Lieutenant-Colonel D. *137*
Milosavljevic, Lieutenant-General D. *92*
Misserey, Lieutenant-General M. *41, 55*
Mlot-Fijalkowski, Major-General C. *18*
Mole, Colonel *157*
Molinie, Major-General *42*
Molle, General M.E.A. *183*
Mond, Major-General B. *17, 19*
Monsabert, Lieutenant-General J. ed *183*
Montagne, General *41*
Montgomery, Lieutenant-General Bernard Law
  British Expeditionary Force *46*, 47
  Germany, assault on *155*, 157–8, 161, 162, 168, *169*, 171, *173, 174*, 176, 183–4
  Italy 107, *108*, 110, 116
  Normandy landings *131*, 146, *147, 149*, 153
  North Africa *74*, 75, 76, *77*, 78, 86, 89
  pre-war *7, 9*
Moore, Major-General B.E. *185*
Morais, General M. de *122, 126*
Morgan, Brigadier H de R. *29*
Morgan, General Frederick 131, 132
Morris, Major-General W.H.H. Jr. *166, 182*
Morton, Lieutenant-Colonel R.E.A. *137*
Moulton, Lieutenant-Colonel J.L. *137*
Mountbatten, Lord Louis 129
Moutouses, Major-General S. *94*
Mozdyniewicz, Colonel M. *17, 18*
Murray, Major-General H. *122, 126*
Murray, Lieutenant-Colonel I. *142*
Murray, Brigadier T.D. *8, 11*
Murrogh, Brigadier W.F. *11*
Musse, Major-General *42*

Naumovic, General J. *93*
Nedeljkovic, General P. *92*
Nedic, General M. *92, 93*
Nichols, Major-General J.S. *77*
Nichols, Lieutenant-Colonel W. *136*
Niezabitowski, Colonel T. *17, 18*
Nijnatten, Major-General *32*
Noel, Lieutenant-General *41, 50*
Norrie, Lieutenant-General C.W.M. *9, 69*

O'Connor, Lieutenant-General Richard N. *7, 10, 65, 66, 147, 149*
O'Daniel, Major-General J.W. *85, 116, 118, 144, 182*
Odzierzyfski, Brigadier-General R. *117*
Olbrycht, Colonel B. *19*
Oliver, Major-General L.E. *164, 185*
Olry, General René-Henri *41*, 57
Osborne, Major-General E.A. *7, 9, 46*
Ostrowski, Colonel M. *19*
Oziewicz, Colonel I. *17, 19*

Palmer, Brigadier-General W.B. *134*
Palmer, Lieutenant-Colonel *157*
Pandurovic, Lieutenant-General D. *92*
Papadopoulos, Lieutenant-General D. *94*
Papagos, Lieutenant-General A. *94*
Papakontantinou, Major-General K. *95*
Papgeorgiou, Major-General G. *94*
Parker, Major-General E.P. *164, 180*
Paszkiewicz, Major-General G. *17, 19*

Patch, General Alexander M. 112, 142, *144*, 175, 178, 179, *182*
Patton, Major-General George S. Jr.
  Germany, assault on 162, *166, 167*, 168, 169, 172, *174*, 175, 176, 178, *181*, 182
  Italy 107, *108*, 110
  Normandy landings 133–4, 145, 146, 151, 153
  North Africa 82, 84, *85*, 86, *88*
Paul, Major-General W.S. *166*, *181*
Peillon, Colonel 55
Peiper, Lieutenant-Colonel Joachim 166
Penney, Major-General W.R.C. *118*, 119
Pepper, Brigadier E.C. *137*
Pétain, Marshal Philippe 58, 84
Petch, Lieutenant-Colonel C. *137*
Peter II, King of Yugoslavia 92
Petiet, Major-General *51*
Petre, Major-General R.L. *7, 9*
Petrovic, General M. *92*
Petrovic, Lieutenant-General V. *93*
Phillips, Lieutenant-Colonel C.F. *137*
Phillips, Brigadier C.G. *29*
Picard, Brigadier-General *42*
Picton-Phillips, Lieutenant-Colonel *130*
Piekarski, Colonel W. *19*
Pienaar, Major-General D.H. *77*
Pierce, Brigadier-General J.L. *181*
Pitsikas, Lieutenant-General P. *95*
Place, Lieutenant-Colonel J. *142*
Podhorski, Brigadier-General Z. *18*
Poett, Brigadier N. *142*
Poole, Major-General W.H.E. *122, 126*
Popadic, Lieutenant-General M. *93*
Pope, Brigadier V.V. *9*
Porter, Major-General R.E. *180*
Powierza, Colonel W. *17, 19*
Predic, Lieutenant-General D. *93*
Preston, Brigadier T. *8, 11*
Prételat, General A.G. *50*
Prichard, Major-General V.E. *122, 126*
Prickett, Major-General F.B. *165*
Priestman, Major-General J.H.T. *7, 9*
Prior, Major-General W.W. *26*
Prior-Palmer, Brigadier G.E. *133, 137*
Prioux, Lieutenant-General *40, 42*
Prugar-Ketling, Colonel B. *17, 18*
Przyjalkowski, Major-General Z. *17, 18, 22*
Purser, Major-General A.W. *7, 8*
Puttick, Brigadier *96, 100*

Radenovic, General M. *92*
Raikes, Major-General G.T. *7, 8*
Raketic, Lieutenant-General R. *92*
Rakowski, Brigadier General B. *117, 123, 127*
Ramsay, Admiral Sir Bertram H. *131*
Ransome, Major-General A.L. *7*
Rawlins, Major-General S.B. *184*
Reeder, Colonel R.P. Jr. *136*
Reid, Major-General D.W. *123, 127*
Reilly, Lieutenant-Colonel Sir B.R. *10*
Reinhardt, Major-General E.F. *180*

Reinhart, Major-General S.E. *181*
Rennie, Major-General T.G. *133, 137, 169, 173*
Requin, General E.J. *41, 50*
Richards, Brigadier C.E.M. *10*
Richards, Brigadier G.W. *77*
Ridgeway, Major-General M.B. *109, 115, 134, 146, 156, 165, 185*
Ries, Captain R.M.C. *137*
Ristic, Lieutenant-General B. *92*
Ritchie, General Neil 70, 71, 74, *147, 171, 185*
Roberts, Major-General F.C. *7, 9*
Roberts, Major-General G.P.B. *147, 149, 172, 185*
Roberts, General J.H. 'Ham' 129, *130*
Robertson, Brigadier *77*
Robertson, Major-General W.M. *134, 146, 164, 181*
Robinett, Colonel P.M. *85*
Robinson, Brigadier H.C.H. *66*
Rochard, Lieutenant-Colonel *40, 43*
Römmel, Lieutenant-General Juliusz 16, *19*, 21, 22, 23
Roosevelt, Brigadier-General Theodore Jr. *85*, 136
Rose, Major-General *94*
Ross, Major-General R.K. *147, 169, 173, 185*
Roucaud, General *43*
Roussopoulos, Major-General G. *94*
Ruge, Major-General Otto *25*, 27, *28*, 29
Russell, Major-General D. *122, 126*
Russell, Brigadier H.E. *65, 66*
Ryder, Major-General Charles W. 82, *88, 115, 118*

Salan, General R. *183*
Salce, Lieutenant-Colonel *51*
Salvagniac, Colonel *50*
Savige, Major-General S.G. *66, 96*
Savory, Brigadier R.A. *65, 66*
Schmidt, Major-General W.R. *180*
Sciard, Major-General *40, 42*
Scobie, Lieutenant-General R.M. *69, 104*
Scott, Brigadier H.B. *169*
Seitz, Colonel J.F.R. *135, 136*
Selby, Brigadier A.R. *66*
Senior, Brigadier R.H. *137*
Senior, Colonel *157*
Simonds, Major-General G.G. *109, 147, 175, 184*
Simonin, Lieutenant-Colonel *50*
Simpson, Air Commodore S.P. *85*
Simpson, General William 162, 171, 172, 176, 178, *180*
Sink, Colonel *156*
Sivot, Major-General *41, 51*
Skaggs, Lieutenant-Colonel R.N. *136*
Skwarczynski, Major-General S. *19*
Slappey, Colonel E.N. *136*
Sloan, Major-General J.E. *118*
Smigly-Rydz, Marshal Edward 15, *18*
Smith, Colonel A. *157*
Smith, Major-General A.C. *181*
Smith, Colonel G. Jr. *135, 136*
Smith, Brigadier K.P. *137*
Smith, Lieutenant-Colonel W. *136*
Smith, Lieutenant-General Walter Bedell *131*, 185

Smyth, Brigadier H.E.F. *29*
Somervell, General Brehon 81
Sosabowski, Major-General S.F. *156*
Southam, Brigadier W. *130*
Spragge, Lieutenant-Colonel J.G. *137*
Spry, Major-General D.C. *175*
Staich, General A. *22*
Stanier, Brigadier A.G.B. *137*
Stanier, Colonel *157*
Stanotas, Major-General G. *94*
Stawarz, Colonel A. *18*
Stefanovic, Lieutenant-General D. *92*
Steffens, Brigadier-General W. *28*
Steliotopoulos, Colonel P. *94*
Steriopoulos, Major-General D. *95*
Steveninck, Colonel de Ruyter van *157*
Steward, Brigadier K.E.S. *8, 11*
Stewart, Lieutenant-Colonel G. *142*
Stone, Lieutenant-General R.G.W.H. *74*
Stosic, Lieutenant-General A. *93*
Stroh, Major-General D.A. *181*
Strzelecki, Colonel L. *18*
Sudre, General A.M. *183*
Sulik, Major-General N. *117, 123, 127*
Switalski, Colonel S. *17, 18*
Szafran, Colonel J. *19*
Szylling, Major-General Antoni 16, *19*

Taitot, Lieutenant-Colonel *42*
Taylor, Colonel *157*
Taylor, Colonel G.A. *135, 136*
Taylor, Major-General M.D. *134, 156*, 160
Teacher, Lieutenant-Colonel T. *142*
Templer, Major-General G. *118*
Tence, Brigadier-General *41, 55*
Terrell, Major-General H. *150*
Thomas, Major-General G.I. *147, 157, 169, 171, 172, 185*
Thommée, Major-General W. *19, 22*
Thompson, Lieutenant-Colonel *156*
Thorne, Major-General A.F.A.N. *9*
Tidbury, Brigadier O.H. *10*
Timberlake, Brigadier-General E.W. *134*
Todd, Brigadier R. *127*
Tonic, Lieutenant-General L. *93*
Tribolet, Colonel H.A. *136*
Trifunovic, Lieutenant-General D. *92*
Troubridge, Commodore T.H. *84*
Truscott, Lieutenant-General Lucian K.
  Germany, assault on 178
  Italy *109, 118*, 120, 125, *126*
  Normandy landings 142, *144*
  North Africa 84, *85*
Tsakalotos, Colonel T. *127*
Tsolakoglou, Lieutenant-General G. *94*
Tucker, Colonel *156*
Turkowski, Colonel M. *17, 19*
Twaddle, Major-General H.L. *180*

Upham, Lieutenant-Colonel J.S. Jr. *136*
Urquhart, Major-General R. *156*, 161

Van Fleet, Major-General J.A. *136, 166, 181*
Vandeleur, Colonel *157*
Varjacic, Brigadier M. *93*
Vasey, Brigadier *96, 100*
Vauthier, Brigadier-General *43*
Vernejoul, General H. de *183*
Vigier, General J.T. de *145*
Villiers, Major-General I.P. de *69*
Vokes, Major-General C. *123, 150, 175, 184*
Vries, Colonel A. de *33*

Walker, Major-General F.L. *115, 118*
Walker, Major-General W.H. *181*
Walton, Colonel *157*
Ward, Major-General A.D. *104, 123*
Ward, Major-General O. *88, 182*
Watson, Major-General L.R. *146*
Wavell, Lieutenant-General Sir Archibald *10*, 62, 65, 71
Welborn, Lieutenant-Colonel J.C. *136*
Welsh, Air Marshal Sir W. *84*
Werobej, Colonel J. *17, 18*
Weston, Major-General C.E. *100*
Weygand, General Maxime 52, 55, 56, 57
Wharton, Brigadier-General J.W. *134, 136*
Whistler, Major-General L.G. *147, 149, 172, 185*
White, Major-General I.D. *180*
Whitehead, Brigadier *77*
Whitfield, Major-General J.Y. *123, 127*
Wieronski, Colonel W. *150*
Wiley, Brigadier H.O. *8, 11*
Williams, Lieutenant-General *9*
Williams, Major-General H. *9*
Wilson, Major-General R.T. *7, 8*
Wilson, Field Marshal Sir Henry Maitland *10*, 65, *74, 96*, 98
Wimberley, Major-General D.N. *77*, 109
Windsor-Lewis, Colonel *157*
Winkelman, General Henri *32*, 33
Witts, Major-General F.V.B. *7, 9*
Wlad, Major-General F. *17, 18*
Wogan, Major-General J.B. *181*
Wolf, Lieutenant-Colonel *51*
Wrigley, Brigadier *77*
Wyche, Major-General I.T. *146, 180*
Wyman, Brigadier R.A. *133, 137*
Wyman, Major-General W.G. *181*

Young, Lieutenant-Colonel P. *137*

Zakrzewski, Colonel A. *18*
Zivanovic, Lieutenant-General D. *93*
Zivkovic, General D. *93*
Zoiopoulos, Major-General K. *95*
Zongollowicz, General E. *19, 22*
Zubosz-Kalinski, General A. *17, 19, 22*
Zugic, Lieutenant-General I. *92*
Zugoures, Major-General K. *94*
Zulauf, Major-General J. *17, 22*

General Index

Page numbers in *italics* refer to tables and illustrations

7TP light tank *15, 16, 17*

Aisne, River 56, 57
Alam el Halfa Ridge 75, 76
Albania 91, *94*
Alexandria 61
Algiers 82, 84
Amsterdam 33
Antwerp 49, 155, 162
Anzio 116, 118–20
Ardennes
  1940 34, 37, 46, 47, 54
  1944 162, *163*, 164–9, 171
Arnhem 33, 158, 160, 161
Arnim, General Jurgen von 86, 88
Arras 49, 51, 52–3
Australia
  Balkans 91, 98, 100

enters war 11
  military expansion 11
  North Africa 76
Austria 125, 176, 178, *181*, 183

Baghdad 64, 65
Balkans *90*, 91–6, *97*, 98–105, 107
Baltic Sea 28
Bardia 67
Bastogne 162, 165, *167*, 168–9
Beda Fomm 66, 67
Belgium *24*
  Ardennes Offensive 1944 162, *163*, 164–9, 171
  German invasion *31*, 33–4, 46–7, *48*, 49, 54
  liberation 155
  unpreparedness of 25, 33
Belgrade 96, 102
Berlin 176, 178, 182
Bir Hacheim 72–3

Bizerte, Tunisia 88, 89
Blitzkrieg 38, 47
Bologna 125
Bosnia *90, 94*
Boulogne 53
Boys anti-tank rifle 11
Breda, Holland 33
Bren gun 11
Brest 57
Brindisi 112
Britain
  Ardennes Offensive *169*
  arms production 185
  Balkans 91, 96, 98–100, 101, 104–5, 107
  Battle of France 45–7, *48*, 49–54, 57–8
  declares war 11
  Dieppe Raid 129–30
  East Africa 62, *63*
  Germany, assault on *173*, 174, 175, 176, 183–4

Italy *113*, 114–15, 119, 120, *121*, 122–5
  Middle East 64–5
  Normandy landings *128*, 131, *132*, 133–7, *138–9*, 140–1, *142*, 147, 155
  North Africa *60*, 61, 62, 65–8, *69*, 70–*1*, *79*, 82, 83, 86–9
  Norway 27, *29*, 30
  Operation Market Garden *156*, 157–8, *159*, 160–1
  and Poland 15
  rearmament 10–11
  Sicily 107, 110, *111*, 112
British Army
  casualties 58, 61, 62, 70–1, 73, 89, 100, 161, 169
  improving firepower 107
  mechanization 10–11, 45, 61
  strength 10–11, 45, 61, 66, 68, 76, 136, 185

British Somaliland 61, 62, *63*
Brussels 155
Bulgaria 91, *97*, 102
Bulge, Battle of the 162, *163*, 164–9, 171

Caen 135, 141, 147, 149
Calabria 112
Calais 38, 53
Canada
  casualties 130
  Dieppe Raid 129–30
  enters war 11
  Germany, assault on 171, 174, *184*
  Italy 120
  military expansion 11, *13*
  Normandy landings *133*, 134, *138–9*, 140, 141, *150*, 151, 152
  Operation Dragoon 144–5
  strength 11, *13*, 136
Carden-Loyd tankette 11, 33, 34

Index

Casablanca, Morocco 82, 84, 131
'Cauldron,' North Africa 72–3
Char B tank 38
Char D2 tank *29*
Cherbourg 57
Chetniks 101, 102
Churchill, Winston 57–8, 75, 102–3, 112, 129, 131, 142, 178
Churchill tank *128*, 130
Compiegne, France 58
Copenhagen 26
Crete 91, *97*, 98–100
Cromwell tank *179*
Cruiser tank Mk I 67, 68
Cruiser tank Mk II 67, 68
Cruiser tank Mk III 45, 67, 68, 70
Czechoslovakia 15, 176, *181*, 182, 183

Denmark
  German invasion 26, *27*, 28
  strength 26
  unpreparedness of 25
Dieppe Raid 129–30
Dinant, Belgium 168, *169*
Dönitz, Admiral Karl 183–4
Dunkirk 38, *43*, 49, 51, 53–4
Dyle, River 47

East Africa 61, 62, *63*
Eben Emael, Belgium 34
Egypt 61, 66, 67, 74
Eindhoven 158
El Alamein 61, 74–6, *77–9*
Elbe, River 176, *177*, 178, 183
Ethiopia 61, 62, *63*

Falaise 149, 151–2, 154
Finland 25, *29*
France
  Allied southern invasion 112, 142–6
  Battle of 45–7, *48*, 49–58, *59*
  casualties 58, 72
  Dieppe Raid 129–30
  Germany, assault on 174, *182*
  Italy 116
  Middle East 64–5
  Normandy landings *128*, 131, *132*, 133–7, *138–9*, 140–1, *142*, 147, 150–5
  North Africa 72–3, 83, 84–5, 86
  Norway 27, *29*, 30
  and Poland 15
  Saar Offensive 30, 38
  unpreparedness of 37–8
French Army
  organization 38, *40–1*
  rearmament 37
  strength *37*, 38, 42–3, *44, 52*, 153

Gabr Saleh 68, 70
Gazala Line 71, 72, *73*
Germany
  Eighth Army 21
  Tenth Army 112, 119
  XXIII Corps 56–7
  352nd Infantry Division 136
  716th Division 140–1
  Afrika Corps 68
  Allied assault on *170*, 171–3, *174*, 175–6, *177*, 178–9, 182–5
  Ardennes Offensive 1944 162, *163*, 164–9, 171
  Army Group B 176
  Army Group E 104
  Balkans 91, 93–4, *97*, 98–100, 101, 102, 104
  casualties 47, 58, 87, 89, 100, 152, 154, 169
  Denmark, invasion of 26, *27*, 28
  France, invasion of 45–7, *48*, 49–58, *59*
  Italy 112, 114–16, 118–20, *121*, 122–5
  Low Countries, invasion of *31*, 33–4, 46–7, *48*, 49, 54
  Normandy landings 136–7, 140–1, 146, 153, 154
  North Africa 61, 68, 70–6, 78, *79*, 83–4, 86–9
  Norway, invasion of 26, *27*, 28–30

Operation Market Garden 159, 160–1
Poland, invasion of *14*, 15, 17, *20*, 21–3
Sicily 107, 110
strength 86, 162
surrender 183–5
see also Panzer Armies; Panzer Corps; Panzer Divisions
Gibraltar 61
Gothic Line 120, 125
Grant tank 71
Grebbe Line, Holland 30, 33
Greece 91, 95–6, *97*, 98, 104–5
Guderian, General Heinz 38, 47
Gustav Line 112, 116, 117

Haakon VII, King of Norway 27
Habbaniyah, Iraq 64, 65
Haile Selassie, Emperor 62
Halfaya Pass 68, 70, 71
Heraklion, Crete 99, 100
Hitler, Adolf
  Ardennes Offensive 162
  Balkans 91, 98
  death 183
  France and the Low Countries 30, 33, 53, 58, 153
  Italy 125
  North Africa 67
Holland
  German invasion *31*, 33, *48*, 54
  Operation Market Garden *156*, 157–8, *159*, 160–1
  unpreparedness of 25, 30
Hotchkiss H-35 tank 17, 38, *39*
Hungary 91

India
  East Africa 62
  Italy 116, *122*
  North Africa 65, 68, 72, 75, 87, 88
  strength *11*
Iran *64*, 65
Iraq *64*, 65
Ireland 11
Italy
  Allied invasion 91, *106*, 107, *113*, 114–16, 118–20, *121*, 122–5, 182
  Ariete Division 70
  Balkans 91, 95, 102
  casualties 68, 89
  declares war 57, 62
  East Africa 64, 65
  North Africa 61, 65–6, *72*, 83–4, 87, 89
  strength 61
  surrender 103, 104, 125
  Trieste Division 72

Kasserine Pass 86
Kenya 62
Koblenz 171, 175
Koryzis, Alexandros 98
Kraków 21

Laon, France 49
Le Muy, France 143, 144, 146
Lebanon 64
Leipzig 176, 182
Lend-Lease 70
Libya 61, *65*, 66
Light Tank Mk IV 67
Lillehammer 30
Losheim Gap 165, 166, 167
Luftwaffe
  Balkans 99, 100
  France 49, 53, 54
  North Africa 72
  Poland 15, 21
  Scandinavia 27
M4 Sherman tank 75–6, 88, *128*, 137, *141*, 148, 150, 160, *179*
M5 Stuart light tank 68, 70, 71, *151*, 168
M8 Greyhound armored car 168
M8 Howitzer Motor Carriage 168
M10 Wolverine tank destroyer *106*, *117*
M24 Chaffee light tank 168
Maas, River 158

Maas-Waal Canal 158, 160
Maginot Line *31*, 37, 38, 45, 47, *51*, 55
Maleme, Crete 99, 100
Malta 61
Manstein, General Erich von 39
Mareth Line 86, 87, 89
Marne, River 57
Matilda tank 45, 52, 68, 70, 71
Mersa Matruh 74
Messina, Sicily 110, 112
Meuse, River 47, 162, 168, *169*
Middle East 64–5
Mihailovic, Draza 101, 103
Monte Cassino 91, 116, 117, 119
Montenegro 102
Moselle, River 175
Mulde, River 182
Mussolini, Benito 91, 95

Narvik 27, 28, 30
Neder Rhine, River 158
New Zealand
  Balkans 91, 98, 99, 100
  enters war 11
  Italy 91, 116
  North Africa 68, 71, *74*, 75, 76, 78, 87, 91
  strength *11*
Nijmegen 158, 160, 171
Normandy landings *128*, 131, *132*, 133–7, *138–9*, 140–1, *142*, 147, 150–5
North Africa *60*, 61, 62, 65–8, *69*, 70–6, *78–9*, 82–9
Norway
  German invasion 26, *27*, 28–30
  strength 26
  unpreparedness of 25, 28

Operations
  Avalanche 112, 114
  Baytown 112
  Blackcock *171*
  Bolero 131
  Charnwood 147
  Cobra 149, 150–2, 154
  Compass 65–8
  Crusader 68, 70–1
  Diadem 116, 119
  Dragoon 112, 142–6
  Dynamo 53–4
  Epsom 147
  Fall Gelb 30, 46, *48*
  Fall Rot 55
  Fall Weiss 102
  Goodwood 147
  Grenade 171, 172
  Husky 107, 109, *110*
  Jubilee 129–30
  Lightfoot 76, *78*
  Market Garden *156*, 157–8, *159*, 160–1, 171
  Mercury 98–100
  Overlord 116, 129, 131, *132*, 133–7, 142, 147
  Plunder 173, 175
  Roundup 131
  Shingle 118–20
  Slapstick 112
  Sledgehammer 131
  Strangle 116
  Supercharge 76, *79*
  Torch 61, 82–5, 86, 125
  Varsity 175
  Veritable 171, 172
  Wacht am Rhein 162
  Weserübung 26
Oran, Algeria 82, 84
Orne, River 135, 141
Oslo 27, 30

Palermo, Sicily 107
Panzer II tank 52
Panzer IV tank 52, *60*
Panzer V Panther 147–8, 150
Panzer VI Tiger 148, 150
Panzer Armies
  Fifth 86, 88, 168
  Africa 71, *72*, 76, 88

Panzer Corps
  II SS 161
  XVI 57
Panzer Divisions
  7th 47, 52, 57
  9th SS 161
  10th SS 161
  15th 68
  21st 68, 86
  29th Panzergrenadier Division 114
Paris 49, 55, 56, 58, 153, 154–5
Partisans
  French 145, 153
  Greek 91
  Yugoslav *90*, 94, 101–3
Paul, Prince of Yugoslavia 93
Pearl Harbor 80
Peiper, Lieutenant-Colonel Joachim 166
Phoney War *31*, *36*, 38, 46
PIAT (Projector, Infantry, Anti-Tank) 11, 161
Po, River 120, 125
Poland
  casualties 23
  German invasion *14*, 15, 17, *20*, 21–3
  Italy 116, *117*, *122*
  Normandy landings *150*, 151, 152
  North Africa 68
  Operation Market Garden 158, 161
  strength 15, 16–17, 117
Port Lyautey, Morocco 84, 85

Red Army
  Germany, assault on 91, 125, 171, 176, 178, 179, 182–3
  Poland, invasion of 21, 23
Remagen 173, 174, 176
Renault
  ACG-1 tank 34
  FT-17 tank *15*, 17, 33
  R-35 tank *15*, 17
Rethymnon, Crete 99, 100
Reynaud, Paul 58
Rhine, River 171, 173, 174, 175
Roer, River 172, 174
Romania 91
Rome *106*, 116, 119, 120, 125
Rommel, General Erwin
  France 52–3, 57
  North Africa 61, 68, 71, 72–3, 74, 86, 87, 89
Roosevelt, Franklin D. 75, 131, 178
Rotterdam 30
Royal Air Force 45
Royal Navy
  Dunkirk 53, 54
  Mediterranean 91
  North Africa 84
Ruhr 171, 176, 178

Saar, River 171, 174
Salerno 107, 112, 114–15, 125
San, River 15
Sardinia 107
Scheldt, River 49, 155
Sedan, France 47
Seine, River 57
Serbia 101, 102
Sicily 107, 110, *111*, 112
Sidi Barrani 66, 67
Sidi Rezegh 68, 70
Siegfried Line *31*, 172, 175
Somme, River 56
Somua S-35 medium tank *39*, 42–3
South Africa 11, 68, 71, 75, 76, *122*
Soviet Union
  Iran 65
  Poland, invasion of 15, 21, 23
  Yugoslavia 102, 103
  see also Red Army
Stalin, Josef 103, 129, 178
Student, General Kurt 98
Sudan 61, 62
Suez Canal 61
Sweden 25
Syria 64

T-13 and T-15 tanks 34
Taranto 107, 112

Tito, Josip Broz *90*, 101, 102–3
TK and TKS Tankettes *15*, *16*, 17, *23*
Tobruk *65*, 67, 68, *69*, 70, 71–3
Torgau, Germany 176, 182
Transjordan 64, 65
Tripoli, Libya 61
Trondheim 25, 27
Tunisia 76, 78, 84, 86–9

United States
  Ardennes Offensive 1944 162, *163*, 164–9, 171
  arms production 185
  Germany, assault on 171–3, *174*, 175–6, *177*, 178–9, 182–5
  Italy *113*, 114–16, 118–20, *121*, 122–5, 182
  Normandy landings 131, *132*, 133–7, *138–9*, 140–1, 153–5
  North Africa 82–9
  Operation Dragoon 142–6
  Operation Market Garden *156*, 157–8, *159*, 160–1
  Sicily 107, 110, *111*, 112
United States Army
  casualties 86, 89, 115, 135, 150, 161, 169
  combat engineers 175–6
  organization 137–8, 178
  pre-war 80
  reorganization 80–1, 112
  strength 80, 131, 136, 153, 185

Valentine tank 70, 71
Vichy 58
Vickers
  6-ton Mark E light tank 17
  Light Tank *6*
Vienna 176
Vietinghoff, General Heinrich von 112, 125
Vistula, River 15, 21

Waal, River 158
Warsaw 21–3
Wasp flamethrower 107
Wesel, Germany 171, 174
Weser, River 176

Yugoslavia 91, 92–4, *97*, 101–3